Merry Christmas 1977
To: Bob and Happy
From: Mother

Old Homes
And Buildings
Of Fredericksburg

Old Homes
And Buildings
Of Fredericksburg

By Elise Kowert

Elise Kowert

Old Homes
And Buildings
Of Fredericksburg

By Elise Kowert

Photography by Art Kowert

Fredericksburg Publishing Company
Fredericksburg, Texas

Preface

Fredericksburg, Texas, is steeped not only in German-Texan traditions, customs and heritage, but its Old World architecture is also being preserved for future generations.

"Old Homes and Buildings of Fredericksburg" began in April 1975 as a weekly series in the **Fredericksburg Standard** as a Bicentennial feature, continuing through 1976. Two buildings are added in this book that appeared in the 1977 series. The stories were compiled for this book with minor corrections to bring each one as up-to-date as possible by publication time.

The 1975-76 series was based on an earlier one I had researched and written that appeared in the **Standard** during the years 1954-57. Many older people, owners of the homes, descendants of the builders, and others, were interviewed then and much of the information contained in those stories would have been lost for posterity had it not been preserved in the series.

The 1975-76 stories embodied much of the family history concerning the old homes and buildings, but brought up-to-date the facts concerning them, as many of them have been restored, renovated or remodeled, with several finding diversified uses by the 1970's.

A deserted courthouse became a library, an old hotel a lawyer's office and home, a millinery store which was later a bakery became a savings and loan branch office, an old log cabin found use as an antique store, a building that was once a bank and then a saloon is now a book store -- and so the list goes on and on.

Of invaluable help were the records in the office of the Gillespie County Clerk, as well as the naturalization papers in the office of the District Clerk. Early issues of the **Fredericksburg Standard** and its sister newspaper, the German-language **Fredericksburg Wochenblatt**, helped in piecing together missing links of information or supplied real "jewels" among the obituaries or news columns.

An attempt was made to include only information obtained in personal interviews or correspondence by the author or which was found in official records or published accounts, with the temptation resisted repeatedly to say, "It is thought" or "It is believed." If there was doubt about a date or a fact, it was omitted, rather than give credence to something that could not be substantiated.

The 1954-57 series was given an Award of Merit by the American Association for State and Local History for its distinctive contribution to preservation of local history.

The Gillespie County Historical Society presented an award of merit to me in 1974 in recognition of my efforts in researching and publicizing the history of many old homes in Fredericksburg for a series of newspaper articles.

In 1976 the series was selected as the statewide newspaper category winner of the prestigious Sixth Annual John G. Flowers Award given by the Texas Society of Architects at their state convention in Dallas. The TSA cited the series in recognition of outstanding contributions to the profession of architecture through journalistic endeavors.

Over forty years of interest in and working with the history of the city's old buildings provided inspiration to write the stories of the structures and the people who built, lived in and owned them. First, in working on abstracts of title to the lots on which they were built, and later as a writer on the staff of the **Fredericksburg Standard**, this interest found fruition in the publication of the stories which are included in this book.

The help of my husband, Art Kowert, the editor of the **Fredericksburg Standard**, was invaluable. He made all of the current photographs that appear in this book, but most of all, his encouragement and expertise made possible the week-to-week work on the project and publication of this book. Nathan L. Cytrin of San Antonio and the staff of the **Fredericksburg Standard**, especially Marcus and Nora

Wehmeyer, Terry Collier, Vickie Klier and Peter Nixon, are due their share of credit for the mechanical production.

This book is dedicated to the memory of the early colonists and settlers of Fredericksburg, to the pioneer builders of these interesting structures whose ingenuity, craftsmanship and wise use of materials made possible the erection of buildings, most of which have stood for over one hundred years.

It is a tribute also to the people who have restored and preserved them, as well as to the present owners, many of whom have adapted them to present-day use while retaining the dimensions of charm these old structures have given to Fredericksburg.

May you, as you read these stories and look at these pictures, gain a new appreciation for the heritage of Fredericksburg, as these old homes and historic buildings reflect a living history of its people.

Elise Kowert
1977

Mr. and Mrs. Raymond Kneese, Owners

JOHN RUEGNER HOME—NOW KNEESE LAW OFFICE

A pioneer stonemason built a home for his own family overlooking Fredericksburg's Courthouse Square, and now almost 125 years later it serves as a law office for Raymond Kneese and for Kneese Abstract and Title Company.

Mr. Kneese and his wife, Eugenia, bought this property September 7, 1968, and began their renovation of it in 1972, finishing in 1973.

The old house at 105 West San Antonio Street is located on a lot granted by the German Emigration Company to Daniel Weiershausen, listed as "D. Weyershausen" on the original list of allottments of Townlots and Outlots to the original settlers. Weiershausen began to make improvements on his lot, as they are mentioned in a March 1, 1852, mortgage, and hauled rock to this site. He was the Gillespie County treasurer from 1850-52. His name is also listed among the original petitioners who on December 15, 1847, requested the Legislature to create Gillespie County out of Bexar County of which this area was then a part.

Weiershausen sold the lot to Johannes (John) Ruegner November 5, 1854, for $200. Ruegner, a stonemason, built the original two-room limestone rock home for his family, and it stands today as an example of the skill of these pioneer craftsmen who had only crude tools, native stone, and hand-hewn or sawn timber to work with.

Ruegner was one of the stonemasons who worked on the old two-storied "college" which is now the middle building on the old Public School campus and for the 1974-75 school year houses the 5th and 6th grades. He also built the stone wall which encloses the lower side of the oldest part of the City Cemetery. He used a two-wheeled cart and a "schimmel" horse to haul the rocks for his stone work.

Originally the large front room served as the combined bedroom and sitting room and the back room was the kitchen and dining room. Later owners put up partition walls, making four rooms out of the two large ones. Still later owners made additions to the rear, some of which have been removed entirely.

The Ruegners brought up their family here. Their children sold it after the death of their parents to A. Walter on April 17, 1899, for $1000. The children included John and Henry Ruegner of Mason; Edward Ruegner; Bertha and husband, G. A. Pfeil; Emma and husband, Carl Durst; and Anna and husband, Alfred Peters.

A. Walter, pioneer Swiss jeweler who founded the Walter Jewelry firm, lived in this house for several years with his family. Walter sold it to Louis von Hagen on January 12, 1904. The Hagens lived here for several years and later moved to Austin.

Louis von Hagen's daughters and devisees under his will, Olga Hagen of New York and

Else Mayer, wife of prominent Austin jeweler, Carl Mayer, sold it to Gus Malchow July 9, 1920.

Malchow owned a furniture store located in an old two-story building that stood where Ward's Catalog Agency is now located. He sold this house on West San Antonio Street to B. R. Bailey in 1928, and a year later Bailey sold it to Marie Calsen. Mrs. Dora Maurer bought it from her on October 21, 1929, and lived here with her family. Her children included Louise, Mrs. Theodore Kunz; Alma, Mrs. Werth Sweatmann; Henry, Erwin, William and Edward Maurer.

Raymond and Eugenia Kneese bought the property from Mrs. Maurer's estate and began their renovation work in 1972.

They had the assistance of Tyrus Cox and James King, who worked with major restoration projects in this area, as well as in Austin. One of the big jobs involved revealing the beautiful old rock work that had in later years been "plastered over."

The large front room now houses the reception room for the law and abstract of title firm at the west end, and at the east end is the law library. During the restoration work, several interesting details were revealed as layers of plaster and boards were removed. The window in the west wall of the reception room was once a door, and later closed up with rock at the bottom below the window panes. The windows in the front are artistically arched at the top.

Some changes were made to facilitate the more modern use of the building, such as closing up a window between the reception room and Mr. Kneese's private office, and leaving a hall between the offices to the back.

Behind the reception room is Mr. Kneese's private office, and back of that the rest room and kitchenette.

Behind the law library on the east side of the building is the secretary's office, and behind that the large fireproof vault. Back of this is Mrs. Kneese's private office.

The new construction was carried on so that it blends harmoniously with the original structure.

Some of the interesting little details were left, such as the trap door in the ceiling of the law library which leads to the loft. There is a good floor in the loft and a small window opens out of the west wall of the loft.

What more appropriate place could be used by a lawyer and a title business dealing with the history of land in Gillespie County. Raymond and Eugenia Kneese have preserved not only an historic pioneer home, but in doing so have provided for themselves a very comfortable, and distinctive office.

RICHTER BUILDING—NOW DOMINO PARLOR

The face of Main Street is constantly changing, but fortunately many of the fine old rock buildings that have brought acclaim to the city remain and, better still, many are being restored for commercial or residential use.

Such is the case with the old Richter Building, known for years as the "Domino Hall." The building now belongs to William A. and Nancy Wareing, who moved to the Fredericksburg area from Houston several years ago. Mr. Wareing, a retired stock broker, is assisted by Diana Hahne in operating the restaurant and bier garten.

Wareing has added the attractive bier garten behind the building, and it really gives a touch of "the old country" to a modern-day business. It's Fredericksburg counterpart of Austin's Scholz Garden and will, no doubt, become just as popular once the word gets around.

The building is located on part of Townlot 177, which was allotted by the German Emigration Company to Adolph Schildknecht, but was deeded by the company to his assignee, John Schmidtzinsky, December 13, 1849. That was the date of the original deed, but fire destroyed the store that housed the county clerk's records in 1850, so a new deed was made, acknowledged and filed for record Nov. 15, 1852. Schmidtzinsky, for $29, also got a quitclaim from the man to whom the survey on which it is located was patented, John H. Herndon, dated July 16, 1859. This covered three townlots he owned -- No. 177, No. 88 which is immediately behind it fronting on East Austin Street, as well as No. 232 which is located directly opposite No. 177 on the other side of Main Street, then known as San Saba Street.

In all probability John Schmidtzinsky built the front part of the house, because there is

Mr. and Mrs. William A. Wareing, Owners

evidence in a side wall that it was built in different stages. When he sold this lot and the one behind it to John A. Alberthal on April 10, 1858, the purchase price was $500. Alberthal and his wife, Wilhelmina (Minna), deeded the same two lots to Ottocar Mueller and Christian Frantzen July 25, 1860. They paid $1100 for the property.

It is known that Mueller was a druggist, and in later legal papers reference is made to the "firm of Mueller and Frantzen." Frantzen died, and his widow, Hedwig, as administrator and surviving wife, transferred the property to Ottocar Mueller Jan. 28, 1865.

The firm owed F. W. Schnerr $360 and on February 9, 1865, Mueller gave him a mortgage payable "within one year after close or termination of the present war between the United and Confederate States of America." Frantzen also gave a mortgage to secure payment of a $400 note dated July 1, 1870, to "Wm. Kramer, legal administrator of the heirs of Dr. Keidel, deceased," payable in three years.

On Sept. 10, 1873, Mueller and his wife, Elisabeth, sold the property to Adolph Dreiss. In the deed reference is made to conveyance of "our dwelling house and a small space between the same and the house adjoining the same on Lot 176 known as Alberthal's bar room."

From Adolph Dreiss ownership passed to Albert Dreiss on May 1, 1876, and from him to

his daughter, Bertha Eisenlohr on June 2, 1890. Bertha Haye (the former Bertha Eisenlohr) and her husband deeded it to H.R. Richter April 29, 1901, however, before that date there were others who lived in it.

Max von Reinbach conducted a drug store in the building and his family also lived there. His two daughters married Christian Stehling and Friedrich Lochte, and his son, Felix, married Elise Henke. The Felix Reinbachs also lived in the house for a while.

The Richter family moved into the house and Mr. Richter operated a jewelry store and sold musical instruments in the western end of the large front room, using the special bay window as his "show window."

H. R. (Henry) Richter was born in Baltimore, but spent most of his boyhood in Staunton, Va. His mother died while he was young and he came to Texas to stay with an uncle near Marble Falls. He married Hermine Stuckert, a native Texan, and they reared their family in this house on Main Street.

A musically talented and culturally inclined man, Richter played several musical instruments, his favorites being the violin and classical guitar. He was also a composer and corresponded with Anton Dvorak, whose music gained international fame.

Concerts were often presented in the large "front room" of the Richter home. He organized the "Philharmonische Geschellschaft" which included a mixed

3

chorus and an orchestra.

At the time they lived here the large room at the west side of the front was Richter's jewelery store, just as it had been the drug store before his day. There were two entrances, each with two large double doors and between them a bay window. The third front entrance, also with large double doors, led into the Richter's front bedroom. Behind this was another bedroom, and the partition wall between these two bedrooms was removed by Knoche when he bought the place.

There were three rooms in the back part of the house. Right behind the bedroom was the Richter's living room, at the northeast corner. In the center was their dining room and at the northwest corner. In the center was their dining room and at the northwest corner their kitchen.

Mrs. Richter kept her eggs, milk and cream in a hanging wire-screened cabinet suspended in the cellar. Steep, narrow stone steps led to this cellar.

There were four girls and one boy in the Richter family. Reinhold, their son, died at the age of 19, two months after the death of his father in 1913. Cecilie married Charles Wenmohs and they lived on a ranch in Blanco County. She died in 1938. Carolyn (Carrie) married Col. Edwin R. York and lived in Austin until her death in 1952. The oldest sister, Mercedes (Mercie) married Fritz Fuchs of Cypress Mills and they later lived in El Reno, Okla. Leilet (Lettie), the youngest, taught for many years in the San Antonio high schools and then lived in Austin. She is now also deceased.

The Richter heirs sold the property to Walter Knoche February 6, 1945. They had not lived here for many years. In the years after which they left here and before Knoche bought the property, it was operated chiefly as a Mexican cafe by various tenants. Knoche made several structural changes in the interior and had plans for establishing a "teen center" here during the years when that was the "in" thing to do, but that use of the building was short-lived.

Prior to Wareing's acquisition it was operated as a "domino parlor and pool hall." Cold drinks and "short orders" of food were available, with Henry Ransleben being one of the tenants for many years.

Knoche's widow, Elsie Knoche, sold the property to William A. Wareing January 10, 1973. Wareing also owns the adjoining Schaefer House, and following his renovation of that building, he began work on the Domino Hall.

Furnishings in an old-fashioned motif are used in the restaurant, with a number of antiques and memorabilia of earlier days adding to the decor.

Sandwiches, hamburgers, light lunches, salad plates, homemade stew and chili, and Reuben sandwiches are now being served in the restaurant. They also have keg and bottled beer and soda water.

The biergarten back of the rock building is the real "charmer." Red cedar lattice work forms a partial roof over the paved area. On one side a native rock fountain and pool and a small garden are enclosed with a rock ledge on which customers may sit.

The rocks Wareing used in the wall and fountain are some that made their way from Main Street to the country and back to Main Street. They are some that were hauled away when an old rock home on Main Street was razed several years ago.

The area can be entered through the restaurant or through the passageway between it and the Schaefer House which has a cedar shingle and lattice work entrance.

If that is not enough "atmosphere," there is a wine cellar under the front part of the building which is reached by steep rock steps. This is one of the few cellars in Fredericksburg with a solid, domed rock ceiling. Since its construction is so similar to the one in the Kurt Keidel home in the same block which was built by "Hermit" Berg, it is taken for granted that he built this, too.

Construction of the domed rock ceiling was made possible by sand fill to hold it in place while masonry work was completed.

The Richters and other families kept their sausage, meat, canned goods and preserves here, but Wareing has stocked his 1975 cellar with handmade wine cabinets which hold choice wines, to be sold in bottles or consumed on the premises. There are tables in the cellar where guests may also be served food.

How nice for Fredericksburg -- to have restoration-minded persons like Bill and Nancy Wareing to preserve one of the city's oldest and most historic buildings in such a practical way -- proving that there is lots of charm and use in the old buildings of Fredericksburg.

Mr. and Mrs. Walter Tatsch, Owners

JOHN PETER TATSCH HOME

If you had to pick the most widely-known old home in Fredericksburg, it would have to be the "Tatsch home." Long before it was the "in" thing to do to admire, restore, preserve or renovate an old home, people here and visitors to the city were fascinated by this old rock home with its two fireplaces, one of unbelievable size.

Because the size of the biggest fireplace staggers the imagination when viewed from the West Schubert Street side of the house, it intrigues visitors who want to see more. Located at the corner of North Bowie and West Schubert Streets, the Tatsch home is only two blocks off Main Street.

It is built on Townlot No. 12, with Peter Birk as the original grantee on the official list of allotments made by the German Emigration Company to the original settlers. Birk's deed from the company was dated December 29, 1849.

The numbering of the original Townlots of Fredericksburg began one block northwest of this lot -- at the corner of West Schubert and North Cherry Streets, continuing in successive numbers southeast along Schubert Street to No. 22 at the corner of Schubert and North Milam.

Peter Birk sold Townlot 12 (an area of 20,000 square feet) to Peter Tatsch on October 9, 1854. The builder of the house was Johann Peter Tatsch, whose name is also given as John Peter Tatsch or simply as Peter Tatsch.

From some of the other original grantees of Townlots in the block, Tatsch also brought a number of the adjoining lots.

Tatsch was a "Tischler" or cabinet-maker and turner. The Texas State Historical Survey Committee medallion and accompanying plaque on the building give a brief history of this house:

"John Peter Tatsch Home. 1856.

"Built by Tatsch (1822-1907) using local stone. A cabinet-maker and turner, did woodwork himself. At first floored only front rooms, using wide boards. North front room had one fireplace.

"Rear gallery kitchen, fireplace and oven added later. Tatsch, from Germany, during Civil War was a Minute Man.

"Wife was Maria Elizabeth (1828-1885). Children: Elizabeth, Sophie, Caroline, Wilhelmine, Richard.

"Recorded Texas Historic Landmark 1965."

Not only is this house a Recorded Texas Historic Landmark, but detailed floor plans of it were placed in the Library of Congress during the Texas Centennial when outstanding landmarks in the state were so recognized.

Originally Tatsch had only planned on building one room with an outside stairway, but then added the second room in front out of which the stairway leads to the attic. The stone walls are almost two feet thick.

Large double wooden doors, with interesting hardware, lead into the larger of the two front rooms. It is furnished with a bed, table, rocker, dresser, trunk and "Schrank" or wardrobe. In one wall is a small built-in cabinet where the Tatsches kept the family Bible, important papers and medicine. Now it holds colorful German dolls brought from Germany by Miss Esther Mueller. There are casement windows in the east and south walls for cross ventillation.

The other front room is furnished now as a living room, with the smaller fireplace used for heating it. In the front wall are two casement windows and the stairway to the attic leads along the inside wall. There is also a built-in shelf in one wall and a pegged board against another wall behind the doors provides room for hanging coats and hats.

Of interest is the fact that in the attic some of the beams still have bark on them.

The huge fireplace is in the "rear gallery kitchen" which was added later. This room originally had only a dirt floor, but in later years a floor was added. Here they did their cooking, and even the family washing.

One end of the big fireplace had an oven built into it so it could be used for baking at the same time that it was used for cooking and heating the room. The fireplace is approximately 13 feet wide, five and a half feet high, with a knee-high hearth running about two thirds the width of it.

The family could also hang their sausage, bacon and ham for curing in this room, using the fireplace to "smoke" it. A mantel was added later and it now holds old china plates and pewter, most of which belong to Miss Esther Mueller.

Ownership of the house has stayed in the Tatsch family since it was first built. After the builder, John Peter Tatsch and his wife, Maria Elizabeth, died, in a partition of their property, ownership of this house passed to one of their daughters, Caroline, who remained single during her life time. She lived here, and after her death her heirs sold it to Walter Tatsch of San Antonio on Oct. 14, 1930.

In addition to Caroline, the other John Peter Tatsch children were Sophie, who married Julius Klingelhoefer; Elise (Elizabeth), who married H. Kuenemann; Wilhelmine, who married Anton Kunz; and Richard Tatsch.

For a number of years the Girl Scouts used this house as a troop meeting place, and the Mueller sisters, Esther and Emmie, lived here for many years. They added some of the modern conveniences, such as the bathroom at the south end of the kitchen and a small kitchen sink and cabinet.

The present owners are very gracious hosts, opening the old home to the public on many occasions when tours are held by the Gillespie County Historical Society or when other groups want to visit there.

KAMMLAH HOUSE—NOW PIONEER MUSEUM

Pioneer Museum at 309 West Main Street, popularly known as "the Kammlah house," is one of the city's oldest buildings and its story is that of a house that grew and grew, was both a home and store for four generations of the Kammlah family, and was once in danger of being sold and razed to make room for a modern business.

Fortunately for Fredericksburg, members of the Gillespie County Historical Society got busy, raised the funds and bought the property from the Kammlah heirs July 9, 1955, for $10,000. The restoration, like its original construction, has been in different stages.

Now the Kammlah house serves as the nucleus for a group of buildings that comprise the museum complex acquired by the society over a number of years. On the front porch is an official Texas State Historical Survey committee medallion and marker.

It has a history in capsule form, but with some discrepancy in the dates, however, the interesting part of the building is the many stages in which the home was enlarged to take care of the several generations and their growing families.

The house is built on Townlot 249 which was granted to Heinrich Kammlah by the German Emigration Company in its original list of allotments to the first settlers. He is hereinafter referred to as Henry I as there are by now five Henry Kammlahs in his direct lineage, four of whom lived in this house. The family claims he built this house in the first year or two after he settled in Fredericksburg.

Henry I and his wife, Auguste, lived in the front four rooms. The present big front room of the museum was originally the two rooms of

the store, while the east room behind them with the first fireplace was their kitchen and the room adjoining it was their bedroom. There is a small attic above the front room with entrance doorway at the west, but no longer any stairway.

Now on display in the large front room are shelves holding early day items that could have been sold in the Kammlah store and other memorabilia and furniture, while on the other side of the room are modern day crafts sold by the society.

The second step in construction was the second (and largest) kitchen which connects the two wings of the house. The cooking fireplace hearth is 10 feet wide -- the full width of the room and it is a little lower than average waist-height, just comfortable for cooking. Now this room is filled with all sorts of kitchen and cooking paraphernalia and furniture.

There is a small window at the left side of the fireplace and originally a frame structure adjoined it on the east side where the stone patio is now and it was here the family ate their meals. Later the Kammlahs tore this down. The stone patio remains, with outdoor fireplace for heating water in the black iron washpot, and there is also the old well with wooden frame for pulling up the water bucket.

The third addition to the house included the next four rooms and the large attic. This adjoined the second kitchen and gave the house a U-shape. In this third addition there

was the third kitchen -- also with a large fireplace, but not as large as the second one. It has a window in the outer wall over a part of the hearth which was also waist-height. The floor in this kitchen, like in the second one, is of native stone.

The large room next to it, facing the patio, was where the family ate their meals, gathered around a long table with the customary bench against the wall. They needed a lot of room for Henry III and wife had four girls and two boys and also cared for six of his nieces and nephews after their parents' deaths.

This long room recently got a new floor of old boards that blend in well with the rest of the house.

Steps lead to the big cellar out of this big room which has slanting double doors above the steps. Nooks in the wall were used for storing wine and whiskey barrels, two of the beverages sold in the Kammlah store. The Kammlahs also had a large butcher block table in here and the cellar was used for storing cured meats, sausage and other staples sold in the store.

Next to the cellar steps are worn stone steps which lead up into the back two rooms which were built at this same time. These have an ingenious partition wall which can be unlatched and swung back to make one big room out of the two which the Kammlahs sometimes did for dances. The rest of the time it is stationary, with one small door in the center for convenient passage from one room to the other.

The east room is now the "Meusebach room" and holds several pieces of furniture which the founder of Fredericksburg used in his home and store at Loyal Valley. There is also a beautiful old organ and some other pieces of furniture, typical of an old-time parlor.

The room next to it is furnished now as a bedroom, and the "kleiderschrank" holds some beautiful antique white baby clothes, elaborate undergarments and aprons which have been washed, starched and ironed -- ready for "Sunday best" dressing.

A narrow stairway leads to the large attic -- really a large room on the second floor where most of the children in the family slept. Several small windows provided good cross-ventilation.

In later years, two additional bedrooms, also of the same stone construction, were added to the rear, bringing to a total of eleven the number of rooms in the house, plus the large attic.

Behind the house is a large stone smokehouse and adjoining it a wooden shed built to house the family car. Part of the original Kammlah property, too, is the large barn on the Pioneer Museum complex.

Amalia Anna Kammlah died December 21, 1941, and her husband, Henry Kammlah (III) died June 24, 1942. His four daughters inherited the house and store property in town and the son, Henry, the farm. The store goods were sold out soon after that, although some of the family continued to occupy and use the house from time to time until it was finally sold in 1955.

Within the past twenty years, many improvements have been made by the society in the property -- at first just to stabilize construction and make needed repairs. A new shingle roof was added over the second kitchen, heating and air conditioning were provided. The barn was renovated and a cement floor put in. The grounds were leveled and sodded.

Now the Kammlah house is a museum -- but not one with everything in display cases -- it is a living museum. Most of the displays are out on shelves or arranged attractively, while the antique and period furniture gives it the true look of being "lived in."

FASSEL HOME

An old Fredericksburg home that has served many purposes during its long life, saw "new life" as this nation's Bicentennial year began. The old Fassel home in the 300 block of West Main Street now belongs to the Gillespie County Historical Society, and is part of the Pioneer Museum Complex.

Restoration work was completed in time for the 1975 Founders Day observance May 10 which launched the Bicentennial year in Fredericksburg.

Townlot 250 on which the house is located was allotted to H. Winkel by the German Emigration Company and the adjoining Townlot 251 was granted to Frdr. Winkel. Since early deed records were destroyed by fire, there are often missing links in the chain of title, and we find Fr. Winkel selling Townlot 250 to Heinrich Kammlah, who had received adjoining Townlot 249 from the Company on which he built his home which is now Pioneer Museum. This deed was dated April 5, 1852, with the purchase price being $60, of which

$30 was cash and $30 was due November 1, 1852. Heinrich Kammlah, as assignee of H. Winkel, however, also got a deed from the Company dated November 18, 1852, and acknowledged February 21, 1853, conveying title to Townlot 250 to him.

The home was built in three different stages -- almost as many as went into construction of the adjoining Kammlah house.

It is very likely that either the first Henry Kammlah or his son, Henry II, built the oldest part of the house, because when Heinrich Kammlah conveyed "one-half of the SW one-half of Townlot 250" to Franz Koehler on October 31, 1871, he sold this 25-foot frontage on San Saba Street (now Main Street) for $300 gold dollars, indicating improvements were on the land. H. Kammlah in a deed dated July 19, 1871, deeded the SE one-fourth of Townlot 250 to Moritz Hartmann, also for $300 coin -- $100 cash and $200 due in three years. On October 9, 1876, H. Kammlah Jr., assignee of H. Kammlah Sr., quitclaimed the SE one-

fourth of the lot to Moritz Hartmann.

Mathias Fassel bought one-half of the SE one-half of Townlot 250 from Franz Koehler and wife, Magdalene, July 14, 1876, and the SE one-fourth from Moritz Hartmann December 8, 1884. He paid the Koehlers $350 for their one-fourth and the Hartmanns $250 for their fourth of the lot.

Mathias Fassel, from whose descendants the Gillespie County Historical Society bought this property Feb. 4, 1967, was a native of the Duchy of Nassau in Germany. He left there in 1871, and came here to make his home. He married Mary (Maria) Baumann on November 3, 1875, and they moved into the small house which was on this lot.

Before the Fassels bought the house, someone had a butcher shop in the small building, according to the family.

Even a casual inspection of the old home from the outside shows that it was built in different stages. The oldest part is the little room at the southwest corner which has a good-sized attic, or half-story, above it. This room has a back door in the south wall, with one window in the west and north walls, and a window and door in the east wall opening into what is now the kitchen. Upstairs there is a window in the back wall, and narrow steps led up the front to a small doorway to the attic.

Behind this one-room rock house was a small frame structure which was the kitchen

and workroom.

The first addition the Fassels made was the addition of the present kitchen which is the room at the southeast corner. It is also of native stone construction and has a door and window in the back wall and a window in the east wall.

The third step in construction was the addition of the front two rooms and porch by the Fassels. The outside walls are also of the same limestone, however, the partition wall separating the front two rooms was of wood laths. This partition wall has now been removed, making the front part of the house one lovely big room, just ideal for small social functions.

Mr. Fassel was a skilled wheelwright and had his shop in a frame building which stood between the house and Main Street. Here he made wheels, axles and assembled buggies and wagons. The floor of the shop was covered with wood shavings and chips which the youngsters gathered for their parents to use in starting the fires in the wood stoves in the house.

For the story on the house which appeared in the June 6, 1956, Standard, Mrs. Lina Dupray, one of the Mathias Fassel daughters, and her niece, Mrs. E.E. Eckert, both of San Antonio, recalled highlights of life in the house.

The Fassel children were Sophie, Mrs. J. R.

9

Kimbrough; Lina, Mrs. Joe Dupray; Anna, Mrs. Wm. Roeder Jr.; Albert Fassel; Alma, who died when she was seven years old; and William Fassel, who was deceased at the time of the conveyance to the Roeders, and his children were Margaret, Mrs. Melvin Woods; Helen Monica Fassel; William Fassel; Patricia, Mrs. James Hood; and James Fassel.

Mrs. Dupray recalled what a familiar sight it was to see their friends, in their long skirts and petticoats, coming up to the house through the shop, and then pausing on the porch to shake the shavings off their hems.

Mrs. Dupray also recalled that the path through the shop was also a short-cut to St. Mary's Church for persons on their way there from the main street (Haupstrasse). The house was also the gathering place for relatives and friends at such times as Easter and Christmas. After midnight mass, a large group usually gathered for coffee at the Fassel home. Mrs. Dupray could remember the top of their wood stove being almost covered with coffee pots as it was being brewed for visitors.

Other times the Fassels would help out relatives when someone who lived in the country became ill and had to stay in town to be near the doctor, this was the place for them. A sadder use the Fassel home saw, too, was that when there was a death in the family of someone who lived in the country, the body would be brought to the Fassel home where the funeral services were held since there were no funeral homes in those days.

After the death of the parents, the other Fassel children sold their interest in this property to Anna Fassel and her husband, Mr. and Mrs. Wm. Roeder Jr. After Mrs. Roeder died, Mr. Roeder and the members of his family used this home as their Sunday house. The Roeder heirs sold the property to the Society February 4, 1967.

Just as there were many more happy days than sad ones in the Fassel home, so there are bound to be only happy days ahead for the house now that it has found a new life on the Pioneer Museum Complex.

Arranged in the large front room now is an old piano, a large spinning wheel which belonged to Lottie Thomas, a library table which Temple D. Smith used in the Bank of Fredericksburg, two "Kleiderschranke" and a chest which belonged to the John O. Meusebach family, some chairs donated by the late Flora Eckert, and several pieces of furniture which belonged to the Fassel family and were used in this house.

The black iron Majestic range in the kitchen is one that belonged to the Hugo Kallenbergs. It cooks and bakes beautifully, using stove wood for heat.

Plaster was knocked off the walls in the house to expose the stone and the walls were painted white. One wall in the kitchen was left plastered to show the same color blue the old-timers obtained by using bluing as the coloring agent. In doing it over, they used bluing, too, in 1975.

The oldest room in the house is now furnished as a bedroom.

In later years, a sink and kitchen cabinets were added, since there was only one shelf in the kitchen. It had formerly been a window before the front room was added. At the cabinet glass doors are crocheted shelf liners; and early-day kitchen utensils, as well as old furniture, some of it the Fassels', furnish the room.

As the Fassel house was once a house where hospitality and "gemuetlichkeit" were a way of life, now it has become a "showcase" of life in earlier days in Fredericksburg where the Gillespie County Historical Society will display much of the memorabilia and many of the furnishings it has acquired over the years.

WEBER SUNDAY HOUSE

An old home that made its way mechanically to Fredericksburg's Main Street is the Weber Sunday House that now sits at the back of the Pioneer Museum Complex. Here it joins the Kammlah and Fassel homes and their outbuildings in giving visitors a glimpse into the interesting history of Fredericksburg, showing a bit of how the people in them lived, worked and played.

The Gillespie County Historical Society was the grateful recipient of this Sunday House for its museum complex when Mrs. Adelbert Weber, a native Gillespian who now lives in New Braunfels, donated it to the society and it was moved to the present site in 1972. It made its way to Main Street from its former location near the corner of West San Antonio and South Cherry Streets by means of a mechanical housemover and was shown to the public for the first time during the Founders Day celebration held at the Pioneer Museum Complex on May 1972.

It was built in 1904 by Mr. and Mrs. August Weber on a lot which Mrs. Weber inherited from her parents, Mr. and Mrs. Conrad Wehmeyer. Wehmeyer was among the first settlers in Fredericksburg and for years conducted the first bakery in town in the middle of the 100 block on the north side of East Main Street. Alwina was one of their nine children.

Mr. and Mrs. Weber had a farm about seven miles out the Kerrville Road where they made their home. They built this small frame house, with one room of dimensions approximately 16 by 20 feet, on this lot in town to use as their Sunday house.

Sunday houses were as much a part of early day Fredericksburg history as people's lake homes or country cabins are now. Those who lived in the country would build these tiny houses in town to use when they came to town to attend church services and Sunday School on Sundays and other church holidays. They were a place to eat and rest when they came to town to shop, to see the doctor or to visit for a brief time.

This was how the Webers used their house. They were members of Zion Lutheran Church, and that was not too far away. Also, they lived near enough to town so they could make the trip in and back the same day. They would come in for church services, and then eat a

Gillespie County Historical Society, Owner

leisurely dinner in the house, staying over in the afternoon for Sunday School and to visit with relatives and friends.

It is furnished in much the same style as it was when the Webers and their two children, Bertha and Adelbert, used it. They had a third son, who died as an infant.

They had no running water in the house and there was no well near it, so they brought their water to drink and to cook with from their home in the country in jugs.

There was no electricity, so lamps and candles were used, but the Webers usually did not stay overnight, as they departed for home before dark.

Mr. and Mrs. Weber died in 1929. The house belonged to their daughter, Bertha, for a while, and later Mr. and Mrs. Adelbert Weber bought it, but none of them ever lived in it.

After the deaths of Adelbert and his sister, Mrs. Weber decided it would be a nice gesture and tribute to the early pioneers who used this type of house to donate it to the Gillespie County Historical Society. Her offer was gratefully accepted. She sold some of the furnishings in the house, giving the money to the church, but several of the original pieces of furniture and some of the dishes used by the Webers went with her gift and are in the house now.

The little house has a small front porch supported by four turned posts. At center front above the porch is a wooden opening into the attic. There is only one door into the room,

11

flanked by a window at each side under the porch. Each side has one window with solid wooden shutters, but there is no opening in the back wall. Now unbleached domestic curtains with red print ruffles hang at the windows.

On the bare wooden floor in front of the small bed used by the Webers is a crocheted rug. The bed is covered with the original white coverlet used by the owners. The Webers' old kitchen "schrank" with its glass doors has crochet-edged shelf liners and here some of the Weber dishes are displayed.

Typical is the long wooden table along one wall with one bench against the wall and the second bench along the other side. The Webers always had a white oilcloth over it, and a similar one is on it now.

Other furnishings include a small child's high chair, one cane-bottom and one rawhide-bottom chair, a small table on which their drinking water bucket stood, and in one corner is a large black kitchen stove. It is not the one the Webers used, but is one the society provided that is similar to those used at that time.

An oil lamp on the wall, another on the table alongside a white candle in a tin candleholder, dishpans hung against the wall, and some large framed family pictures add to the furnishings of the house.

Now when the Sunday house is open to visitors, they have a chance to see what these looked like in the early days. Too many of them have been remodeled, enlarged or changed completely with the passage of years and when the need for them no longer existed once the automobile and paved road era got here.

Mrs. Weber's generous gift of the old home is something that all generations can now appreciate as they come here to look at one that is typical of Fredericksburg's Sunday Houses.

At the front of the Pioneer Museum Complex rock fence is an official Texas State Historical Marker which "capsules" their story. The inscription reads:

"Sunday Houses

"Small townhouses built by German settlers who lived in distant rural areas. Used over weekends by families while they traded or attended church.

"A typical early Sunday House had one room with a lean-to kitchen and a half-story above, which was reached by attic stairway or ladder. Built during 1890's-1920's, most Sunday Houses were frame, but some were rock.

"Houses found use during school sessions, periods of religious instructions or serious illness.

"Some of the larger ones made comfortable retirement homes for elderly German farmers. 1970."

OLD JAIL

Since Gillespie County was formally organized February 23, 1848, it has had six jails.

The oldest jail still in existence is the fourth jail, built in 1885. It stands across the street from the new Law Enforcement Building that houses the sixth jail. The fifth was on the third floor level of the present Gillespie County Courthouse.

Of the first three jails, one burned down and two were razed when better ones were needed.

At the July 1852 session of the Commissioners Court it was voted that a jail be built, to be 18 by 18 feet wide, with stone walls 8 feet high and 2 feet thick. On July 19, 1852, the contract was awarded to John Ruegner and John Walch for the sum of $413.50.

Ruegner was the stonemason who built the present home of Kneese Law Office and Walch built the home which now belongs to Oliver and Nell Betty Harrison at 402 E. Austin St.

John Kleck received the contract for the "necessary ironworks" at 37½ cents per pound. According to "Fredericksburg, Texas...the First Fifty Years," this jail "stood near the east corner of the fence around the old school building on the market place." That would place it near the present City Hall site.

At the January 31, 1853, session of the Commissioners Court, a contract was given to Christ. Durst for laying a stone floor in the county jail at a cost of $26.

So, Gillespie County had a jail before it had a courthouse, as its first courthouse was authorized October 3, 1854, when Jacob Arhelger was given a contract in the amount of $2200. This stood where the present post office is now located and was razed in 1940.

By April 11, 1859, the need for a new jail had been shown and a contract was let for $900 to Ludwig Schmidt to build the second jail at a location behind the first courthouse -- approximately where Nimitz Parkway now intersects with South Crockett Street. According to the Commissioners Court Minutes, the first one was badly built and several prisoners had broken out without an effort.

This second jail was to be 30 by 14 feet of "hard rocks with vaulted ceiling", with four rooms -- three above ground, and one "underground." This second jail proved to be inadequate, too, as the records show it lacked sanitation, was too damp and improperly ventillated -- especially in the summertime.

As early as 1870 plans were underway to build the third jail, but lack of funds and various controversies caused changes in plans and building was stopped. Finally on Aug. 10, 1874, a contract was awarded to Louis Doebbler for the sum of $1645 for a jail to be erected on the "South side" of the courthouse.

This third jail is the one that burned down 10 years later. About daybreak January 7, 1885, fire broke out and the prisoner, Wm. Allison, lost his life. He had been indicted for the murder of John Braeutigam November 17, 1884, and one source states he started a fire, hoping to burn his way out of jail, but it got out of control. According to "Fredericksburg, Texas...the First Fifty Years," Penniger states "The real cause of the fire was not known, but it was assumed that somehow while the prisoner was reading, the oil lamp caused the conflagration."

Gillespie County had built its second courthouse by that time in the middle of the square. This is the building that was beautifully restored as the McDermott Building in 1967 and now houses Pioneer Memorial Library. The contract for it was awarded in January 1882 at a cost of $23,000.

On March 23, 1885, a little more than two months after the jail fire, the county closed a contract with C. F. Priess and Bro. for the construction of a new county jail (the fourth) at a cost of $9,962. It was completed in December 1885 and is still standing.

The site chosen was on a part of Townlot No. 352 in the middle of the block directly south of the Courthouse Square. The Townlot was originally granted to Justuss Herber, and title passed to Ottocar Mueller, as assignee of Justus (also spelled "Julius" at one place) Herber by deed dated November 15, 1850.

County of Gillespie, Owner

On May 16, 1855, Mueller sold this Townlot to Wilhelm Leilich, a cabinet maker, and the County of Gillespie bought the South one-half of it from Leilich on February 10, 1885, for a price of $150 to be paid for in monthly installments of $10, without interest, the deed containing the condition that it was to be used "for the purpose of erecting a jail thereon."

The contract for the fourth jail stipulated that it was to be 25 feet wide, 35 feet deep and from 20 to 22 feet high, and to have two stories. The ground floor was to have four rooms, one to be used as a lockup, and the others for the jailer. On the second floor were to be the steel-clad cells or cages.

The contract also called for "waterclosets, privy, sinks, wash sinks, water tank," etc., and advertisements for bids were placed in the San Antonio Express, Austin Statesman and Friederichsburger Wochenblatt.

The bid of C. Priess and Bro. for $9,962 was accepted. When Priess completed the job he asked for more money, however, as he said he had to dig the foundation deeper due to heavy rains and on account of having to use more rocks. After some controversy he was allowed an additional $100.

John Kollett, pioneer well digger, had the contract for digging the well for the jail at the sum of $2.75 a foot. It was to be five feet across "well walled out" (gut ausgemauert) with all the material to be furnished by Kollett. After he had worked on it a while, he petitioned the court, stating that due to heavy rains it was unsafe and dangerous to continue the first well, so he was paid $20 for his trouble, was instructed to fill up the hole and dig another well according to the original contract.

N. Ankemann was hired by the county to superintend the building of the jail at a cost of $200, but was later given an additional $120 when work continued during September, October and November, three months longer than the original contract called for.

A few changes have been made over the years since the jail was finished in December 1885, but basically it remains the same, especially the second floor.

The jail had a heavy solid steel plate door and another one with bars as the front entrance. All the windows had bars, but the ones on the lower floor and the two front doors were removed after its use as a jail was discontinued in 1939 when this building became a home for the custodian of the new courthouse, William (Bill) Heimann, and his wife.

The room at the northeast corner on the ground floor was the original "lock-up," but was used in later years as the women's cell. The door between this and the other front room is a solid steel plate, with a heavy brass key used to work the massive lock.

The rooms in the back on the ground floor were those originally intended for the jailer. The door which led from the front room into the back was a heavy steel plate, with steel frame.

Each of the back rooms has a door leading outside, and there are two windows in the outside walls. (These never had bars.) For many years, the county used these rooms as quarters for indigent persons who were dependent upon the county for their upkeep.

Iron steps lead to the upper floor out of the west front room. Part of the ceiling in this room is open, with the rest of curved corrugated steel upon which concrete was poured on the second floor.

Upstairs the front room has an open space at the head of the stairs. Against the east wall are two steel cells, each with a crude iron

lavatory and commode, and at one time there were steel cots riveted to the walls. The doors are of heavy flat crossbars, while the floors and ceiling are of solid steel plates.

Going through a solid steel door, with an opening resembling a bird cage through which food could be passed, one reached the back room.

Maximum security was provided in the back part of the second floor in the large cell and two cages in the center.

There is a "run-around" around the two cells where prisoners who were incarcerated for long periods of time could get their exercise.

The massive door leading into back room has several bars and locks. An ingenious device is the P. J. Pauly and Bro. Lever Lock which was used from the outside to open the doors of the cages into which the prisoners were to retreat, then the doors of the cages were closed again, and the officer or jailer could go in to leave food in the cell. Once he was outside of the cell door again and had barred it, he used the lever lock to open the cages and the prisoners went back into the larger cell where they ate and slept. The crude sanitation facilities were also in the larger cell.

The only heat for the upper floor was a wood heater in the corner of the back room in the "run around." When there were prisoners in the front part of the jail during bitter cold days in winter they would often have to be moved in with the others in the back cell, often crowding the quarters.

A high stone wall was built surrounding the jail, with iron pickets along the front part. The solid rock fence was topped with pieces of broken glass, designed to make escape over its walls painful. John Dietz had the contract to build the fence for $348 and Chas. Ahrens was paid $5.25 for the iron gate at the front.

When its use as a jail ceased with the dedication on August 10, 1939, of the new courthouse which contained the fifth jail, a new era opened for this old building. After it was no longer used as a residence by the Bill Heimanns, it was used for many purposes -- chiefly storage. At one time the Gillespie County Historical Society had custody of it.

Now the Fredericksburg Historic Federation is undertaking its renovation for use as a depository for historic county archives.

_____

Mr. and Mrs. Joe Bolin, Owners

BETZ-KAMMLAH HOME—NOW TULIP AND BIRD

"The Tulip and The Bird" located at the corner of West Main and North Bowie Streets may be one of Fredericksburg's **newest** businesses, one dealing in antiques and collectibles, but it is housed in one of the city's **oldest** buildings.

Built in the mid-1850's, it was first a combination store and dwelling, then for many years a home, then a rent house, then a home owned and occupied for many years by the Louis Kammlah family -- a branch of the same family that first owned what is now Pioneer Museum.

Now it belongs to Mr. and Mrs. Joe Bolin, formerly of Houston, who for several years have owned the Carl Lindig farm in the Albert area. They bought this old rock house and the entire lot on February 19, 1974, from A.N. Denton and his wife. The Dentons had owned it for only a few years, having bought it from Oliver C. W. Kowert October 9, 1970. Kowert, a real estate dealer, had bought it from the Louis Kammlah heirs November 21, 1968.

The Louis Kammlahs owned this property since May 23, 1923, when Mr. Kammlah acquired it from his brother, Henry Kammlah Jr., who on the same date had acquired the interest of his sisters and their spouses, Auguste and Louis Heimann, Lina and John Heimann Sr., Louise and Henry Henke and Emilie and Henry Marshall.

The property had been in the Kammlah family relationship ever since the father of Mrs. Henry Kammlah Jr., Peter Betz, bought if from Geo. Goehmann and wife, Maria, on May 10, 1854, paying the sum of $110 for this entire corner Townlot No. 144 and adjoining Townlot 143 (100 by 200 feet each). On that same date Goehmann had bought the same two lots for $46 from Mathias Bonn and wife. Townlot No. 144, on which the house is located, was granted to Mathias Bonn, and the adjoining No. 143, to his brother, Peter Bonn, by the German Emigration Company. Mathias must have acquired ownership of Peter's lot, too, for the deed states specifically that he conveys his and his brother's interest in the two lots.

Henry Kammlah (referred to as Jr. in this chain of title) was the second Henry Kammlah, a son of Henry I. He married Amalia Betz, Jan. 21, 1859, and for a number of years they lived here with her parents, Peter and Elizabeth Betz, who had a store in this old home that is now "The Tulip and The Bird." The Betzes partitioned some of their property, and various references are made in the deeds to the care that the Henry Kammlahs were to provide for him and for her, but there is nothing of record that shows just what kind of a store they had in this house.

Betz, the builder of this house, was a native

of Nassau and according to the 1860 U.S. census, was a blacksmith.

When the present owners bought it -- about 121 years after Betz first owned it -- they found a structurally sound building, and with only a few modifications, the house is basically the same.

Built of native limestone, the porch abuts on the sidewalk, and there is a narrow walkway between the house and the long rock fence that runs along the eastern boundary of the lot. Originally the house had no front porch -- that was added later, according to earlier owners.

Inside, the Bolins removed the plaster from the walls, repointed the rocks and cleaned them, leaving them exposed so they make a beautiful background for the lovely old antique furniture and collectibles they have for sale.

The large front room has a front entrance through large double doors, the originals of which are still in use. Flanking it on each side is a window and there is a window in the east wall. The original floor is still in this room, too, the wide, solid boards worn smooth by the footsteps of many customers, occupants and visitors in the home.

Behind this big front room is the kitchen, and though you can't tell it from the outside, there is a good-sized fireplace in the east wall of the room. This was originally used as a cooking fireplace, as well as for heating, with a waist-high raised hearth, just like those in the Kammlah House that is now Pioneer Museum. It also furnished warmth for the kitchen and the large upstairs room to which a stairway ascended out of the kitchen.

Originally the area in the front of the fireplace was paved with large field stones and the rest of the kitchen floor was board. Later occupants covered the stones with boards and closed up the fireplace chimney, putting in a stovepipe for a conventional heating and cook stove.

Now the Bolins have opened up the chimney again and restored the fireplace, with many of their beautiful copper pans, including several German "Eierpfanne" adding warmth and color to the wall surrounding it.

A frame screen porch and bathroom had been added behind the kitchen by the Kammlahs, however, the Bolins took out the bathroom fixtures, and closed up the walls with rustic boards for what is now an additional sales and display room.

Upstairs there is a large open storage space over the kitchen ceiling and here in the early days they hung their cured meats, sausage and bacon.

The front part of the second floor is a large airy room which was used as a bedroom. When the original Old Homes series was begun in 1954, Mrs. Louis Kammlah recalled how the seven sons of their family had slept up here. They were Albert, Edwin, Erwin, Felix, Louis, Ruben and Walter. An eighth son had died at the age of two years.

This room is now an ideal display space for more of the Bolins' antiques. It has two casement windows under the front roof line, and a large window in each the west and east wall. There is also a small window in the west wall, halfway up the stairway, providing light on the steps.

Outside in the yard the Kammlahs had a wood structure, part of which was the garage and a storage and wash-house. This the Bolins have incorporated into the restaurant building they put up on the west side of the old house. It is known as the "Immigrants Landing."

A fireplace has been built in the restaurant and the Bolins use some of their old furniture and antiques to add to the atmosphere, using period tables and chairs to keep the "old look."

The random flagstone paved area under the tree was extended to the entrance of the restaurant.

Helping the Bolins in the store is her mother, Mrs. Mimi Willard. She had been living on their place in Albert since they opened their business here last year and took care of it for them, as they did not move up here permanently until in January 1975. They have a married daughter, Jody, and a son, Greg.

Mrs. Bolin majored in interior decorating in college and is putting her artistic talents to work now in restoring furniture, in decorating the old home and the restaurant.

Mr. Bolin was a manager of Luby's Cafeterias for the past 14 years, most of them in Houston with a few in Corpus Christi. He put his expertise in food preparation and restaurant managements to good use.

From the days when immigrants made their home here, to the present day, this is one old house and store that has come full cycle -- it is beautifully restored and filled with furnishings of yesteryear. By its side is a modern eating place that in its name takes note of the immigrants who once lived here.

KLOTH-LUDWIG HOME—NOW THE COMPANY STORE

Most of the old homes in Fredericksburg are steeped in history and tradition, and the building at 414 East Main Street is no exception. Throughout its history it has been both a home and a store, and even a combination of both. Now its picturesque name is "The Company Store" and the owners, James R. Waldrip Jr. and his wife, Janet H. Waldrip, are operating their sewing factory, "Thee and Me," in it.

Prior to their purchase of the building, Dean and Barbara Joyner, lived here when he operated the Haversack Wine Company business, and they made many of the interior renovations.

Now the Waldrips use the large front room for their retailing of distinctive children's wear and stylized jeans, with the cutting room behind the curtain that separates the two areas. From it steps lead to the second floor and two rooms filled with sewing machines where skilled seamstresses turn out their finished garments.

Below these two rooms, on a lower level than the front retail and cutting room, are two large rooms now devoted to sorting, packing and shipping.

The shipping room was once the kitchen and steps lead out of it to what was formerly a bedroom on the upper level where the ladies now sew. The upper room at the east has two

double doors which now have a small balcony in front of them put there during the Joyner occupation. A gable above the doors adds a distinctive touch to the lines of the house.

What is interesting about its construction is that the roofline is of the same height and pitch, in spite of the fact that the house is built on three levels. This left room for a large attic with a window in front.

Its early history reflects a number of different uses for the building.

The house is built on Townlot 190 which the German Emigration Company granted to George Plehve in its original allotment and for which he received a deed from them dated January 9, 1851, but not acknowledged until May 16, 1852. Prior to that, however, in 1849, Plehve entered into contracts for sale of the lot to Cuno D. v. Schuetz, who in turn contracted to sell it to Gottlieb Fisher. Apparently these transactions came to naught, for George Plehwe (written with a "w" here) of Bexar County sold the lot to Lewis Donop of Blanco County September 6, 1860. Witnesses to the deed were John O. Meusebach and F. Wendler, the latter acknowledging on January 19, 1862, that he saw Plehwe sign it. The deed was not filed of record until June 9, 1897. Meusebach was granted Townlot 189 which adjoins 190 on the west.

Caroline V. Donop, the surviving wife of

17

Lewis Donop, deceased, conveyed the Townlot to John Adam Alberthal November 4, 1867, for the sum of $22, indicating that there was no construction of value on it.

Alverthal had owned what is now the Domino Parlor and had sold it by this time, however, he operated a "barroom" adjoining it. It follows that he built this old house when the "post Civil War" building boom took place here. Many of the larger rock homes can be dated to this period in the last years of the 1860's or early 1870's.

That the house served as home and place of business for Alberthal is evident for when he bought additional land next to this lot, in the description of it reference is made to "Alberthal's workshop."

Alberthal and his wife sold this place to Christian Kloth December 31, 1878. Mr. Koth was the grandfather of Johanna (Hansie) Ludwig, a later owner, and who with her sister, Bertha Ludwig, is in the florist business next door. They started their business, however, in this old house.

The Kloths had two daughters, one of whom married Richard Ludwig and later made her home next door. Mrs. Kloth died while quite young, but her husband continued to live in the rear of the house, renting out the front part of the building.

Different families lived in and conducted businesses here.

Arwed Hillmann, who printed Penniger's Festausgabe in 1896, and which was translated into English in 1971 as "Fredericks-burg, Texas...the First Fifty Years," operated a print shop in this building. He was also one of the editors of Fredericksburg's German newspaper, the Wochenblatt.

Among the families who rented the house were the Casper Molbergs, the Heinrich Stoffers family and Mrs. Jacob Hirsch and two daughters. For many years, the William Bruns family also lived in a part of the house. Mrs. Bruns was a sister to the Ludwig sisters.

Ownership passed to Johanna Ludwig, Kloth's granddaughter, who on January 8, 1966, sold the house and property to Midwestern Development and Realty Company of Fort Worth. The owner had his friend, Milton Moseley, do some renovating, including the adding of heating and air conditioning.

The Joyners, however, were the ones that made a showplace of the old rock house. With its several floor levels, they kept the charm of the old, but added personality and convenience.

Now it has undergone a transformation again since Mr. and Mrs. Waldrip, formerly of Houston, bought this place from the Fort Worth company for which Elton M. Hyder Jr. signed as president on April 21, 1976. Now it is their place of business, and the garments that go out under their labels to such prestigious stores as Saks Fifth Avenue and fine children's clothing stores everywhere carry on a tradition in Fredericksburg of utilizing the old houses for useful purposes and, as in this case, for promoting fashion, too.

KRAUSKOPF BUILDING—NOW OMA KOOCK'S RESTAURANT

The O. Krauskopf building at 312 West Main Street in which "Oma Koock's Restaurant" opened in June 1975 was the home of Fredericksburg's oldest business for almost 75 years. Now Guich Koock has a restaurant and beer garden here.

The Krauskopf firm had its beginning in the earliest years of Fredericksburg, when Engelbert Krauskopf, a cabinetmaker and gunsmith, plied his trade after arriving here in 1846.

The present building was erected in 1900 by Engelbert's son, Oscar, but the building in which Engelbert and later his son, Oscar, worked for many years is unfortunately one of those removed in 1961.

Engelbert Krauskopf was one of the remarkable pioneers whose inventive genius prompted by necessity, coupled with his interest in the beauties of nature, make his story and that of his home and business so fascinating. Although his old home is no longer standing, the part it played in Fredericksburg's history is worthy of having it included in this series.

Engelbert was born Aug. 21, 1820, in Bendorf on the Rhine near Coblenz. He had trained as a cabinetmaker in Germany, but since guns were his first love, he became a gunsmith. He reached the Texas coast on New Year's Day 1846. On the frontier he became a hunter for Meusebach and also did some cabinetwork

Mr. and Mrs. William Faulk (Guich) Koock, Owners

and gunsmithing.

The building and adjoining property bought by Koock includes parts of Townlots 160 and 161 which front on West Main Street and Townlot 105 which is directly behind 160 and faces on West Austin.

Engelbert Krauskopf bought Townlot 161 on December 20, 1851, from Gottlieb Fischer, paying him $35 for it. Fischer was the assignee of Jacob Wurzbach, to whom the townlot had been granted by the German Emigration Company. It was deeded to Fischer by L. Bene, Trustee for the company, on December 17, 1849.

Townlot 160, which is the farthest west of the two, was bought by Englebert Krauskopf from F. Wrede April 12, 1858, for $100. This townlot was granted by the German Emigration Company to John Mahr, and his deed from them is dated April 2, 1852. George Schneider and wife, the former Catharine Mahr, the original grantee's heir, deeded it to Wrede June 2, 1856.

These two townlots fronting on San Saba Street (now Main Street) were where Engelbert Krauskopf built his first home and had his first shop.

His first home was a log cabin which he built behind the two-story limestone house and store he constructed in 1856. He had his first workshop in a long, log lean-to which adjoined the rock house.

Meeting two of the necessities of the frontier, furniture for homes and guns to use in providing wild game for food and as protec-

tion against the Indians, Krauskopf was kept busy in these early buildings. He built and operated one of the first saw mills in Fredericksburg on this present site. Later he also added a cotton gin run by a horse-powered treadmill on this property. There was a campyard on the premises where farmers could spend the night who had come in to have repairs made or to buy supplies.

As a gunsmith, the only readymade parts Krauskopf used were the barrels which were shipped in. These came with a crude hole drilled in the middle of each, and it was up to Krauskopf to "rifle" the barrel. He also made the triggers, guards, hammers and firing mechanisms. The stocks he made out of walnut and other native wood.

The rifle he made was a general improvement of the Kentucky rifle. In later years he also made buffalo rifles. Gunsmithing became such a vital part of his life, he even used a pistol as his cattlebrand as recorded in the county records.

During the early years of the Civil War when sources of ammunition were cut off from the outside by Federal blockade of Texas and supplies from Mexico could not always be depended upon, Krauskopf faced a real challenge. He could make a gun, now could he make ammunition? His friend, Adolph Lungkwitz, a coppersmith and silversmith who lived in downtown Fredericksburg, worked with him on perfecting two machines for this purpose.

Krauskopf got the saltpeter, one of the chief

19

ingredients for making the black explosive powder, from the bat caves in Gillespie County, and for the quicksilver or mercury he made a trip to Galveston.

The small machine that formed the caps was screwed to a table and then thin, flattened strips of copper were fed into it. With each turn of the handle, a small copper cap was formed, cut from the sheet, and dropped from the machine.

Two of Engelbert's daughters, Amalia and Minna, helped fill the caps which were set up in lines on long slats of wood, grooved to hold the caps and to keep them from falling over.

They used a round stick, dipped in water occasionally, to make the powder adhere better, to fill the cups. They pressed this stick down upon the powder until enough stuck to the end, and then pressed into each cap, and then they were run through the second machine which made them waterproof and left the impression of the Texas star upon each cap.

Krauskopf was also a captain of a Home Guard company of 57 men under the command of Gen. McAdoo and Maj. D'Armand, Confederate officers stationed here.

As the years passed and the economy improved after the Civil War, Engelbert added hardware lines to the business. He sold Winchester rifles after they came on the market, and after selling 1000, he earned a silver-barreled Winchester from the company.

He made basic improvments in the original design of the rifle, inventing a dustproof loader and discharge and automatic cartridge and hull extractor. He showed the improvement to the Winchester agent, who promised him recognition and remuneration for his work, but instead the Winchester company got the patent and Krauskopf got nothing. He was so disgusted he gave away his silver-barreled Winchester and dropped the dealership.

His name, however, remains forever in the botanical records of Texas. On one of his wagon trips to West Texas where he traded, hunted and prospected for freshwater pearls, he noticed a plant with beautiful red flowers. He gathered some of the plants and took them home in his wagon, however, he could find no one that could identify them.

He sent part of the plant to Washington, asking for identification and after a long time received word that he had "discovered" in the botanical sense a new plant and that it would be named for him. Listed in Cory and Parks, Catalogue of the Flora of Texas, under the Liliaceae plant family is: "HESPERALOE var. Engelmanni (Krauskopf) Trel. Red-Flowered Yucca."

This is the plant that dots so many yards and roadsides in this area of Texas, so while he received no recognition for his improvement in the Winchester rifle, his name forever will be recorded in the botanical annals of plant-life.

Engelbert Krauskopf and his wife, Rosa, had six children: Oscar and Max; Amalia, Mrs. David Crockett Riley; Sophie, Mrs. C.E. Buchholz; Minna, Mrs. John M. Comparet; and Olga, Mrs. C.G. Hall. He died July 11, 1881, and his wife on June 27, 1884.

Their son, Oscar, carried on the family business here, building a large frame house surrounding a smaller residence he had added behind the two story stone house and store. Here the family lived which included Edward and Lawrence who had joined their father in the business; Lottie, Mrs. A.L. Cunningham; Nettie, Mrs. Emil Hahne; Irene, Mrs. F.E. Crouch; Edyth, Mrs. M.L. Bogisch; and Pat Krauskopf.

In 1900 Oscar built the structure which now houses "Oma Koock's." With the exception of this building, all the others were torn down when Community Savings and Loan Association bought the property and put up their building.

After the deaths of Oscar Krauskopf in 1940 and his sons, Edward and Lawrence, the fourth generation, Edward's three sons, Oscar, Victor and Ben Robert Krauskopf, own and operate the firm now known as Krauskopf Bros. They sold this property on Main Street to William Faulk Koock, better known as "Guich", on February 13, 1975, after moving their business headquarters to the large new structure they completed on the outskirts of the city on Highway Street.

Though the old home in which Engelbert Krauskopf lived and worked was torn down, his spirit lives on. Guich Koock has done a great job of remodeling the commercial building Engelbert's son, Oscar, put up in 1900, and it joins the Fredericksburg scene now as an eating place in which everyone can take pride.

Here Fredericksburg's pioneer heritage and architecture is being **preserved** while good food is being **served.**

20

PETER ITZ LOG CABIN—NOW ANTIQUE STORE

Until renovation was begun, you would never have thought that one of Fredericksburg's oldest log houses was almost hidden behind a giant chinaberry tree and grapevines on Main Street almost in the middle of the city. After William Faulk (Guich) Koock started restoring the old house that is part of the property he acquired earlier in 1975 from Krauskopf Bros. on the north side of the 300 block of East Main Street, the antiquity of the old building became evident.

Unless you knew it was there, the house would have escaped your attention altogether, and if you had looked behind the greenery that almost obscured it from view, you might have thought it was just another mediocre old house because its real age was covered up with a frame room in front and a porch.

Now that the old log house and the adjoining stone addition are exposed you see what a "jewel" this old place really is.

Koock was assisted by Larry Fancher in restoring the old building and now his wife, Jo Fancher, runs their antique store, "Antiek", in it.

That the old home has remained in the midst of this block on Main Street and was not torn down is fortunate, for interwoven into its history is one of the most fascinating stories concerning a pioneer settler, Karl Itz Sr.

Fortunate, too is the fact that the Fredericksburg Wochenblatt, a German newspaper published here, carried such complete and interesting stories about a couple who owned this house, Karl Itz and his wife, Henriette, both on the occasion of their golden wedding celebration in 1906 and when he died in 1908. In the latter the writer referred to his life story as being so interesting it would make a good "novel."

The story of the house and the land on which it is built goes back earlier, however, than the Itz ownership.

In the original list of allotments of Townlots to settlers by the German Emigration Company, Townlot No. 159 on which this house is located and three others that adjoined it were given to a father and his three sons. The corner lot, 157, was given to Martin Mahr; 158 to Johan Phil. Mahr; 159 to Andreas Mahr; and 160 to Johan Mahr.

All of them died in the early years of the colony, probably during the cholera epidemics, because when on June 2, 1856, George Schneider and his wife, Katharina (some places spelled Catharina), sold the four Townlots to F. Wrede, then County Clerk of Gillespie County, the deed stated that she was the daughter of Martin and that Johannes, Andreas and Johan Philipp were her deceased brothers from whom she acquired the title.

On April 12, 1858, Wrede sold No. 160 to E. Krauskopf for $100, and on March 29, 1865, he

21

sold Nos. 157, 158 and 159 to Peter Itz for $800. This purchase price indicates that there must have been a house on them, and that was probably the small log cabin, the oldest part of the house.

Peter Itz and his wife, Christine, and children came to Fredericksburg December 7, 1852, from Germany. They lived in Fredericksburg for about a year, according to the newspaper story, and then they moved to the Palo Alto community where they began to farm. To supplement the meager income from the farm, Peter and his three sons, Karl, who later owned this house in town, and Jacob and Heinrich, found additional employment in making shingles on the Guadalupe River for several years.

Karl Itz married Henriette Evers, a sister to Ludwig Evers, on October 5, 1856. He also farmed in the Palo Alto area.

When the Civil War began, Karl Itz was not in favor of slavery and rather than take up arms with the Confederate Army, he chose to join the group of Union sympathizers under Jacob Kuechler that was bound for Mexico when most of them were killed in the Nueces River massacre. A bullet fired at Itz was deflected by his hunting knife which he wore in his belt. Afterwards he wandered around in the hills, wounded and starving, healing his wounds as best he could with cactus poultices.

Karl finally made his way to his parents' home where his mother brought him food as he hid in the brush. He had taken his wife and children to live with the Evers family. His brother-in-law, Ludwig Evers, warned him, however, to leave as it would be too dangerous for everyone if he were found in the neighborhood. People were searching for him as they wanted news about the fate of the others engaged in the Nueces affair, information he did not have since a few of the survivors were still in the vicinity of the massacre, lying hidden in the Nueces hills, trying to heal their wounds with cactus leaves.

So Karl left at night, walking westward, and remained for sometime with acquaintances and friends near Llano. Then he went to Cherry Springs where his brother-in-law, Ludwig Evers, had settled. For eight months he lay hidden in the brush near the Evers home, being supplied with food which was left in a designated place from which he took it at night.

In the meantime, his two brothers, Jacob and Heinrich, had suffered a terrible fate.

They were taken by Confederate soldiers from their parents' home to Fredericksburg, under the impression that they were to be conscripted. Their father, who was not at home at the time, rode to Fredericksburg the next day to attempt to consult with the military authorities. When he came to town he heard the terrible news that they had been "summarily shot" that morning. The news story said that they were shot at the site of the "negro church" which is the small white church on East Main Street across from Super S Foods Store. This news came to Karl while he was still in hiding.

Finally, as the result of a pardon for him and his comrades, he could come out of hiding and "appeared before the authorities in Fredericksburg. From then on he was unmolested in his affairs."

While he was in hiding one of his own children and one of the Ludwig Evers children had died of diptheria.

Karl and Henrietta Itz had 13 children, five of whom died in childhood.

The Gillespie County Deed Records also throw some interesting sidelights on this property. Peter Itz and his wife, Christine, contracted to sell to their son, Karl Itz, and his wife's brother, Ludwig Evers, Lots 157, 158 and 159 on October 23, 1867. The consideration included the usual "love and affection" clause, but added "also for the consideration of the faithful help and assistance rendered to the erecting of some buildings and still to be rendered by them in furnishing material and contributing money and labor." Karl Itz and Evers were to get possession of the property after the death of the survivor of either Peter or Christine Itz; they were to furnish them necessary firewood and also "render them all childlike attendance in their helpless and eventual sick days"; they were to make payment of certain sums of money to Ad. Arhelger, minor son of Heinrich Arhelger, deceased, and his other minor children, Louise, Karl, Albert and Heinrich; also to the children of Ludwig Jung (not named) -- all grandchildren of Peter Itz. The money was payable when the children attained full age or married, however, if the two events came about before the Peter Itzes died, the payment was not due until the grandparents had died.

On August 6, 1887, Ludwig Evers and his wife, Pauline, and Karl Itz (then written "Carl") partitioned their three townlots, with Evers taking the corner lot, No. 157, and Itz

Nos. 158 and 159. Of interest is the fact that in this deed reference is made to the street that is now North Milam as being named "Susan Street."

Karl and Henrietta Itz, after he became too "infirm" to farm, moved permanently into this house in town and were living here when they celebrated their golden wedding anniversary October 5, 1906. Their children, in secrecy, planned a celebration at this home on Main Street in their honor. In the October 10, 1906, edition of the Wochenblatt, there is a short story telling about their anniversary, however, over two months later, for the December 19 issue, the paper ran a complete story with a picture of the couple. Reference is made to the celebration being a "rare event" and it probably was in those days because people's longevity was not what it is now and one or the other of a couple rarely lived long enough to celebrate a 50th wedding anniversary.

For the celebration, since the couple was so "special," the news story stated, Klaerner's Kapelle (Band) came to serenade in the evening. Earlier the choir of the Evangelical Church (as Bethany Lutheran was known then) and the Concordia Choir came and sang "several appropriate songs." The guests "were served with excellent food and drink. The table groaned under the weight of the delicacies."

Karl Itz died January 31, 1908, but his widow, Henrietta, continued to make her home here until she died September 27, 1923.

Two of the couple's sons, Rudolph and Charles Itz, inherited this property. A larger, two-story, stone building had been built adjoining the old log cabin on its east side and here Rudolph Itz conducted a saloon and his family lived in part of it until 1918.

The Rudolph Itz family and others used the little house as a "Sunday house" after their mother's death whenever they came to town from their homes in the country.

Charles Itz and his wife, Louise, and the children of Rudolph and Emma Itz, sold this property to Paul Pfiester October 26, 1944. He made considerable renovations in the two-story Rudolph Itz building, but fortunately did not alter the little old house. Pfiester sold this property to Krauskopf Bros. November 14, 1949, and they used the old house for storage. Koock acquired it February 13, 1975.

When the carpenter crew he hired began restoration work on this old house it was like

pealing off layers. The different stages of construction were easily discernible.

The oldest part is the one room log cabin, built rather high off the ground, so the cellar below it had "windows" in the back and two side walls -- about a foot or more above ground. There were also several shelves, some open and others with doors -- in recesses in the thick stone walls. The floor is dirt.

Steps of stone to the cellar were placed at the front west corner, and next to them steep, short steps led to the front door. This room had one window flanking the front door and a window in the east wall which has been made into a door way because the logs are so deteriorated. There was also a door in the back and the west side wall.

As restoration progressed, the mode of building the earliest log cabins was clearly visible. So often they were in such a hurry to get their homes built that they did not take the time to strip all the bark off the logs, and such is the case with many of these logs in the little room. The ceiling beams are pegged, and the long, stout pegs can be seen as new beams replaced those that had rotted. This roof was repaired with some cypress logs which Ty Cox located and had "ripped" (sawed into boards) at a mill. Windy Goff, head of the restoration crew, cut them in two to use as the roof supports which were later covered with cedar shakes.

Behind the log cabin is a small room with solid rock outer walls, and the back of the log cabin serving as the fourth wall of this room.

Through the doorway in the west wall of the log cabin, you step down into the later rock addition to the house. The larger of the two rooms, in front, had apparently once been partitioned, and later a room of frame construction was added at the front. This has been torn away, leaving the aged limestone which blends well with the adjoining logs.

How fortunate for Fredericksburg -- that through all these years -- this little log cabin built by an early settler and its rock additions have been left untouched while many similar "jewels" have been torn down because they were considered "too unsightly." Its survival is almost as fantastic as that of one of the men who once lived in it.

William Faulk Koock and his wife sold this property to his brother, Tim Koock, October 15, 1976, and "Antiek" is no longer located in the log cabin.

Lucille and Fred Dietel, Owners

EVERS BUILDING—NOW GALLERIE OF FINE ART

Because its early history is so closely interwoven into that of the old Itz home in the same block, the story of the corner building at 342 West Main Street adds its interesting chapter to the history of old homes along Fredericksburg's Main Street.

Now occupied by an art gallery, the building has been used for many purposes, but was built as a combination home and store.

Following publication of the story on the Itz home, some interesting information came to light when a great-grandson of the man to whom the corner Townlot on which it is built called at the Standard office. He was Chester Schneider of Prairie Mountain Route, Llano, who was a grandson of George and Catharina Schneider, and a great-grandson of Martin Mahr, the father of Mrs. George Schneider, and to whom the German Emigration Company originally granted this lot.

Mr. Schneider pointed out that the family name was "Mahr" -- spelled with an "a". He knew from family history that Martin Mahr and his three sons died in the cholera epidemic, leaving only his grandmother, Catharina, the daughter of Martin Mahr, as their survivor. An uncle, Philipp Klaerner, reared her, and from the very early Probate Records in the county clerk's office, interesting information on Martin Mahr's estate was learned.

Philipp Klaerner was appointed administrator of the estate, and his account showed that April 3, 1847 he paid $10.75 "for

goods and boards for a coffin." The inventory showed four Townlots on San Saba Street (now Main Street) rented to Frederick Pape, valued at $50. Among the other items listed were 12 yards linen cloth, $1.50; 11 yards cotton cloth, $2.30; 3 bed sheets, 50 cents; 1 watch, $5; 6 pewter plates, $1; 6 teaspoons, 30 cents, 1 spinning wheel, 20 cents; 1 cow and calf $10; 1 steer, $4; and other household items. There was also a claim against the German Emigration Company for $108.63.

Klaerner's account also showed that May 8, 9, 10, 1847, he paid $3 for labor done on lots; May 17-20, mending fence, $3.50; on July 3, 1847, for "15 days going and coming to bring a cow from Santa Clara," $15; October 18, for 3 load bricks, $3.75; Oct. 21-28, repairing the house, $4; for boards, $3; and on November 11, two doors to the house, $2; nails and boards for the door, 35 cents, hooks and hinges, $1.50; November 12-17 for six days work, $6.

January 1 to May 1848 he was allowed $16 for boarding minor (Cath. Mahr -- later Mrs. Schneider); two trips from Llano to be sworn in as guardian, $6; and on December 17, 1848, $4 for making a trip to San Antonio to get the claim of Cath. Mahr recorded in County clerk's office.

Among his receipts for May 1847 to November, 1850, were $12 house rent; $4 rent for the hut; $24 for house and hut; and additional sums of $8, $6.55 and $4 for rent.

The term "hut" used here is English for the German word "Huette" used often in describing a very small house that was evidently located on the corner lot.

Philipp Klaerner was discharged as administrator June 28, 1852. Chester Schneider recalled that his grandmother, Catharina Schneider, had been reared by her uncle by the name of Klaerner.

He must have been a good business man, because when the original county records were destroyed by fire in 1850 he had duplicate deeds made from the German Emigration for these Townlots the Mahrs were entitled to as well as some he was entitled to, and filed them for record.

George Schneider and his wife, Catharina Mahr Schneider, sold this corner lot, No. 157, together with the three adjoining ones along Main Street, to F. Wrede, then County Clerk of Gillespie County, on June 2, 1856. This deed stated that she was the daughter of Martin Mahr and that Johannes, Andreas and Johan Philipp Mahr were her deceased brothers from whom she inherited the title to the other three.

Two years later Wrede sold the easternmost townlot, No. 160, to E. Krauskopf for $100, and on March 29, 1865, sold Nos. 157 (the corner lot), 158 and 159 to Peter Itz for $800.

From Peter Itz and his wife, Christine, ownership passed to Karl Itz and a brother of Mrs. Karl Itz, Ludwig Evers, by deed dated October 23, 1867. In this deed reference is made to "some buildings" on the property and still to be erected, for which Karl Itz and Ludwig Evers agreed to furnish material, money and labor, with the Peter Itzes retaining the right to live there with the grantees to get possession after the death of the older couple.

Ludwig Evers and his wife, Pauline, and Karl Itz, partitioned their three lots on August 6, 1887, with Ludwig Evers and his wife taking the corner lot, No. 157, and Itz the other two. In this deed reference is made to Susan Street -- the street now known as Milam Street.

The corner lot has remained in the same family ever since. In a partition of the Ludwig Evers property after his death, one of the daughters, Lina, Mrs. Hy. C. Keyser, received the Northwest ½ of Townlot 157. Lina Keyser died November 1, 1936, and her daughter, Lillie Bierschwale, wife of Walter F. Bierschwale, inherited this Northwest ½ of this lot on which this building stands. On March 30, 1972, Mr. and Mrs. Bierschwale deeded this property to their daughter, Lucille, and her husband, Fred E. Dietel.

Mr. and Mrs. Ludwig Evers farmed and ranched in the northwestern part of the county, but in their old age moved to town, settling in the little log and rock house which was adjacent to this place.

A simple floor plan was followed by the original builders of the structure. Downstairs there was one large room, with a thick stone wall dividing it from the smaller back room. Underneath this is a large cellar.

At one time the steps led up along the east wall on the inside of the building, but these have been removed and an outside stairway put in their place.

The upstairs was originally one large room, which was later divided with frame partitions, but these were removed by later tenants. When the building was renovated by Mrs. Keyser, the front was knocked out and show windows added and additional windows were added upstairs. There are no openings of any kind on the west side of the building.

At one time the John Knopp family lived upstairs and he operated a saloon downstairs, selling groceries and also some staples, too. During these years this place also figured in the "beer war," a fact mentioned in Knopp's obituary. At that time Probst was brewing beer here and selling it for 10 cents a glass. Knopp imported it from San Antonio and sold it for 5 cents. Tales were told long after of the rush on his bar.

Once a doctor who felt that goat's milk would cure most people's ills occupied the building and kept a lot of goats here to supply the demand. It was not great, however, so he did not stay long. A dentist office, a millinery store operated by Mrs. Louis Henke, Otto Schneider's grocery store and Schneider Produce, Walter Knopp's grocery store, Haversack Wines and W-K Electric were other tenants.

Now that the Gallerie of Fine Arts' owners, Mr. and Mrs. Karl B. Guiney, occupy the building, visitors can see and buy their art and gifts attractively displayed in one of the city's oldest buildings.

Mr. and Mrs. John Cotter, Owners

WILLIAM C. HENKE HOME

Carved in the limestone rock above the doorway of the old William C. Henke home at the corner of West Main and North Milam Streets is the year "1886", the year in which the house was built.

It is now owned by a native of Fredericksburg, Dorothea (Doris) Weinheimer Cotter, and her husband, John, who lived in San Antonio, but spend much time in Fredericksburg. They were two of the 1975 recipients of awards given June 12 by the Gillespie County Historical Society for their research in the history of this area and for their generous donations of books and the research data they have compiled on people, places and buildings.

The house has an interesting early history, and for almost 60 years it was in the William C. Henke family.

Townlot 156 on which it is built once belonged to Sophie Spaeth, the widow of Ludwig Spaeth who was murdered by the Indians in 1870 at age 39 while at work in the fields on his place near Enchanted Rock. Mrs. Spaeth was a daughter of Peter Behrens, who was granted Townlot 155 which adjoins 156 on the west.

No. 156 was granted by the German Emigration Company to P. Friess on the original list of allotments. Behrens acquired Friess's claim to the corner lot and on November 21, 1849, signed a paper authorizing the company to make title to Townlot 156 to Julius Splittgerber. On September 24, 1851, a deed was signed by the GEC conveying No. 156 to Splittgerber as assignee of Behrens.

Splittgerber and his wife gave Sophie Spaeth, widow of Ludwig Spaeth, a mortgage on this lot as security for a $1000 note, due in 1874. He defaulted on the note, so following a judgment dated October 26, 1876, and foreclosure, Mrs. Spaeth bought it at sheriff's sale for $120 on August 7, 1878.

Sophie Spaeth and some of her children, Heinrich, Louis, Frank and Mary, sold the Southeast one-half of Townlot 156 for $350 to William C. Henke on April 4, 1885, with the provision that her minor children, Jacob and Wilhelm, would quitclaim their interest when they became of age, and they did so December 27, 1890.

William C. Henke was one of seven sons of Fredericksburg's pioneer butcher, Heinrich Henke, who founded the first Henke Meat Market "downtown" at the corner of East Main and South Lincoln. Five of these sons followed their father's trade and went into the butcher business. Richard and Hugo con-

26

tinued in the downtown location founded by their father; William founded the Uptown Henke Meat Market; and two brothers, August and Henry, moved to Kerrville where they opened a meat market. The other two brothers, Alfred and Otto, were farmers and ranchers.

Their five sisters were Anna, whose first husband was Chester B. Nimitz, (parents of Fleet Admiral Chester W. Nimitz), and after his death, she married his brother, William Nimitz; Lina, Mrs. Adolf Weber; Sophie, Mrs. Otto Evers; Mina, Mrs. Henry Hirsch; and Elise, Mrs. Charles F. Kiehne.

When William Henke founded his butcher business uptown he had his shop at first on the front porch of this old home. Butchering of the animals was done at various locations near town, and then the meat, sausage, bacon and ham was sold from the front porch.

The porch was enclosed with "Laden" (shutters) and wooden flaps which could be raised. It made an ideal place to sell meat to customers who could walk or drive right up to it. They also had a delivery wagon which was used for making the rounds in the city selling or delivering meat.

Later, Henke erected a frame structure back of the house over a huge cellar. The butcher shop was then housed in this building. The cellar under it was so large that the entire family could gather around a table for meals here when the inside of the rock house was being painted. Still later, William Henke's sons erected a concrete block building next door in which they carried on the meat market for many years. This building now houses Hill Country Marine Sales.

All of the William C. Henke children were born in this house, and all of the boys helped "papa" in the butcher shop with most of them making this their livelihood in adulthood. The shop was closed in 1949.

There were 10 children, of whom one girl, Dora, died in infancy. The others who grew up here were Louis; Walter; Albert; Alex; Bertha, Mrs. Arthur Kuenemann; Felix; Ella, Mrs. Albert Kordzik; Emil; and Fritz.

The house has double, glass-paned doors over which is an ornamental transom with unusual-shaped glass panes. Originally the front hall extended back to the kitchen at the northeast corner. At the south side was the parents' bedroom, and across the hall their living room. Behind this was the "spare" bedroom.

Upstairs the floor plan was much the same, except that there was one large room at the west side and there were two rooms at the east side, with a central hall. The Henkes used the second floor as sleeping quarters for the children.

The William Henke heirs sold the house to R.B. Reissig and Max E. Schneider October 24, 1944, and they in turn sold it to Hans E. Lindenberg October 22, 1945. From Lindenbergs the title passed to Henry Pfeiffer April 30, 1947, and the Pfeiffers then sold it to the Cotters June 19, 1948.

After the Cotters bought the house, they made some changes, doing a lot of the construction work themselves when they came here on weekends and during vacations. They have converted it into a duplex and many people have rented it during the years that followed their purchase, most of them using it for residential purposes while some also put it to professional or business use.

BESIER HOME—NOW SUNDAY HOUSE RESTAURANT

The large two-story Sunday House Restaurant was never a "Sunday house," as its name seems to imply, but the nucleus of the structure was once an old rock home of Fredericksburg. When it opened to the public in June 1967, the business provided this area with facilities not available before--a restaurant with atmosphere, a private club, and a large convention center and meeting room. Now it's a place to go for a good time, for good food and good fellowship.

The old house which forms part of the building has seen other aspects of life, however, for its history shows the hardships that early inhabitants endured.

It is built on a lot granted by the German Emigration Company to Johan Heinrich Behrens in the original list of allottments, and his deed from the company is dated January 12, 1850. Title passed from his daughter, Anna Elisabeth, who married Chr. Althaus, to Daniel Garrison on July 18, 1866, for the price of $60. On August 17, 1867, Garrison and his wife sold the lot for $70 to F. Dambach.

Dambach made improvements on the lot, possibly the rock house, for when he sold it on May 31, 1869, to Elizabeth Itz, the consideration was $450 paid to Dambach on behalf of the grantee by Peter Itz.

Little is known as to who lived in the house for the next few years, for the house was rented to strangers, and for a while was also vacant. On August 18, 1881, Elizabeth Itz sold it to Mrs. Anna Besier for $400. She was the widow of George Besier, and it was from the daughter of this couple, Mrs. Theo. Heep, who later lived in the block behind this house, that information on the old home was gained for the original series in 1956.

Mrs. Heep recalled that after her father died, her mother was left with four young children and no place to go. For a while they made their home with her parents, the John Schmidtzenskys, but when time came for the oldest child, Mrs. Heep, to go to school, it was deemed advisable to buy a house in town. When Mrs. Heep was seven years old, her mother bought this house and lot, and she started to school in the old "Schwester Schule" as St. Mary's School was commonly called.

Mrs. Heep also had one brother, Joe Besier, and two sisters, Amalia, Mrs. Ad. Weinheimer; and Bertha, Mrs. Weigand.

Mrs. Heep, in 1956, recalled how her mother helped support herself and her small children. When they moved to town, they brought with them their livestock which included several cows and four horses. Mrs. Besier traded four horses for three lots across the street and kept the cows there. Through the sale of milk, butter and cheese, she was able to earn a little money.

She recalled how the children would trudge

off early in the morning with three or four buckets on their arms as they delivered milk to the Nimitz Hotel and other customers up the street. Then they returned home to get their school satchels and would carry some more milk as they went up the street to school.

They also had a large vegetable garden here from which they sold surplus produce. By hand they had to pull up the water from the old "dug" well to water their garden.

Mrs. Heep also recalled another childhood experience. She was allowed to help with candlemaking. Eight tallow candles would be made from the mold at one time, and her chief delight was being allowed to pull the string through for the wicks.

The house in 1956 had changed very little, with the exception of some improvements inside, and the addition of a small porch in the front. It is one of the few old two-story rock homes built in an L-shape.

The wing that extended to the street had one large bedroom at the front with a door which led out under the porch. Behind it was a smaller bedroom with a frame partition separating the two rooms. The steps ascended out of this smaller bedroom to the upper floor.

The other wing of the house had one large room with front door which the Besiers used as a bedroom and later occupants as living-dining room. The crude steps led from here into the cellar which is one large room extending the entire length of the front wing. This is now the restaurant's wine cellar, but renters who lived here before the Besiers kept their chickens in there at night for safekeeping. People were often so desperate for food that they stole chickens at night.

Behind the side wing was a small one-story addition which Mrs. Heep recalled as their kitchen. It was so crudely constructed that during the winter the cold winds blew through the cracks. Mrs. Heep recalled that often her mother would bundle up on cold mornings, go into the kitchen to cook breakfast and then bring it into the warmer rooms for the family to eat.

The upper story had the same floor plan as the lower floor, with three bedrooms which were well-lighted and ventilated. There was a door at the east bedroom to which a stairway must have been planned originally.

Mrs. Besier deeded the house and lot to Joe J. Besier April 9, 1924. Robert Besier bought the house and lot from the other Besier heirs February 6, 1962. Through the years it was rented by different families, with Mrs. Willie Mae Merz as the occupant at the time of the 1956 feature story.

Robert Besier and his wife sold the property to Sam Parker December 27, 1966, and he in turn conveyed it on May 8, 1967, to Fredericksburg Enterprises, Inc., the corporation which built the Sunday House Restaurant.

The entire outer structure of the house was retained as the front for the restaurant building. The plaster on the interior of the old home was chipped off, the rocks were repointed and the rough finish on the walls makes a perfect background for the front of the restaurant. Extensive additions provided the rest of the space that now serves as a gathering space for conventions, meetings, wedding receptions, other social events and for intimate dining in the restaurant or club.

Mr. and Mrs. Udo Henke, Owners

HENKE HOME—ADMIRAL NIMITZ BIRTHPLACE

Houses are often best known for the role the owner or builder played in the community, or because of a well known person who was born there. Both cases apply to the Henke home at 247 East Main Street, also known as the birthplace of Admiral Nimitz. An historical marker at the site gives the history in capsule form:

"Typical early Fredericksburg home built 1866 by Carl Basse. (**Author's note:** this may be inaccurate, as Carl Basse never had title to the land) Property of Henke family since 1873. Heinrich Henke, early settler, Confederate freighter, had butcher counter on front porch; meat processing was done in back yard; there the horses that pulled meat vending cart were stabled. Shop later built on foundation of stone walls surrounding lot.

"Henke and his wife, Dorothea (nee Weirich) added the long dining room and kitchen with sloped roof to accommodate the 12 children. Many of the furnishings are preserved by Udo Henke, a descendant.

"In small room to rear of front bedroom, on February 24, 1885, their daughter, Anna Henke Nimitz, gave birth to Chester William Nimitz, destined to command the greatest Naval Armada in history.

"A 1905 honor graduate of the U.S. Naval Academy, Nimitz was chief of staff to Commander, Atlantic Submarine Fleet, WWI, installed first Naval ROTC unit in US Navy,

1926; selected Commander in Chief, Pacific Fleet, after attack on Pearl Harbor; appointed Fleet Admiral, U.S. Navy 1944. As representative of the U.S. he signed Japanese surrender documents on his flagship, USS Missouri, September 2, 1945, in Tokyo Bay. Admiral Nimitz died in San Francisco on February 20, 1966."

While this property has been in the Henke family for over 100 years, during the years that preceded their ownership many transactions took place. This was a choice location and it is significant that the Townlot on which the house is built, No. 229, was one of two allotted to L. Bene, a trustee for the German Emigration Company. The company, by another trustee, Gustavus Dresel, formally deeded the lots to Bene April 10, 1848, and he sold the corner lot to James Ferguson and Henry Hesler on the following day. Afterwards it was inherited by James Ferguson, according to Comal County Probate Records, and in a partition was allotted and transferred to Alexander Ferguson, the surviving partner of the firm of "Ferguson and Brother", on June 8, 1859.

Alexander Ferguson's estate, by its administrator, on September 24, 1860, deeded Townlot 229 to Louis Weiss. A year later, September 24, 1861, Weiss sold the lot to Edward Tips for $125 cash.

30

Tips sold the lot to Charlotte Basse February 12, 1866, for $175. She was the wife of Henry Basse, a Lutheran minister, but who is listed as a "merchant" on both the 1850 and 1860 US censuses. During her ownership the main part of the house was built.

Charlotte Basse, as principal, and Carl Basse, as surety, made a bond for title, agreeing to sell the property to Heinrich Henke on October 1, 1873. He paid $1050 cash and agreed to pay the balance of $3000 which was due to August, Wilhelm and Carl Koennecke as a claim against the lot. This was done and Henke received a warranty deed dated March 4, 1876 from Mrs. Basse.

Heinrich Henke, born June 23, 1837, in Braunschweig, Germany, came here in 1856. He married Dorothea Weirich here in 1861. She was born in Coblenz, Germany May 20, 1844. They had 13 children, one of whom, Max, died in infancy.

The twelve who lived in this home were William C.; Anna, whose first husband was Chester B. Nimitz, the father of Adm. Chester W. Nimitz, and who married his brother, William Nimitz, after his death; Otto; Lina, Mrs. Adolf Weber; Henry Jr.; August; Alfred; Richard; Sophie, Mrs. Otto Evers; Mina, Mrs. Henry Hirsch; Elise, Mrs. Charles F. Kiehne; and Hugo.

He founded the first meat market in Fredericksburg in 1867, according to his published obituary, so he must have rented these premises at that time as he did not get title to it until 1873.

The butcher shop at first was in a small wooden shed attached to the east side of the front porch. The front had a wooden flap which was propped up with an iron rod, and the customers stood on the sidewalk to make their purchases.

The kettles used for heating water and making "kochwurst" were at about the same location they are now in the building next door, however, they were not enclosed in the early days because of the danger of fire.

The boys in the family helped butcher, tended to stock and worked in the market. The girls helped their mother in the home, but they also had duties in connection with the meat market. They scrubbed out the meat delivery wagon each evening, and the next morning spread a clean cloth on the floor on which were laid the steaks, chops, roasts and other meat. This was then topped with another clean cloth before the wagon made the rounds in the city to sell meat.

The long front porch was used in the evening when the chores were done and they could sit here to relax and visit with company who came by. Thursdays, "der schoene Tag", the mother and girls would often sit here, too, as they patched and mended clothes after the week's washing and ironing and baking was done.

The front entrance is through a double door with a very special lock and hardware. The brass key for the lock is almost five inches long. Originally there were only two rooms in the front, but the Richard Henkes (later owners) put up a wood partition wall to make a hall between the living room at the west and the front bedroom at the east side.

There is a small bedroom behind the front bedroom in which the future admiral, Chester W. Nimitz, was born. Across the hall is a bathroom, but originally the Henkes used this as a bedroom.

Behind these rooms is the dining room and the kitchen which were added later. The rock walls of the old home are almost two feet thick and are covered with plaster. Originally the house had a shingle roof, but this was covered with tin later.

Upstairs is a large attic or half-story where the boys slept. Originally the entrance to this was by way of a stairway on the outside of the west wall, but when this property was sold, the stairway was moved to the east side. In this side yard at the west was where the Henkes kept the horses.

When Richard Henke, one of the sons, married, the Heinrich Henkes and the unmarried children, moved t to their farm. The Richard Henkes made their home in this house while he conducted the business in the meat market that had been erected at the corner of the lot. The other Heinrich Henke heirs deeded the property to Richard Henke September 27, 1926.

After her husband's death, Mrs. Richard Henke continued to make her home in this house, while her son, Udo, ran the meat market. She and her daughter and son-in-law, Helen and Ralph Gold, deeded the home and market to Udo Henke January 2, 1947, and he still owns the house. It has been vacant since his mother's death, and most of the furnishings are preserved intact. The meat market was closed several years ago when Henke retired.

————

Fleet Adm. C.W. Nimitz Memorial Naval Museum Commission, Owner

NAUWALD HOUSE

The old Nauwald house on East Main Street next to the Admiral Nimitz Center literally made a cycle of ownership when it passed into the possession of the Nimitz Commission October 18, 1974.

It was built in 1874 on Townlot 185 which Admiral Chester W. Nimitz' grandfather, Charles H. Nimitz, bought at a sheriff's sale June 4, 1855, along with the two adjoining lots.

In the intervening years, there were several other owners and many different tenants who used it for many different purposes.

Now, however, the old building is destined to have a part in telling the Nimitz story to all who visit the Center.

The townlot was allotted to J.L. Ransleben by the German Emigration Company, and ownership passed to Joseph Martin. To satisfy a judgment against him, Townlots 184, 185 and 186, were sold at sheriff's sale June 5, 1855, to Chas. H. Nimitz for $385. Of interest is the fact that what is now Washington Street which adjoins the Nimitz Center on the east was referred to as Kleine Creek (Little Creek) Street in the deed.

Nimitz was the builder of the Nimitz Hotel. One of his daughters, Bertha, married Charles Nauwald on January 23, 1868. She was his second wife and he had a son by his first wife, Charles Nauwald Jr.

After Bertha and Charles were married,

they at first lived in San Antonio where he worked for Hugo and Schmeltzer. Their oldest children, Anna and Albert, were born there. Her father deeded part of Townlots 185 and 80 to the Nauwalds, June 17, 1874. When they moved back to Fredericksburg they located in the Weber building which stood at the corner of East Main and South Lincoln Street where Weidenfellers now operate a Magnolia service station.

Mr. Nauwald was in the commission business, buying potatoes, corn, wheat and such commodities from local farmers which he in turn sold to the government for use at such places as Fort Mason and Fort McKavett.

When this building next to the hotel was finished, the Nauwalds moved in and he expanded his business to include a complete line of general merchandise as well. He conducted his business under his own name, "Charles Nauwald."

The Nauwalds also lived in this building, and even today, it shows what a complex structure it was, with three different levels for the original thirteen rooms. Alterations and additions were made over the years, but from Mrs. W.H. Schaefer, the former Ella Nauwald who was a daughter of Charles and Bertha Nauwald, a good "picture" of the house in the early days was obtained for the time this house was featured September 7, 1955, in the original series.

The store was in the big room at the front, the plate glass windows having been added by later owners. Originally there was only the large front double door. There is one large window in this portion facing the Nimitz Hotel and here the Nauwalds had their office, and for the children, the window was a favorite exit from which they jumped into the Nimitz courtyard to play.

One doorway in back of the store leads into the driveway at the west side, another exit from the store leads to the lower level, a semi-basement, and another leads to the upper level of rooms. This last entrance had been closed by a more recent owner, but has now been opened again with the small steps leading from the large front room to the upper level rooms.

The room on the lower level behind the store on the east side was used as a warehouse for store supplies. The smaller room with arched ceiling on the west of it was the storage bin for perishables, such as potatoes, which were kept in the large sand bins.

Behind the warehouse room is a very large room which the Nauwalds used as their dining room and everyday sitting room. Three large windows face the hotel and afford ample light and air for this. The outside doorway led into an open space or gangway in line with the rest of the building.

At the corner of this part of the building is a small room which originally was a pantry, but later became a kitchen. At first the kitchen was divided from the dining room by a frame partition which was later removed. The steps led out of the dining-sitting room to ground level. From here the rooms are strung out -- one behind the other.

The first was a "durchgang" the old-fashioned counterpart of our modern breezeways. The wall towards the driveway was closed up, however, that side facing the hotel originally had green wood lattice-work set above the knee-high rock wall. The rest of the wall was later closed up with hollow tile with two windows in the center. The Nauwalds had their well in this part of the house. Often, this part of a house, when a well was located in a room, was called the "Brunnenhaus".

Behind it was the servants' room and behind that the washhouse and general utility room. In much later years a small frame addition was added behind here for use as a kitchen and bath.

The upper level of the house was reached from the store via the short steps. The first room was a large bedroom with windows opening towards the hotel. The Nauwald children slept here, and next to it on the west, was their parents' bedroom.

Behind the bedroom was a spacious hall with double doors of paneled wood which opened towards the driveway. Above them is a fancy glass transom.

The original steps which led down to the ground level were wide and imposing with bannisters at each side. The entrance was recessed for a width equal to the bedrooms at each corner.

Behind the hall was the family "parlor" and at the corner was another bedroom. From here steps also led up to the upper floor above the store building. This was used for storage, and has two small windows in the east and west walls, and two larger ones in the wall facing the street. In chipping away the plaster, there is also evidence now that once there were also steps leading to the attic along the back wall of the store.

All this added up to a lot of rooms for the Nauwalds (and later tenants partitioned some to make the number even larger). The space was all needed by the family, however, for there were seven children, and since Mrs. Nauwald helped her husband in his business by assisting with the bookkeeping and in waiting on customers, she always had "live-in" household help and to assist in making all the children's clothing.

Getting them ready for school was no small task, Mrs. Schaefer recalled. Mrs. Nauwald would cut the garments, using the store counters for most of this work. She would be joined by a seamstress, one of whom was Miss Cornelia Lungkwitz, who would do all the machine sewing and finishing at the Nauwald home.

The Nauwalds used Grandpa Nimitz's hotel bathhouse for their bathing. The bathhouse, which is still standing, was close to the Nauwald living quarters. Huge boilers heated the water for the four large tubs in the compartments in the bathhouse.

In later years two bathrooms were added to the Nauwald house by partitioning some of the original rooms.

The children of Bertha and Charles Nauwald included Anna, Mrs. Fritz Luckenbach; Albert Nauwald; Lina, Mrs.

Peter Schramm; Sophie, Mrs. Emil Toepperwein; Dora, Mrs. Tom Gott; Ella, Mrs. W.H. Schaefer; and Bertha, Mrs. E.H. Riley. Two died in infancy.

The Nauwalds conducted their business here until sometime after 1890 when they moved to Burnet where he ran the Burnet Hotel.

After this, Richard Burrier and F.J. Maier conducted their store here under the name of "Burrier and Maier", and the Burrier family resided in the living quarters. Still later, Emil Riley and his father ran a grocery and general merchandise store here under the name of "George Riley and Son".

The Nauwalds moved back into the house after a few years. Mr. Nauwald died Sept. 1, 1900, and on January 17, 1913, Bertha Nauwald sold the property to Otto Braeutigam. Mrs. Nauwald died October 30, 1933. Braeutigam did some of the remodeling, as the granite stone in front indicates: "O.H. Braeutigam 1931."

Braeutigam's widow sold the property to Eddie Grobe September 27, 1944, and five years later on October 1, 1949, Grobe sold it to Paul Pfiester. While it had been used as a grocery store in some of the intervening years, Pfiester used the premises to conduct his second hand furniture store.

Pfiester sold the property to Wade E. Basemore October 27, 1964. He had grandiose ideas of a tourist and visitor center adjoining the Nimitz Center, but these never materialized and A.L. Myrick eventually acquired the Nauwald house. Through his generosity, it now belongs to the Fleet Admiral Chester W. Nimitz Memorial Naval Museum Commission who acquired it October 18, 1974.

The front of the building is once again a store, appropriately named "The Nauwald Mercantile Company." Here, in miniature, various rooms have been arranged, some with authentic furnishings, of the rooms to be restored within the Nimitz Center when it once more assumes its steamboat-shape. Souvenirs, toys and candy are for sale.

There's room for other exhibit areas and administrative offices, and plans are to use the basement for research area.

It's good to have the Nauwald building back in the "Nimitz family" helping to tell the story of the illustrious World War II Naval leader, Fleet Admiral Chester W. Nimitz.

RUFF HOME—NOW PART OF NIMITZ CENTER

An old home that was in the Schmitz family and their descendants from the time it was built in 1872 until it was sold to the Rodolphs Smiths in 1971 is now a part of the assets of the Admiral Nimitz Foundation and the Admiral Nimitz Center development. This is the two-story Ruff home that sits majestically on a high corner lot overlooking Town Creek at 502 East Austin Street.

The Ruff home was in the long-range development plans for the Nimitz Center, but when funds for its purchase were not available, the Smiths bought it, restored the exterior and renovated the interior. When funds were available from the Moody Foundation, Houston, it was purchased by the Admiral Nimitz Foundation March 19, 1975.

It is being used by the Nimitz Center now as a guest house. The townlots facing on Austin Street which adjoin it where all the wartime relics have been moved from their former location at the Center on East Main Street will "tell" the story of Nimitz and his part in winning World War II in the Pacific. Tall pines have been planted, a rustic security fence is under construction, the relics are in place on concrete pads or in natural surroundings, and the trail to be laid out will take visitors through the meaningful display.

These same visitors can glance at the cornerstone of the rock house Peter Schmitz, a stonemason, built on the corner lot and see that they are back over 100 years. He carved his initials and those of his wife, "P.S.-T.S." on the top line, and below that "L.A. JAN. TEN 15, 1872." Who the L.A. refers to is not known, however, it may have been his helper. He misspelled the German term, "den," as "ten" in the date line, meaning for it to be "JAN. THE 15, 1872."

Peter Schmitz and his wife, Therese, at one time owned all of the entire block bounded by East Austin, North Lee, East Schubert and North Elk Streets. From the German

Emigration Company he received as his allotment Townlot 487 at the northeast corner of the block nearest the City Cemetery entrance. On the list his name is given as "Peter Schmidt." He and his first wife, Anna Maria, lived in a log house on this lot, and in the years that followed he, in his name, or in the name of his second wife, Therese, acquired title to all the other lots in the block. Therese was the widow of Edward Moritz and had five children, one of whom, Clara, married Johan Petri and was the mother of Mrs. Jim Ruff from whose heirs the Smiths bought the property.

Behind his two-story home, Schmitz also built a rock smokehouse and next to that later added frame barns. Since he was also a freighter, this block gave him enough room to keep his animals, and enough space for a large-scale garden or a bit of small-scale farming.

In the years that followed various changes were made in the house, with restoration by the Smiths after they bought it bringing back the original lines on the exterior. This included taking out the two large gables that had been built into the front roofline, and closing up a small window on the west side that had been hewn out of the wall by later owners.

The Smiths also made extensive changes in the interior. The upper floor had never been "finished" and here they made a large bedroom with ample closet and storage space under the eaves towards the back, together with a tiny bath and dressing room.

The steep stairs that led out of the kitchen were left "as is", but some partition walls were removed, and a commodious bath was added at the west corner on the first floor.

Next to it is the kitchen area, complete with "dry sink" and modern conveniences, such as plumbing, were artfully worked in without destroying the character of the old home. There is now one large room in the front with the front door leading out onto a raised set of steps.

At the time the Smiths bought the property, descendants of the builder recalled that for a long time there were two huge beams behind the house which were used as benches. These came out of the Vereins Kirche when it was dismantled late in the 1800's. Efforts to locate them failed.

Schmitz also built a rock fence around part of the west side and front of his block, but some of these rocks were removed by Mr. Ruff for Mrs. Leroy Denman when she made improvements in the Walch house and its surrounding rock fence which she owned at the corner of the block immediately to the west of the Ruff house.

A number of other people owned Townlot 481 on which the house is built before Peter Schmitz acquired it. It was granted to George Goehmann by the German Emigration Company. John Schmidt and his wife, Caroline, sold it to Gottfried Ottmers November 12, 1858, for $65, and by deed dated December 12, 1857 (a year before his own deed is dated unless a mistake was made in the records) Gottfried Ottmers and his wife, Wilhelmine sold it and the adjoining Lots 482 and 483 to George Leineweber for $325. On February 9, 1860, George Leineweber sold the three lots to Jacob Schmidt, together with other property. Jacob Schmidt deeded Nos. 481, 482 and 483 to Therese Schmitz on July 12, 1867. There's also another deed to Therese Schmitz from Anton Maier for Nos. 481, 482, 483 and 491 on February 6, 1871. Maier's interest in this property was vague as he acquired from Chr. Doebner on Aug. 10, 1869, that undivided one-fourth interest in the unsold portions of the survey on which these lots are located which was sold by the bankruptcy trustee for John H. Herndon (to whom it had been patented) to Doebner on July 6, 1869.

On May 7, 1883, Peter Schmidtz and his wife, Therese, made a conditional gift deed to their "minor children," Peter and Ferdinand Schmitz, of several lots in this block, among them the one with the house on it. It was made on the condition that the parents had the right to live there for the rest of their lives, men-

tioning that the children of Edward Moritz, deceased, had been given real and personal property on Palo Alto Creek.

On March 27, 1902, the two brothers, Ferdinand and Peter Schmitz, partitioned the lots, with Ferdinand getting title to Nos. 481, 482, 483 and 484. It remained in his name until April 17, 1926, when Ferdinand Schmitz and his wife, Annie, sold to James Ruff Townlots 481, 482, 483, 484 and 485, the lots now owned by the Nimitz Foundation. Ferdinand Schmitz had acquired title to some of the other lots under the will of his father, Peter, "concurred in" by his mother, Therese. The father, Peter Schmitz and builder of the house, died in 1888.

As the Ruff children married, they moved away from their old home, and after the death of both parents, the children, Werner Ruff, Marvin Ruff, Norma Boos, Dora Fritz, Wanda Birck and Annie Grobe, sold it to the Rodolph Smiths September 4, 1971.

Now the house sits as a symbol of peace, tranquility and pioneer skills at the corner of the half-block extension of the Admiral Nimitz Center with wartime relics of the 1940's to the east of it. The windmill in front of the house will soon be operative and pump water from the old well to be used in irrigating the landscaping of the area, thus its usefulness continues in this Bicentennial year.

SCHNEIDER-KLINGELHOEFER HOME

One of Fredericksburg's well-preserved old homes along the city's main thoroughfare is the old Schneider-Klingelhoefer home at 714 West Main Street. With its front porch adjacent to the sidewalk, it was built in the style of homes in Europe which were usually built that way. Now dense shrubbery in front of the porch provides privacy for the occupants.

The house was the home of Mrs. Arthur (Lilly) Klingelhoefer and her late husband for many years, but she sold it to Rudolf F. Huber of Cook County, Illinois, March 25, 1976.

Townlot No. 133 on which it is built was granted by the German Emigration Company to Christian Aug. Hahn. Title to it shows up, however, in the name of a minor, listed variously as Daniel Conrad Ch. Hahn, Daniel Hahn, and Wilhelm Daniel Hahn. An affidavit filed at one time states that the last was his

"true Christian" name.

While tracing the ownership of these old buildings and the lots on which they are built is relatively simple, in some cases, as with this, there are voids, but a knowledge of early history helps to fill the "blanks".

During the early years of the colony, many Fredericksburg settlers died during the two cholera epidemics that hit the settlement. Townlots and Outlots were allotted to the original settlers and when they died, their survivors, often orphaned children, fell heir to them. Such was the case here, and a number of different applicants petitioned to be his guardian as he was entitled to a Townlot, an Outlot (or Ten-Acre Lot) and a land certificate for 640 acres in Fisher and Miller Colony in the Giddings District issued to Wilhelm Hahn.

The lot was sold at "public outcry" July 3,

Rudolf F. Huber, Owner

1855, for $9 payable half in cash and half in 12 months.

Who built the house is not definitely known, but this Townlot and four others, Nos. 133, 134, 136, 137 and 138, being all of those facing on Main Street in this block, with the exception of No. 135, were sold by Andreas Jaeger to Ludwig Schneider, along with an Outlot and a section in the Fisher & Miller & Grant on January 2, 1869, for $370 cash.

It is known that Ludwig Schneider lived in this house, as recalled for the 1954 series by Albert Henke, a grandson of the Ludwig Schneiders. Mr. Schneider was an ''uhrmacher'' and ''maurer'', a watch repairman and a stonemason, two unrelated trades, but typical of the pioneers who often, through necessity, become proficient in several trades.

From the Schneiders title passed to H. Habenicht by trustee's sale January 4, 1879. He paid $575 cash for Townlot 133, 134 and Outlot 584. Habenicht sold the lot to Charles F. and Louis Priess November 24, 1883, and Charles F. Priess sold his interest to Louis Priess September 6, 1887. Priess sold it to Mary Neal Brodie, May 8, 1890, who lived here with her husband, S.L. Brodie. They sold it to Aug. Koennecke June 30, 1894, and the Koennecke heirs conveyed it to A.W. Klingelhoefer of Salt Lake City August 27, 1914, who in turn conveyed it to A.H. Klingelhoefer, July 31, 1924.

At various times in its early history the house was rented, among early occupants being the August Zinckes and the Ad. Wehmeyers.

The house, as remodeled by the Arthur Klingelhoefers, still has the original doors with immense locks and heavy brass keys. In their renovation they made their bedroom on the west side of the front two rooms and their living room in the east end. Behind the living room is a small bedroom which they first used as a dining room.

Originally the kitchen at the back was one long room, however, the Klingelhoefers converted the west end into a bathroom and pantry. A small frame porch was added by the Klingelhoefers at the rear of the house.

There is a large attic with two windows at the east end and a window and ''laden'' at the west end. There is no outside stairway, and no one could recollect that there had ever been one, however, access to attics like this where often the boys in the family slept, was by means of a ladder or short, steep interior steps.

The beautiful oak tree at the west end of the lot is typical of the stately trees that grew in great profusion at the site of the colony when the settlers arrived here. Most of these were felled to provide logs for construction of the first homes.

But it is trees and homes like this that give Fredericksburg its charm and appeal .

J.J. KLINGELHOEFER HOME

The oldest home built in Fredericksburg still in existence and use is the Johann Jost Klingelhoefer home at the corner of West Main and South Acorn Street.

It is built on Townlot 271 which the German Emigration Company assigned to "Klingelhoefer" when the original allotments of Townlots and 10-acre Outlots were made. His granddaughter, Lyne Klingelhoefer Lewis Harper, now owns the property, and though she no longer resides there, she maintains the old home, using the back part of it as her art studio. She frequently shows the house during the old home tours and pilgrimages sponsored by the Gillespie County Historical Society.

Until her marriage to J. Watson Harper, Mrs. Harper lived here -- the same house in which she, her brothers and sisters, and her father were born.

Julius Klingelhoefer, Mrs. Harper's father, married Sophie Tatsch, a daughter of John Peter Tatsch, the man who built the old Tatsch home with the big chimney. This Klingelhoefer house was their home, too, with Mrs. Klingelhoefer surviving her husband and dying at age 92 in 1949.

Because this place has been home to three generations for all of their life in Fredericksburg, there is so much family memorabilia and so many furnishings preserved in it that its story is almost endless.

Johann Jost Klingelhoefer (later known simply as "John") was born July 11, 1802, in Eibelshausen, Nassau, Germany. In Germany he had trained as a professional surveyor, but because he wanted to leave that country and seek freedom from the political and economic conditions that prevailed there, he decided to migrate to Texas. By his first wife, Elisabeth Weil, he had four children: August, Louise, Elizabeth and Henrietta. After her death he married Elisabeth Heiland and with her and the children sailed to America on the Johann Dethardt. By oxcart they came to Fredericksburg in the spring of 1847.

Providing a home for the family was his first concern, and he pitched a tent on his Townlot and set to work building his new home in this new land. This is the oldest part of the present house -- the front rooms.

It had two rooms with a "durch gang" (breezeway) between them which was later enclosed to make the third room. Above this was a half-story or attic in which the boys slept. Originally access to this upper level was by a narrow, steep set of stairs. Below the front room on the west side, he excavated a huge cellar which is still in use.

The outside stairway was added in later years.

In building the house, the first Klingelhoefer used the fachwerk style so familiar in Germany, and finding the logs was no great task as immense trees grew all around. To fill the space between the horizontal and vertical logs, he made his own handmade bricks, and these were later covered with plaster.

In this new home in Texas two sons were born to the family, Julius, the father of Mrs. Harper, in 1851, and William in 1853.

The elder Klingelhoefer interested himself in the affairs of the new colony and was elected as the third Chief Justice (the equivalent of the present office of County Judge) in 1851; he took steps to become an American citizen soon after his arrival here; and he was a charter member of the first Democratic Club formed in this county. His wife died in 1881 and Johann on May 1, 1886.

Julius brought his bride to this old home in 1886 and the couple's children were all born here. They were Olga, Mrs. Otto Dittmar; Nellie, Mrs. August Stahl; Lyne, who after the death of her first husband, H. Welge Lewis, married J. Watson Harper; Robert W. Klingelhoefer and Gus Klingelhoefer. A grandson, Robert Dittmar, was also born in this house.

Some remodeling was done by the Julius Klingelhoefers. The open area between the front two rooms was closed and a cypress wood door was installed as the front entrance in 1900. Originally the bedroom was where the present living room is at the west end, and the east room was used as the living room and is now a bedroom.

Behind these two front rooms, the "leanto" addition was added after the Civil War. There was a small bedroom at the east end and a larger kitchen and dining room at the west end. The entrance to the cellar which had been outside the original two rooms was covered with a trapdoor over the steps which is still in use in the kitchen floor.

A bathroom was later added at the west side behind the kitchen and the rest of the area behind the house is a big room with windows in the two outer walls which Mrs. Harper uses as

her art studio. Her oil paintings and sketches are prized possessions in many collections and galleries.

Although the house was continuously lived in and cared for, renovations and repairs finally had to be made, so in the late 1950's the owners moved out so the restoration could be carried out. Some of the good wide boards in the floor were utilized in rebuilding the front entrance, and new flooring was added in the front rooms.

The fireplace in the front room at the west end had been closed, but this was again opened and made operative. In the very early days, there had also been a fireplace in the east room. The ceiling beams had to be replaced, although ones just like those in the original rooms are still in place in the ceiling above the cellar.

While the construction details of the old home are interesting, of just as great interest are the furnishings. Mrs. Julius Klingelhoefer's father, John Peter Tatsch, was a cabinet maker and several pieces of furniture he made are in this house. Among them is some child's furniture which was made as a Christmas present for Tatsch's daughter, Sophie, Mrs. Julius Klingelhoefer. There are also some chairs and other pieces, outstanding of which is the large "schrank" (wardrobe) to which he added special touches as he always did for a member of his family. Carved decor on it includes a lyre and a star.

When the Julius Klingelhoefers were married, Sophie wanted a "store bought" bedroom set -- not her father's handmade furniture which is so widely prized now. The bed, dresser and washstand in the front bedroom, therefore, were bought at Kuenemanns' furniture store. In the little bedroom behind it, however, is one of Tatsch's prized handmade beds of walnut that he personally selected from the banks of the Pedernales and aged for several years.

Other handmade furniture includes a chest of cypress and long-leaf pine and another piece made of cypress, walnut and long-leaf pine.

There are so many choice antiques and memorabilia of the early days of Fredericksburg, of the people that lived in this house, and of their relatives and friends, which have been so carefully preserved by the granddaughter of the builder that it can best be described as Fredericksburg's "mini-museum."

Jessie L. Thompson, Owner

KNOPP BUILDING

An old building on Fredericksburg's Main Street that recently underwent change in ownership and some exterior renovation is the one at 410 West Main Street. Here Knopp Insurance had its headquarters before moving across the street into their new building.

Vincent Knopp, the owner, sold it to Jessie L. Thompson October 26, 1976, and she has opened an antique store, "Jessie's Antiques" in it.

This pioneer building is built along lines found in many rock homes, but what sets it apart is that it has an interesting link with Gillespie County history dating back to over 100 years ago when the sheriff and tax collector had to give up ownership of it to satisfy a deficit in the funds of his office.

Built on Townlot 155 which was allotted to Peter Behrens by the German Emigration Company when the original allotments were made, the deed to him from the company is dated Nov. 11, 1852. He deeded it to his daughter, Sophie Spaeth Dec. 10, 1870, and on the same date she conveyed it to F.C. Radeleff for the price of $650, so it is assumed that the house, or part of it, was built by then.

During the time Radeleff lived here, he also conducted a store in the front of this building. He was sworn in as Sheriff and Tax Collector of Gillespie County May 26, 1874, but his term of office was short-lived. On December 21, 1874, John Walter was sworn in, taking over the office of Sheriff and Tax Collector. To make restitution to Gillespie County for the

"deficiency" Radeleff and his wife, Agnes, deeded this Townlot to F. Probst on January 26, 1875. Probst paid them $500 cash and "assumed payment of $1400 to County of Gillespie, being the deficiency of Radeleff in the settlement of the balance of county and school taxes as late Sheriff and Collector of taxes, and the claim of Willis and Bro. and Mrs. Spaeth for $150.

Probst was considered one of the best brewers in this section of the state, but he had his brewery elsewhere and did not consider this his homestead.

He kept this property until March 17, 1896, when he conveyed it to E. Wahrmund. Wahrmund sold it to John Knopp December 16, 1896, for $1,250.

John Knopp was a pioneer merchant who conducted his general merchandise business in the two-story combination store building and home across the street. He also made his home there with his son, Anton and family, so it was logical for his other son, Jacob, to move into this house across the street, so he would be near the place of business.

Like many others, the wide walls of the house are of limestone. Originally the front two rooms were one, probably when the store was operated here by Radeleff. In the days when the Knopp family lived here, the room on the west was a bedroom, and the one on the east was the family parlor. Each room has a front entrance door.

A thick stone wall divides this part from the

rest of the house, with only a door from the west front room to the room behind it. This door and the door leading out of the back of this room were constructed of vertical or upright boards. The Knopps used this as their family dining room, but earlier occupants probably used it as their kitchen.

The Knopps added the frame part on the northwest corner in which their kitchen was located. The room at the northeast corner of the rock building was originally used as a bedroom.

The Jacob Knopp family moved here some time after the property passed into Knopp ownership. Jacob Knopp had married Auguste Knopp, a sister to the girl his brother, Anton, married. He was born in Eitelborn, Germany, on July 2, 1865, and came to America with his father, brother and sister, when he was a child. His mother and a sister had died in Germany.

The Jacob Knopps had ten children, four of whom died in childhood, Max, Benno, Zelima and an infant. The other children were Alvin, Robert, Lawrence, Jacob, Auguste, Mrs. Felix Burg, and Paul.

Jacob helped his father in the store across the street, and after John Knopp's death, Jacob and his brother, Anton, ran the business. Jacob died May 23, 1913, four years after his wife's death, however their children until they married or made their home elsewhere, lived in this old house. After Paul and Jacob married, they also lived here, and for a number of years it also was rented to different tenants.

Ownership passed to Henry L. Ellebracht Aug. 4, 1943, and to Mrs. Lawrence Knopp on Aug. 5, 1943.

Vincent Knopp and his late father, Lawrence Knopp, conducted their insurance business in this building until the business was moved into its present location.

Now antiques, perhaps some dating from the period when this home was in its original use, are sold here.

FRIEDRICH KIEHNE HOME

One Maria and her family lived in the two-story rock home at 405 East Main Street when it was built in 1850 and now another Maria lives there 125 years later with her family. But the coincidence does not end there -- the first Maria was German and the second Maria's background is German, too.

The second Maria probably takes as great pride in the authentically restored house now as the first Maria did when she must have been proud to live in what was Fredericksburg's first solid stone house -- and also the first two-storied house -- when it was built in 1850.

The house was built by Friedrich Kiehne and his wife, Maria Kreinsen, in 1850, and on January 27, 1973, it was acquired by Maria and Ronald Herrmann who restored it.

Built on Townlot 220 which was allotted to Wilhelm Keidel by the German Emigration Company, it was deeded by the company to Friedrich Kiehne as assignee of Keidel. Since early records were destroyed by fire, a duplicate deed was made dated November 14, 1851, and acknowledged April 22, 1853.

Kiehne was a "messerschmied" or cutler by trade in Everode, Germany. His first wife died in Germany when their son, Frederick, was an infant. He then married Maria Johanna Kreinsen. With her, Frederick, and their other children, Maria Johanna, William and Minna, he sailed for America on the ship "Margarethe" along with other immigrants from Hanover.

The two girls died, one at Indianola, and after they came to Fredericksburg. A daughter, Sophie, who died in early childhood, and three boys, John, Carl and August, were born to the couple in Texas.

At first Friedrich Kiehne lived in a log cabin on Creek Street, considered one of the most desirable streets by early settlers because of its fertile soil, but he moved several years later. According to Penniger's "Fest Ausgabe," published in 1896, in telling about the growth of the colony, reference is made to Kiehne's house: "With increasing prosperity came the desire to enjoy the blessings thereof. The primitive houses were replaced by better ones. Mr. Kiehne erected the first stone building, using the soft stone which he quarried at Cross Mountain. The surrounding

Mrs. Maria Herrmann, Owner

hills yielded many kinds of building stone, and the limestone hills supplied good lime.''

The house that Kiehne and his wife built in 1850 emboided many touches of refinement in construction details not seen in any other of the early homes. His two-story structure with large attic under the steep-pitched roof is reminiscent of German homes, however, Kiehne added a two-story porch, a concession to early Texas architecture.

At first he probably built only the four front rooms, two on the ground floor, two on the second floor, and the large attic which was reached by a disappearing stairway from the upper porch. That he built the back four rooms (two on each floor) about ten years later was determined by the workmen who restored the house under Mrs. Herrmann's supervision. The rear one-story portion was added sometime in the 1930's.

The walls of the old house are 24-26 inches thick and in order not to disturb them one air-conditioning unit was installed for the first floor and another was put in the attic for the second story.

All of the restoration work was done slowly and deliberately so that which was still good of the old would not be disturbed and that those parts that had to be rebuilt would be authentically restored. W. K. Perrett did most of the work and Tyrus Cox, who has become quite a restoration specialist, helped with the project.

The two front rooms each have large double doors, arched gracefully at the top and with glass panes in the tops of the panelled wood doors. Kiehne, the builder, in addition to being a cutler was also a blacksmith, a skill greatly needed on the fronter. He made most of his own hardware used in the house, and when fire years ago almost destroyed the front doors, the massive key was lost for a while in the rubble under the floor. Maria Herrmann found it, however, and had duplicates made by Arthur Kneese.

The two front rooms are furnished as a parlor (on the east) and the living room is on the west side. In the latter room the fireplace was re-opened that had been closed up by later owners.

All the old floors, which had deteriorated, were ripped out and replaced with random-length wide planks laid over the carefully-prepared sub-floor where the electrical conduits and air-conditioning ducts are located.

The room behind the parlor on the east is the master bedroom now, and there is an arched doorway between the two rooms. The original double doors were found intact in the attic, complete with the hardware, and were put back in place.

Behind the living room on the west side is the dining room. From it an indoor stairway was added. There is also a stairway outdoors under the front porch.

The part added in the 1930's is what is now the kitchen, providing also a large closet area, a bathroom, and a utility room where the washer, dryer and air-conditioning unit are housed.

The doors to the closet area are some Mrs. Herrmann picked up on the San Jose Mission grounds where they had been discarded to be burned. With their leaded glass tops they look pretty when illuminated from inside.

The kitchen has all the modern conveniences one could wish for, including a microwave oven, but it is so carefully put together with an island counter and serving area that it blends in perfectly with the "old" look of the house.

On the second floor there is a "kitchenette" which the children can use in a room which is also an ideal place to study and play games at an old table of magnolia wood found in the attic of the house. In between the back two rooms is a bathroom, complete with a toilet with raised tank and pull flush chain. The small bedroom in back is David's, the only boy in the Herrmann family. His sisters Karin, Carol and Helen, share the second floor with him.

The two front bedrooms have large doors leading out onto the second floor front porch. These doors have panes in the upper half which can be opened for ventillation, yet with the bottom closed, allowed privacy in the days before air-conditioning. Here again Kiehne, the builder, showed a touch of elegance in the construction. The upper part of the wooden beams over the windows are arched and of choice hewn wood.

The windows throughout the old part of the house are of special interest. The upper part of the window is stationary, but the lower part is a casement-type window, both sides of which can be swung open. To replace a pane is like taking a puzzle apart and putting it back together again, as the various pieces of wood have to be carefully removed.

There are so many features of the house that are distinctive and unusual -- both in the original construction and in the Herrmann restoration that it is impossible to describe them all. As Mrs. Herrmann stressed, the house is very functional and very comfortable, but as far as possible all the original details and design were retained.

There's a lot around, too, to remind the visitor of Friedrich Kiehne. He did blacksmith work at this place, and often the Indians brought their horses to him to be shod. Though he could not understand their language, they communicated by signs and got along well. While digging under the kitchen floor, they found many arrowheads there, as well as in other places in the yard, indicating the Indians busied themselves with their arrowhead-making while waiting for the horses to be shod, or else just used the occasion to toss away some of their less-than-perfect specimen. Mrs. Herrmann has preserved these arrowheads.

From Friedrich Kiehne's heirs title to this property passed to Marius Mathisen August 20, 1904, and reference in the deed is made to its being known as "the old Kiehne place". Townlot 220 fronted 100 feet on Main Street and ran back for 200 feet, and behind that is an "unnumbered townlot" extending to Barons Creek which was included in the transaction.

(This area is now the Herrmanns' garden.) Kiehne had also acquired in the early years title to several lots to the east of his original one.

When Marius Mathisen and his wife, Annie, sold the property known as "the old Kiehne place" to Frank H. Petermann and H. Foerster March 1, 1906, the deed mentions that included in the sale is "one gasoline engine, a wood saw and wood splitter and all appliances to a wood yard that is operated on said lots."

H. Foerster died and the heirs, who included the wife of the other co-owner, Frieda Petermann; Bruno Foerster; Olga Foerster Appleby; R.T. Gliddon, Inez and Marie Gliddon, husband and children of the late Emilie Foerster Gliddon, deeded the property to Walter Foerster on October 4, 1927. When the Herrmanns bought the property January 27, 1973, it was owned by Otto W. Schmidt and Lillie Fischer. The latter had been married to Foerster and lived in this house for many years.

Now there is an official Texas State Historical Medallion and plaque on the old Kiehne house. Carefully preserved under the front porch is the stone in which the original builder carefully carved his name and that of his wife and the year in which he built his house: "1850. Friedrich Kiehne - Maria Kreinsen."

Now a second Maria is the "lady of the house" and once more the house is a home for a family that appreciates the true beauty of the 125-year old stone home. It has been filled with furnishings in keeping with an elegant old Fredericksburg home. It's almost a mini-museum, but one which is functional and lived in.

Mr. and Mrs. Milton Crenwelge, Owners

WILHELM CRENWELGE HOME

"Three In A Row" might be a good title for the three old rock homes in the 400 block of West Main Street. A sub-title might be "...And Once There Were Four!" One old combination log cabin and rock house was torn down many years ago.

The Wilhelm Crenwelge home at 415 West Main Street which now belongs to Milton Crenwelge (no relationship) is located next door to his business, Crenwelge Motor Sales. The old house which was torn down years ago stood west of it.

This is one of the biggest old homes on Main Street, and was built in the 1860's. It is located on Townlot 256 which the German Emigration Company granted to Franz Gross and deeded to his assignee, Gottlieb Fischer, December 17, 1849. Fischer sold it to John (Johannes) Schmidt March 7, 1850, for $30. Schmidt must have built the first log cabin on it, for when he sold it to Jacob Schneider August 4, 1852, the deed states that he is selling his "city lot and home with all improvements thereon."

The deed from Jacob Schneider to Wilhelm Crenwelge in October 1860 is signed by three witnesses and the acknowledgement states that "Jacob Schneider of Bexar County" was "a blind man." The price was $60.

Mrs. Otto Kolmeier, the former Dorathea Crenwelge, a daughter of Wilhelm Crenwelge, was still living when this "Old Homes" series was first published in the mid-1950's

and was full of recollections about this house and the other old homes which are still standing near it, as well as the one which was torn down. Dorathea Crenwelge Kolmeier also wrote her name "Dora," but is affectionately recalled by many who worked with her in Holy Ghost Ladies Aid Quilting Circle as "Doretchen."

The Wilhelm Crenwelge family lived in the combination log cabin and rock house west of this large two-story house and his parents, Mr. and Mrs. Peter Crenwelge Sr. lived in the newer big house after it was finished. Wilhelm Crenwelge was known also as George William, and often wrote his name as G.W. Crenwelge.

He and his father were both wheelwrights and conducted this trade at these premises, having their shop on the front porch of the Wilhelm Crenwelge home -- which faced east towards this two-story house.

The big house had its front porch abutting on the sidewalk, and there are three broad stone steps along the entire length of the porch. This porch was torn down years ago when the lumber rotted. The front entrance is through the large double doors which lead into a hallway. Originally there was only one large room in the front, but when the house was leased to tenants by the Crenwelges, frame partitions formed a hall with two rooms at each side.

Eye-catching are the wide cypress planks in the floor, some as wide as 18 inches. Some of these were taken up from the older Crenwelge house next door when it was torn down.

There are no windows downstairs on the west side, a door opening out of the southwest corner room in the back being the only opening. This corner room was the Crenwelges' kitchen and dining room.

At the southeast corner in back is another small room which has a very small fireplace in the wall. This room has a door which leads out the back. Between these two rooms is a small hallway, which also had a door leading out the back. Out of the hall, steps lead up to the second floor, while another set of steps leads down into the cellar.

The steps leading to the upper floor make three turns before opening into the small hallway in the back. On either side of it are two bedrooms which have a window in each outside wall. The front part of the upper floor is on a higher level and consists of two rooms. The one on the northwest corner is the smaller one of the two. Double doors open out of the large room onto what was one once the large two-story porch that ran across the entire front of the house.

The house is so high that there is still room for a big attic above the second floor. It has small square windows in each the west and east walls.

Below the first floor of the house, all along the east side, is a large cellar, the walls of which are lined solidly with rock. It is divided into two rooms, with an archway between them. Stone steps lead down with a trap door above part of them forming part of the hall floor.

There are seven large slanted openings in the walls of the cellar, so the air is fresh and sweet-smelling, not the least bit musty.

Mrs. Kolmeier recalled in 1956 that they used this cellar space for storing food and staples. Her grandfather Crenwelge also kept his wine barrels here.

Mrs. Kolmeier at the time had a large crock which her mother kept in the cellar and used for storing butter during the winter. In those days they didn't milk the cows during the coldest winter months, so would make a large amount of butter for storage and use during that time. It stayed fresh and sweet in these crocks.

When Mrs. Kolmeier's family lived next door, Mrs. Kolmeier loved to visit with her grandparents in this large old rock home, and since her's was a large family, they used the cellar space below it for storage. Her brothers were William and Adolph Crenwelge, and her sisters were Mary, Mrs. W. L. Surber; Lina, Mrs. Peter Ahrens; and Sophie, Mrs. H.A. Holtzer. One brother, Henry, died in infancy.

This two story rock home was the scene of at least three weddings, one of them that of Otto Kolmeier and Dorathea Crenwelge in 1898. At that time no one was living in the big house, so the wedding ceremony was held upstairs in the large front room, while the sumptious wedding meal was served downstairs.

The other two were those of two teachers. One was that of Alice Tucker and a Mr. Mogford who settled on a ranch near Junction. Miss Tucker was a teacher in the Fredericksburg College, a Methodist school operated in the middle building on the old Public School campus. Professor Chas. F. Tansill, principal of the school, and his wife were renting this house during the early 1880's and Miss Tucker lived with them.

The other was that of another teacher, Belle Anderson, and Charles Morris of Morris Ranch. Mrs. Kolmeier recalled that one afternoon she, Miss Anderson and Grandmother Crenwelge were sitting on the back steps of the house shelling peas. Miss Anderson asked them to watch for a pod containing nine peas. They found one, and she hung it over the front doorway, saying that she would marry the first single man who walked under it. That was on Wednesday, and on Friday, Mr. Morris, a stranger to her, came to see Prof. Tansill on business. He and Miss Anderson became acquainted, and when he called on her the next week, the family started teasing her. Sure enough, the old superstition came true, for the two were married in this old house.

After the Tansills moved away, the house was vacant for a number of years. A Dr. Stammer lived here for a while and R.M. Burrier conducted a store in it at one time.

The heirs of Wilhelm Crenwelge and his wife partitioned their property, and in a deed dated March 14, 1935, Mrs. Surber and her husband, conveyed this house and lot to William and Adolph Crenwelge, Dora Kolmeier, Lina Ahrens and Sophie Holtzer. The two brothers conveyed their interest to the three sisters on June 12, 1939.

The three sisters sold it to Chas. Dolezal September 26, 1945, and a month later, on October 13, 1945, he sold it to Erwin C. Kraus and Paul A. Kraus. The Krauses used the building for storage as their soda water bottling business, Fredericksburg Coca-Cola Bottling Company and Pearl Beer Distributing Company was located nearby at the corner of the block.

The two Kraus brothers sold this property to Mary Crenwelge (no relationship to the earlier Crenwelge owners) January 28, 1966, and she conveyed it to her son, Milton Crenwelge, January 2, 1972. He operates his business, Crenwelge Motor Sales, in the building immediately east of this old home.

Mr. and Mrs. Milton Crenwelge are very conservation-minded, and he had the old roof replaced with an authentic shingle roof as the old one was leaking and he wanted to protect the interior. His interest in conservation has also extended to restoring and preserving a little Sunday house in this same block south of this building, fronting on West San Antonio Street.

———————

CRENWELGE RENT HOUSE

The second old home in a row of three in the 400 block of West Main Street is one that was in the Crenwelge family for 95 years before it was sold by them. When it was built in the late 1860's or early 1870, it was built as a rent house and that's just how it is being used now.

It now belongs to Carl Kraus of Austin.

Located at 419 West Main Street, it is built on the Southeast one-half of Townlot 257 which was granted by the German Emigration Company to Conrad Kolmeier (spelled "Kollmeyer" on the original list). He was the grandfather of Otto Kolmeier, who in 1898 married Dorathea (Dora) Crenwelge, a daughter of Wilhelm Crenwelge, the builder of this house. Her family lived in the combination log and rock house that was formerly located next door.

Conrad Kolmeier and his wife contracted to sell the townlot to Ernst Dannheim January 14, 1851, for $25. On July 7, 1851, Ernst Dannheim conveyed to his wife, Juliane Kalberla, some real estate, including his interest in this townlot for the "consideration that my wife has given me since we are married $800."

The contract between Kolmeiers and Dannheim was never formalized, so on May 31, 1856, both men, for $60, conveyed full title to Louis Martin to Townlot 257, stating that due to "mistake in deed both join in this conveyance." In four months time Martin must have figured its value increased because

September 23, 1856, he sold it to Christian Kraus for $67.

Wilhelm (William) Crenwelge bought the townlot from Kraus April 12, 1865 for $50 and his descendants owned it until 1960.

At the time the original series appeared in 1956, Mrs. Otto Kolmeier was still living and recalled several interesting details about life in this part of the block. Her brother, Adolph Crenwelge, who later owned the house, worked on it as a young boy, and she thought it was built in the late 1860's or early 70's.

This house sits back a little farther from the street than the first two-story Crenwelge house to the east. There is room for a small flower garden between the porch and the sidewalk and over the years, that's just how it has been planted, with big mesquite trees shading the front porch.

The original floor plan was very simple, the house being only one room wide with two rooms downstairs and two upstairs. There are two front doors flanked by a window at each side under the front porch. The room on the east side also has a window in the east and south (back) wall.

There are no openings of any kind on the entire west side of the house, with the exception of a small opening in the wall of the attic above the second floor.

Many of the tenants used the west front room downstairs as the kitchen, and in later years an addition was placed behind it providing a bathroom, small hallway and "washhouse". The east room was used by some as a living room and by others as a bedroom.

The steps lead up through the center of the house. The room at the east side is closed off from the rest of the second floor with a wall and two doors. The other large room has two windows to the north facing Main Street and two in the south or back wall.

There is a big, well-ventillated cellar below this house.

Wilhelm Crenwelge (also known as G.W. or George William) died July 5, 1923, and his wife, Sophie, died January 7, 1930. Their children included William; Adolph; Henry who died as an infant; Mary, Mrs. W.L. Surber; Lina, Mrs. Pete (Peter) Ahrens; Dora (Dorathea), Mrs. Otto Kolmeier; and Sophie, Mrs. H. A. Holtzer.

When they partitioned their property, the Southeast one-half of Townlot 257 on which this house is built was conveyed to William and Adolph Crenwelge, Dora Kolmeier, Lina Ahrens and Sophie Holtzer by the other sister, Mary Surber, on March 13, 1935. On June 12, 1939, Adolph Crenwelge acquired the interest of the others. The Adolph Crenwelges were ranchers, but they used this house in town as a

"Sunday house" when they came to town, and they also lived here for a number of years when their grandchild, Harriet Crenwelge, now Mrs. Martin Schlaudt, attended school in town.

Sarah, Mrs. Adolph Crenwelge, died in 1943, and Mr. Crenwelge on January 16, 1947. Their only child was Werner Crenwelge, who inherited this house from his parents. He rented it out to various tenants, but for many years retained the right to use one of the upstairs rooms as a "Sunday house" when they came to town for services at Zion Lutheran Church and for other purposes.

Werner Crenwelges sold it to Alfred Moellendorf on March 27, 1960, and he in turn sold it to Erwin C. Kraus, a partner in the soda water and beer distributing firm at the "Kraus corner," on February 26, 1963.

Mr. Kraus is now deceased, and his wife conveyed it to her son, Carl, who now owns it. He is a lawyer and an accountant with the accounting firm of Ernst and Ernst and now lives in Austin.

The present owner has done some work on the house to preserve it, and the tenants keep the yard so pretty that is is definitely one of the picturesque assets along Fredericksburg's Main Street.

JOHN SCHLAUDT HOME

The third old house in a row near the "Kraus Corner" of the 400 block of West Main Street does not look like such an "old" house, but part of it is! And its early history is interwoven into that of the two old rock houses still standing to the east of it, but unlike them, this house served as "home" for the builder's family for many years, and his widow lived to a very old age and spent her last years in this house.

At first glance the structure at 421 West Main Street looks like a "not-so-old" concrete block house, but that is only because of the face-lifting given the old limestone rock house that serves as the nucleus for it.

It now belongs to Louise (Mrs. Steven) Montgomery, a daughter of Mrs. Erwin C. Kraus and the late Mr. Kraus from whom she received title December 30, 1974.

The oldest part of the house was built by

Johann (John) Schlaudt, a young blacksmith. It is located on the Northwest one-half of Townlot No. 257 which the German Emigration Company originally granted to Conrad Kolmeier. Up until it was sold to Wilhelm (William) Crenwelge April 12, 1865, its chain of ownership was identical with that of the "middle" house, the Adolph and Werner Crenwelge home. It was even in the present owner's family over 100 years ago when Christian Kraus, her great-grandfather, owned it from September 23, 1856, to April 12, 1865. He was the father of Jacob Kraus Sr., who founded the soda water factory at the corner of this block.

Wilhelm Crenwelge and his father, Peter Crenwelge, conducted a wheelwright business at the combination log cabin and rock house which stood between the big white-plastered two-story rock house at 415 W. Main St., and

Mr. and Mrs. Steven Montgomery, Owners

the rock house now owned by Carl Kraus at 419 W. Main St.

Johann (John) Schlaudt, a young blacksmith, decided this would be a good location for his business, so he bought the Northwest one-half of Townlot 257 from Wilhelm Crenwelge and his wife, Sophie, on April 18, 1871. The Crenwelges included this provision in the deed: "provided that we reserve for our own use the crop which is already planted out for this year." Evidently they got a good early start on their spring garden or corn crop that year.

The price Schluadt paid indicates that there were some improvements on it -- probably the small log house which stood in front of the rock house that is the nucleus for the present house. The purchase price was $340, $100 of which was cash; $100 was due "at or before next Christmas 1871" without interest; and the balance to be paid on Christmas 1872 with eight percent interest.

Business must have been good, for he paid off the indebtedness before it was due.

Johann (or John as he was later known) Schlaudt was born on August 25, 1847, in Fredericksburg. He married Sophie Honig, who was born in Germany on November 17, 1852.

She lived to be 97 years old, spending her last years in this house.

The Schlaudts built their rock house behind the small log house, using the log house as sleeping quarters before it was torn down. The original limestone rock house they built had two large rooms and a second story, all with the traditional thick walls. One room downstairs was their parlor, although it did have an extra bed in it, as so many did in the early days. The other room was the kitchen.

Out of the east room which was their kitchen, steep stairs led to the upper floor. The original part of the upper floor had a narrow hallway and two large bedrooms.

Just like the two houses east of it, this old house had a large cellar below it, providing much-needed storage space.

Although the rooms were large, this old rock house must have been crowded at times. The Schlaudts had ten children, and often Mrs. Schlaudt would care for a friend or relative's child who was sick, or needed a doctor's care.

Also, Mr. Schlaudt's customers would often spend the night with the family if the work they were having done in his blacksmith shop was not finished by nightfall and they would have to wait over for it until the next day.

48

Mr. Schlaudt made his own charcoal which he used in his blacksmith shop. On the side of this lot towards the corner Kraus building, he had his sheds for making the coals which were so important to a "smithy". When they were "coaling", huge piles of wood were laid, then covered with dirt and straw which was kept wet, so that the wood which was smoldering would not break out into flames and ruin the charcoal. This necessitated someone staying with the piles day and night, until the process was complete.

The old rock horse trough in which Mr. Schlaudt kept his water for cooling the irons in his shop was used as a flower planter by the late Mrs. August Itz, one of his daughters.

The John Schlaudt family lived in the rock house until Mr. Schlaudt's death. He died at a comparatively young age of 54, after which his widow and the children moved out to their ranch in the Eckert community.

After the children were married and moved off to places of their own, Mrs. Schlaudt and her daughter, Anna Schlaudt, moved back to town. She lived in this house until her death, with the August Itz family coming to make their home with her during the last fifteen years of her life. Mrs. Itz was one of her daughters.

When Mrs. Schlaudt and the daughter moved back to town, the additions and renovations were made to the old house, giving it the appearance and floor plan it has now. These included adding the wing to the front along the east side which provided one more room downstairs and another above it on the second floor.

Behind the old part of the house at the east side was added a kitchen, a small hall and a bathroom. At that time, the old rock exterior was covered with cement plaster and marked off in blocks to resemble the new concrete block addition. Upstairs another bedroom was added above the kitchen. This room had twelve windows, making it an ideal bedroom.

All of the Schlaudt children were born in this old house. They included Charles (Carl) Schlaudt, Renatus (Rennie) Schlaudt, Arthur Schlaudt; Hulda, Mrs. W. R. Eckert; Celestine, Mrs. August Itz; Constance, Mrs. Albert Kolmeier; Willie Schlaudt; Anna, Mrs. Edmund Eckert; Emil Schlaudt; and Emma, Mrs. Henry Duebner.

After the death of Mrs. Schlaudt on March 15, 1950, the heirs sold this house, deeding it to Erwin C. Kraus November 17, 1951. Since that time it has served a useful purpose as a rent house.

Since two of the Erwin Kraus children now own the two adjoining old houses, they have coordinated the appearance from the front by placing a pretty low white picket fence between both front yards and the sidewalk.

Mrs. Montgomery and her husband, Steven, a linguistic expert with the United States Department of State in Washington, D.C., and their children are now back in the U.S. after having lived in India for a number of years while he was stationed there with the State Department.

Their upkeep and preservation of an historic house in Fredericksburg at "the Kraus corner" is commendable and adds much to the scenery and lore of this city.

David, Frederick and Mrs. Erwin Kraus, Owners

KRAUS BUILDING

One of Fredericksburg's stately old buildings, located at the corner of West Main and South Edison Streets, better known as "the Kraus corner," has served as home and store for many years. It is still in use as a business establishment, housing the Fredericksburg Coca Cola Bottling Company and Pearl Brew Distributing Company. No longer is part of it used as a home.

But home it was for the Kraus family for many years and for others before them. The oldest part of the present structure is that part of the building located at the corner. In later years, in successive stages, alterations and additions were made as the Kraus family grew and their business expanded.

It is located on Townlot No. 258 which was granted to V. Fuhrmann by the German Emigration Company, according to the list of townlot allotments. The next link in the chain of title is when Johann Fuhrmann sold the corner lot to Wilhelm (also known as Wm.) Luckenbach on January 18, 1868, for "100 dollars in gold." This price indicates that at that time there were little, if any, improvements on it.

By then Wilhelm Crenwelge had acquired ownership of the two lots to the east of this and some of the rock homes on them were being built, so it follows in logical order that this two-story one was built around that time -- the late 1860's or early 70's when many of the two-story rock houses were built. After the trauma of the Civil War was over, folks could get down to providing themselves with better homes and places of business.

Not much is known of the building's use in Luckenbach's day, except that the family lived here and that the front part of the first floor was used as a "store." According to Penniger's Fest Ausgabe, "On June 10, 1871, Wm. Luckenbach accepted the office of (county) treasurer."

Luckenbach borrowed some money with this place as security, and on August 29, 1898, deeded it to H.B. Meckel, August Zincke, William Kettner, Louis Kettner and Otto Donop in settlement of the note. A few days later these five men sold it to Jacob Kraus on September 12, 1898. By that time he was operating his soda water bottling plant here. On March 15, 1892, Kraus and Max Blum had bought the equipment for it from Balthasar Blum (B. Blum), who had rented these premises. A few months later, Max Blum sold his interest to Kraus and went back to teaching school.

Today the grandsons of Jacob Kraus Sr. are running the business in the same location, but a lot of things have changed about the "modus operandi" of the soda water bottling industry since 1892.

There are some soda water bottles around yet of B. Blum's vintage which closed with the "Hutchinson stoppers," but they wouldn't meet present-day sanitation standards. From the way they opened, the name "soda pop" originated. To open a bottle you "popped" the metal loop or spring down that was attached to the stopper, forcing it into the bottle. When the bottle was returned to the bottling plant, the bottle was cleaned and this same stopper was pulled up again to "seal" it. The greater the pressure inside the bottle, the better the seal.

The original building was built right on the property line at the corner and had two very large double doors downstairs and two almost as large upstairs in the front, with a two-story porch complete with gingerbread and fancy railing.

There was one large room downstairs in the front, with a somewhat smaller one behind it. The front room was used originally as the bottling plant and the back room was the Kraus' kitchen. It at one time had a fireplace in it. Upstairs there was one large room in front and two in the back. The big room upstairs has the original floor with its random-width boards, some as wide and wider than 12 inches. The front room floor was a step higher than the back two rooms, a plan similar to that of the Crenwelge home which is next to Crenwelge Motors.

Kraus was an astute businessman, and his business must have been successful, for he paid off the purchase price for this building several years before it was due. He bought the building for $1150 on September 12, 1898, paying $150 cash, and executing 10 notes of $100 each, due in successive years, but by July 31, 1901, he had paid off the entire indebtedness.

On February 12, 1901, he married Theresia Segner, a daughter of John and Elizabeth Koehler Segner. She was born and reared in an old home in the block immediately east of the Kraus block.

The old corner building was home to the Jacob Kraus family before they added the second addition -- a limestone rock structure built along the same lines. This was done in 1906 by Weber Bros., Aug. L. C. and Otto Weber, early-day stonemasons who built many of the old rock homes and buildings in the city.

Three of the couple's children were born while they lived in this old house: Dora, Mrs. Hugo Stehling; Erwin, who died in 1968; and Emil, who died at the age of nine years. The other children were all born in the "new house" and included Margaret, Mrs. Henry Reinbach; Theresa, Mrs. Alex Knopp; Gertrude (Trudy) Kraus; Paul Kraus; and two who are deceased, Otto, who died in childhood, and Jacob Kraus Jr., who died in 1948.

The new addition to the house gave the family more room for living as well as for their business. A spacious hallway was built between them with a single door as entrance downstairs and upstairs and the two-story porch with its railing and gingerbread was extended across the front of the new addition. The new addition has a wide double door with a window at each side in the front room which served as the office. Behind this was the Kraus' living room, and back of that the dining room. The kitchen adjoined this and extended under the stairway across to the west wall of the new addition.

The stairway which leads from the front hall entrance to the second floor is a beautiful structure. The handturned balusters of the balustrade on the stairway are accented with some beautiful scalloped woodwork trim. Willie Kuenemann is credited with most of this woodwork, including the grooved and decorative window and door frames of the 1906 addition.

Upstairs this addition originally had four bedrooms, but one of the larger ones was partitioned, making five in all. This space is all used now for storage.

Water for the family and the business came out of a "dug" well near the corner of the 1906 addition. This was topped with a huge stone that John Stehling had brought to town, tied under his wagon. When it had to be removed at the time the newest annex was built, it was so heavy that it had to be broken up. Another well was drilled and topped with a windmill. When electricity was available, an electric pump was installed, and finally "city water" was available through the mains.

Water was important in the bottling plant. In the olden days the bottles were carefully washed by hand, with buckshot added in the bottles as they were shaken to clean away any dirt particles. After several rinsings, they were turned upside down in cases and filled the next day with soda water. Now they are cleaned, sterilized, filled and capped by machinery and then placed in cases.

Long ago the Hutchinson stopper had given way to the crown bottle caps now in use. Though plentiful now, there have been times when they were not and caps had to be salvaged, cleaned, the tops repainted, and new cork fillers added.

In the early days metal trays were used for the soda water cases, then came the familiar wooden ones now in use, but it looks like these will eventually be replaced with the plastic ones that are being used more and more.

The variety of soda water available everywhere now is almost unbelievable, and even at the Kraus plant the flavors number at least eight, several of them in regular or king size bottles. Once there was only "red" and "white" soda water, and then came Iron Brew. The syrup for this comes from the East and the Krauses are among the very few in Texas that bottle it. Flavors now bottled here are Coca Cola, Orange Crush, Sprite, Mr. Pibb, Iron Brew, Frosty Root Beer, Strawberry and Delaware Punch.

Coca Cola came on the local scene around 1910, and at first there was no distinction between bottles it came in and others, however, by 1916, the distinctive Coke bottle was adopted. Now the favorite soft drink around the world, its formula is a carefully guarded secret, and bottlers and distributors of it come under strict scrutiny to insure its uniform taste and "goodness." The Kraus family has received a number of merit awards from Coca Cola for excellence.

Another business conducted here was cigar making. The cigar factory was located in the front room on the second floor of the old building. In 1916 Jacob Kraus Sr. bought the cigar factory from Max Wahrmund and it became known as Jacob Kraus Cigar Factory, No. 43, 1st District of Texas. The cigar makers were Adolph Mergenthaler and Otto Zimmermann, and later Erwin and Paul learned how to make cigars.

To make cigars, the tobacco was soaked in water, and then slung about to remove most of the moisture, after which it was placed on wire racks until it was almost dry, but still moist enough for rolling. The Kraus youngsters helped to strip the coarse veins out of the leaves before they were rolled into cigars.

Tobacco came in different grades, and the inferior grades were used for cut-up filler and for the inside of the roll. Then the cigars were put into presses for shaping, following which the top grade tobacco was wrapped around the outside. Next they were sealed in cellophane or tinfoil and cigar bands attached, indicating the quality and price. The top of the line was "La Palma" which sold for 10 cents and the other two were the "Big Five" and "Kraus Special" both of which were nickel cigars.

The Kraus children helped put the bands on the finished cigars, and on occasions such as for the Christmas market, they would wrap the boxes in holiday gift wrap. This usually took place at night around the kitchen and dining room tables. The Krauses in later years sold the cigar factory to Mergenthaler who moved it away from the Kraus building.

The original building at the Kraus corner had other additions besides the 1906 limestone annex. It was enlarged in the 1940's when that part behind the oldest building was added, other renovations were made in back in the 1950's, and in 1967 the large annex at the east side was built.

When the east annex was added, the Kraus flower garden and lawn that had been a special attraction along Main Street gave way. Here Mrs. Kraus grew beautiful flowers, had a pretty lawn, with honeycomb rock-lined walks and other decor.

In 1928 "Pearl Near Beer" was added to the Kraus products, and in 1933 after the repeal of prohibition, the Pearl Beer agency was established and is known now as the Pearl Beer Distributing Company. Beer was never brewed or bottled here by the Krauses.

Though the business has stayed in the Kraus family, its management has been under several members of the family. Following the death of the founder on May 14, 1922, his widow took over the management of it with the help of the oldest sons, Erwin and Paul, who later became the owners of the business after the death of their mother. In 1938 the firm was incorporated and became known as the Fredericksburg Coca Cola Bottling Company, although there are still many who refer to it today as "Kraus Bottling Works."

Mrs. Kraus died October 28, 1955. Erwin Kraus died in 1968 and Paul Kraus has retired, and now the majority stockholders are two of Erwin's sons, David and Frederick, with their mother still having a small interest.

Helping them with office management of the firm is Gertrude (Trudy) Kraus. She is also active in the Gillespie County Historical Society and all of its projects, so her interest in the history and preservation of the "Kraus corner" is something that is dear to her heart. She had made her home here with her mother, but in 1957-58 built her own home at another location and now all of the building is used commercially for the two businesses, Fredericksburg Coca Cola Bottling Co., Inc., and Pearl Beer Distributing Company.

Business at the Kraus corner now is a far cry from the days of the 1890's when only red

and white soda water was bottled here, bottles were handwashed, cigar making was a sideline, and the owners lived in the same house where all this took place. All of which makes it all the more commendable that the family takes pride in their old building and the great asset it is in preserving Fredericksburg's rich historical and architectural heritage.

Mrs. Oswald Oestreich, Owner

FUHRMANN-OCHS HOME

Modern facades and additions often camouflage an old home but if you look at the lines of some of the simple little houses you can usually spot an "oldie" underneath the plaster, siding or fresh paint. The home of Mrs. Oswald Oestreich lives in at 105 South Edison Street, directly behind the "Kraus corner," is such a home.

Built on Townlot No. 295 which was conveyed to F. Nicholi by the German Emigration Company, it was long in the Ochs family, a name familiar in pioneer circles of Fredericksburg. The list of original allotments shows the name as "Nicolay," however the deed dated July 28, 1854 was signed by William R. Baker, administrator de bonis non for the estate of Francis Nicholi, deceased, of Travis County.

The lot, 100 by 200 feet in dimension, was

bought by Frederick Fuhrmann for $14.50, so there must not have been any improvements on it. On the 1850 census he is listed as a single man, and since his uncle, Johann Friedrich Fuhrmann, owned two townlots fronting on West San Antonio Street in the block west of this block, it is logical that he was the one who built the original little log cabin that is the front room of the present-day Oestreich home.

Fuhrmann sold the entire Townlot, which fronted for 100 feet on West San Antonio Street and ran back for 200 feet along the present-day South Edison Street, to Heinrich Ochs Jr., on January 4, 1870, for $75.00.

Ochs was a stonemason, and since log cabins were no longer the type of construction utilized in town houses by that time, he added the stone addition. Originally there was the front room, the log cabin, and behind that he

53

added two rooms and the adjoining rock smokehouse. Later additions were of frame construction which the Oestreichs used as a kitchen, hall, two bedrooms and screened porch.

The log cabin exterior walls for many years were covered with shingles that blended with the shingle roof. In recent years the roof shingles were covered with tin and the shingles were removed from the side walls and they were covered with siding.

The outside stairway that led up the north side to the attic also has been removed.

On February 1, 1871, Ochs sold the lower half of the townlot to Jacob Hirsch, and this is the property that later was used for the parsonage for the former Edison Street Methodist Church before the two Methodist Churches merged into the present-day Fredericksburg United Methodist Church.

Though the Ochs house was small, it was home for the family until after Mr. Ochs' death, when Mrs. Ochs and daughter, Irma, moved to San Antonio to be near the other two children. They were Frieda, who married J.B. Schrolle, and Herman Ochs, who was a widely known and prominent San Antonio businessman, heading the firm of Wolf and Marx for many years, and was also prominent in Lutheran church circles and civic organizations in that city.

The house was the scene of many special events, among them two weddings that were held here -- those of two of Mr. Ochs' sisters. Mrs. Jacob Treibs married her first husband, Adolph Thiele, in this house; and her sister, Regina, married her husband, William Thiele, there too.

Mrs. Elise Ochs, Mr. and Mrs. Schrolle and Miss Ochs sold the house and the upper half of the townlot to Hilmar Saenger January 8, 1921, for $1500. His parents, Mr. and Mrs. Edmund Saenger, made their home in the house until their death.

Hilmar (H.R.) Saenger and his wife, then of Ollochita Parish, Louisiana, sold the property to Oswald Oestreich January 20, 1943, and his widow continues to make her home here. Mr. Oestreich was for many years a road overseer for Gillespie County. He died May 1, 1974. They had three children, one of whom, Louis, died late last year. The other two are Nolan Oestreich of San Antonio and Myrtle, Mrs. Marvin Honig, of Harper.

So an old house, once only a log cabin, was used and enlarged over the years, and now continues to be a comfortable home for the present owner.

FALSTAFF HOUSE

An old home of Fredericksburg with a fairly new name is that known nowadays as "the Falstaff house" at 112 North Crockett Street. Its "historic" name is the Krueger-Weihmiller house, and since the old rock building located next to it has its history interwoven into the first one, the two used together have a most interesting story to tell.

These two buildings have been put to many different uses, resulting in deterioration of some portions. No efforts at renovation or restoration have ever been made by the owners.

The present tenant, Charles Svatek, distributor for Falstaff beer (hence the name "Falstaff house"), and his helper, Freddie Aguilar, who lives in the house, are doing all they can, however, to preserve and make the best possible use of them.

The houses are located on Townlot 97, which faces for 100 feet on North Crockett Street towards the Market Square, and runs back for 200 feet. It was allotted by the German Emigration Company to Ferdinand Wilhelm, according to the original list, but the earliest owner of record is Franz W. Krueger.

Krueger built the oldest of the two houses, the present-day Falstaff office, and the fachwerk portion at the north side is the oldest and was constructed first. He operated a drug store (it was listed as an apothecary on the probate records) in this house. When he died in 1865, an administrator of his estate, Aug. Schild, was appointed. In the inventory of the estate is given a complete list of the "bottles and medicines" which made up the stock of his "apothecary."

The administrator proposed to sell the medicines and bottles of the apothecary at private sale to O. Mueller, who had offered to pay the appraised amount because he was doubtful that much could be realized by sale at

public auction. In the meantime, the administrator was to try to find a renter for the "townlot and house." Ottocar Mueller, the buyer, operated another drug store in Fredericksburg -- at one time in what is now W. A. Wareing's "Domino Parlor."

By January, 1866, no renter had been found for the house, so the administrator was given permission to rent it himself for six months for one dollar a month, so that he could sell the "remaining few trifling things at private sale."

By January 1867 a buyer was found and the court ordered the "house and townlot fronting on the Market Square" to be sold to Friedrich Weihmiller for $410. Weihmiller married Caroline Kirchner, a widow, on February 10, 1867. His deed is dated July 29, 1867.

The place was known as "the Weihmiller place" through the years, and title stayed in this family until 1938 when Hugo Basse bought it from Annie and Minnie Kirchner, whose mother had been the wife of Friedrich Weihmiller. After the death of her first husband, Henry Kirchner, by whom she had two daughters and one son, she married Weihmiller.

Those who knew her, recall the delight they had as children in hearing and seeing her sing in her native Danish tongue a little ditty as she would gather up her skirts and perform a little folk dance of Denmark.

The Weihmillers lived in the "Falstaff house" and the one used by Svatek now for beer storage was a blacksmith shop.

Here the oldest daughter worked alongside her stepfather as a blacksmith, heaving the heavy hammer with ease.

When they needed charcoal for their work, they went out to their ten-acre Outlot at the northwest part of town and made coals by burning wood and then covering it with sand. After it had "coaled" and cooled, they brought it to their blacksmith shop.

Neighbors recall the daughter often going after the charcoal and bringing it back in the folds of her heavy leather "blacksmith apron." This Outlot is that block of land which the late Rev. O. Lindenberg developed as an addition and is bounded by North Milam, North Orange, West College and West Morse Streets.

In later years, Richard Tatsch also had a blacksmith shop in the same building. After it was no longer used as a blacksmith shop, it was "fixed up" and was occupied by various tenants. When the Saengers rented these premises, they operated a cafe in it. For many years Lone Star Beer distributor, Reinhold Enderlin, used it for the same purpose Falstaff is now using it.

This lower house is of solid rock construction, with no opening at all in the back (west) wall. The front has a double door with glass transom, flanked by a window at each side. The door and door frame match in appearance those of the "wohn haus" or dwelling next to it. There is also a window in the north wall, and in the south wall there is a window and a door.

The present-day Falstaff office building was the Weihmillers' residence and is the older of the two. When her husband had his beer distributorship here, Mrs. Enderlin operated a doll shop in it.

An early mode of construction is evident on the porch. It is not put together with nails, but instead the pegs that hold the beams together are in full view.

There is a large double door in front which has beautiful detailing in the wood. Each door has three beveled panels which are matched in size by the panels of the wood used for the door frame. Above them is a wishbone pattern in the glass of the transom. Flanking the door are two windows, and there is another window in the south wall.

This front room was the parlor, and its floor was laid with a large wool carpet in the Weihmiller days. As parlors of those days were seldomly used when there was enough room in the rest of the house for eating and sleeping, such was the case with this house, too, and neighbors' children recalled standing at the door and merely looking in -- not entering it.

Behind it is a smaller room which was a bedroom. Stairs lead from it up to the second story which has two windows. Small windows under the eaves in front and the larger windows in the side walls made this comfortable sleeping quarters for the boy in the family. There is a small window, too, to throw light on the stairway.

The two-story part of the house is built of solid rock, over 18 inches thick, and the stones were shaped to form arches over the doors and each window. Inscribed on the chimney is the year 1862. The former blacksmith shop building next to it has the year 1883 scratched into the stone at one corner.

From the front room, or the old parlor and now the Falstaff office, you step down into the one story and oldest part of the house. This is partly of fachwerk construction, having rocks and mortar filled in between the upright and cross pieces of logs. Some changes have taken place in this portion, and part of it is in very poor condition. Where the plaster has fallen off, the homemade mortar in which grass was mixed is showing.

There is a window in this room next to the entrance door. Behind it is the old kitchen with a large fireplace, with a doorway between the two rooms.

One of the former tenants tore out the northeast front to make a garage at one time.

Behind this old house is one of the few remaining old iron water pumps over the well which still pumped water until Svatek wired down the pump handle to prevent its destruction. Next to it, the oldest well, one that was "dug" has caved in and was filled with rocks.

Title to this property was conveyed by Weihmiller to his wife, Caroline, on February 4, 1881. The deed states that he is conveying to her this townlot and an outlot he owned for $650 and on the condition "that she relinquish all right and interest and claim to any of my property that I may own or hereafter may acquire."

In later years, Mrs. Weihmiller and her family moved to San Antonio where the girls operated a millinery store. A changing stream of tenants occupied the two houses over the years.

On January 10, 1938, Annie and Minnie Kirchner, the only heirs of Caroline Weihmiller, sold this property to Hugo Basse. His daughter, Alma Connelly, now owns it, as her parents have died.

It is doubtful that there are many other houses in Fredericksburg that attract more attention of passersby than these two. The Falstaff house, especially, is a favorite subject for artists, and it is commendable that the present tenant, Charlie Svatek, takes pride in keeping it as his place of business. His employee, Freddie Aguilar, enhances it with his potted plants and vines, and is a familiar figure as he is often seated on the porch or in the doorway of the house, playing his guitar.

From the first owner's medicine bottles, to the present tenant's bottles of Falstaff, Miller's and Shiner beer, the house continues to serve a useful purpose in the community and is one that is worthy of preserving for future generations.

———————

ZION SUNDAY SCHOOL HOUSE

That different buildings along Fredericksburg's Main Street have had multiple uses is nothing new, because through the years that has been the case with many of them. Such was the case with the little house directly behind Zion Lutheran Church. Built originally as a school house, it also served as a home for a pastor's widow and her family for several years.

It is located on Townlot 151 which was granted to Jacob Hardt by the German Emigration Company, and title passed from him to the founders of Zion Lutheran Church. On October 14, 1853, Hardt sold the 100 by 200 corner townlot for $45 to the trustees of "Evangelic Lutheran Zions Church," although his name is listed in that deed and acknowledgement as "Jacob Harth."

The trustees to whom title was given in the deed were F. W. Schumacher, D.W. Reider, G. Rorig and D. Rode.

The founders of Zion originally worshipped with their fellow Lutherans and those of other faiths in separate worship services in the Vereins Kirche. When doctrinal differences late in 1852 arose among the Lutherans, several families decided to withdraw from worshipping in the Vereins Kirche and conducted their own services in a "mud house" which was not in use at the time.

Zion congregation was organized and plans were made to acquire a building site. Several were available, so a lot was cast to select the site, with the Townlot 151 coming up the "winner."

The cornerstone for the first church was laid March 6, 1854, later a parsonage was built, and the congregation began to grow.

Soon the need for a parochial school was felt, and the first school was conducted in the parsonage. Later the pastors served as teachers in the little church.

Following the Civil War in 1865 this little limestone house, 20 by 30 feet, was erected. During the 110 years that followed some changes were made in the building and it served as a school house, a Sunday School building, a meeting room, and even for a while as a home for the widow of Rev. F. Holzinger, during whose pastorate the little house was built.

Just how long Mrs. Holzinger and her two daughters lived here is not known, and it was probably not a very "homey" place to live since it was a one-room affair planned as a school house, but home it was for her.

The little house was built right behind the first church, with the entrance being a door in the south wall facing the church. There were three good-sized windows in each the east and west walls, just as there are today. In the north wall they placed a large fireplace which was used to heat the building during the winter. This was later closed up and a wood stove was used for heat before natural gas came to Fredericksburg. Now one part of it is even used for the air-conditioning unit.

The pupils in the school were children of Fredericksburg and from nearby in the county, with each year there also being a group who had come to school here during their year of confirmation instruction.

J.J. Weber was the teacher from 1866 to 1867. In 1871 the Lutheran parochial school was discontinued and the building was used thereafter for Sunday School, confirmation instruction, church groups' meetings and other congregational purposes.

At one time there was a driveway between the church and this little house, and the doorway towards the church was closed to prevent children from getting hurt as they darted out of the little house into the path of vehicles using the driveway. At that time the space was made into a bookshelf and at the same time a middle window in the east wall was made into a door. Now one of the west windows has also been made into another door. The loft entrance into the attic remains.

Currently the little house is being used as a Sunday School room for the nursery group, and its exterior appearance has been changed considerably. It was stuccoed white to match the exterior of the many-times remodeled church building. Though dwarfed by the surrounding structures, this little house near Fredericksburg's Main Street has played its vital role in history and the church life of the community.

WISSEMANN-HANISCH HOME

The interesting story of Conrad Wissemann, the builder of the oldest part of the home at the corner of West Main and South Orange Streets, and the additions made to it by the family of the later owner and occupant, Miss Elsbeth Hanisch, combine to make a fascinating account.

Now known as the Hanisch home, the oldest part of the building at 301 W. Main Street was built by Conrad Wissemann soon after the colonization of Fredericksburg. His grandson, the late Dr. Charles L. Wissemann, who made the English translation of Penniger's 1896 "Festausgabe" which was published in 1971 as "Fredericksburg, Texas ... the First Fifty Years," also published a family history entitled simply "Wissemann" in 1970. He did extensive research on his grandfather and his descendants, shedding new light on the builder of the first four rooms of this house.

Conrad Wissemann was the son of a Lutheran minister, Rev. Johann Conrad Wissemann. He was born Jan. 1, 1816, in Raboldshausen, Hessen-Nassau, Germany. Before he came to America, he was employed as a warden on a game preserve owned by some of the German nobility, but he was a carpenter by trade. The 1850 census of Gillespie County lists him as a carpenter, but on the 1860 census he is listed as a cabinet-maker.

Before leaving Germany, he spent some time in Hamburg for treatment of his eyes, and then joined 142 other immigrants to sail for Texas on January 2, 1846, aboard the "Talisman" from Antwerp for Galveston, landing there April 11, 1846. He is thought to have been among the second group of immigrants to reach Fredericksburg in the early summer of 1846.

Wissemann was allotted Townlot No. 247 on which he built his home and a ten-acre Outlot where he farmed. He took an interest in the affairs of the colony, joining 95 other colonists who signed a resolution January 17, 1847, commending John O. Mesuebach for his leadership and urging him to continue in that capacity. On December 15, 1847, he was one of the 150 citizens who petitioned the Texas Legislature to organize a new county with Fredericks1burg as the county seat. This area was originally part of Bexar County.

Wissemann married Luise Spaeth, who came to Fredericksburg from Germany with her mother, Mrs. Elizabeth Spaeth, and brother, Ludwig Spaeth, early in 1847. The

Mr. and Mrs. Thomas E. Alt, Owners

Wissemanns made their home on this townlot and here seven of their nine children were born, and one daughter, who died in infancy, was buried on this lot. There is no evidence now, however, of the grave. The couple's seven children who reached maturity were William, Ludwig Heinrich (later called Louis), Marie, Lisette, Lena, Bertha and Mathilda. Carl died at the age of 15 years.

The family, while they lived in this house, endured the privations experienced by the other early colonists. In addition to his carpentry work, often in working on some of the forts in the area, Wissemann also hauled freight between here and San Antonio or Austin or for construction jobs.

Some fachwerk construction and also limestone rock were used in building the old part of the home -- the front four rooms facing on Main Street. Much of this was probably done by Wissemann himself.

On September 23, 1862, Wissemann traded this corner lot and the house to Frederick Gentemann for two townlots and a ten-acre lot. Gentemann and his wife owned this place until they sold the Southeast part of it to Paul Hanisch April 11, 1879. Gentemann is listed on the 1860 census as a cabinet-maker.

While the Wissemann family history had its interesting sidelights, so does the Hanisch family. Paul Hanisch's daughter owned and lived in this house until before her death at age 95 on July 23, 1976.

Paul Hanisch was born June 4, 1831, on the Isle of Ruegen, said to be one of the most picturesque and beautiful spots on the coast of Germany. Like Wissemann, he, too, was the son of a Lutheran minister. His father was Rev. Peter Hanisch.

After securing a good literary education, Hanisch applied himself for ten years to the study of pharmacy and kindred branches of science. On June 6, 1856, he arrived at Indianola, and then came by cart to New Braunfels, San Antonio and Comfort. He lived in Comfort until 1872 where he conducted a drug store, and then moved to Fredericksburg and opened a drug store here.

He married his fiancee, Miss Helene Siedschlag, Dec. 18, 1878, when she came to Galveston from Germany with the fiancee of Dr. Albert Keidel, a pioneer Fredericksburg physician. The two men met the women in Galveston and after their marriage, they returned to Fredericksburg to make their homes.

At first Mr. and Mrs. Hanisch lived in the little rock house that stood to the rear of their present home. This was torn down several years ago to make a parking lot. Helene Hanisch, the oldest of the three Hanisch children, was born in that house. She died in 1942.

On April 11, 1879, Paul Hanisch bought the Southeast part of Townlot 247 and the house that was on it from Frederick Gentemann.

Here the family lived, with Mr. Hanisch operating his drug store in the front of the building. Another daughter, Elsbeth and a son, Frank, were born to the couple here.

When Hanisch acquired this place, A. L. Patton operated a tin shop in one end of the building and Hanisch had his drug store in the other end. After a while, Patton moved away from this location.

The drug store was in the largest of the front two rooms -- the one on the west side. It has two large double doors flanked by big windows. Next to this at the east corner is the family parlor. This room also has a front entrance through double doors flanked by windows.

Behind the parlor was a large bedroom furnished with beautiful antique furniture. This was the bedroom of Mrs. Paul Hanisch, who lived to be 103 years old.

Next to this bedroom, and directly behind the room used for the drug store was a combination family sitting room and bedroom. It faces the back porch which runs along all the rooms at the back of house.

Additions to this original part of the house were made by Paul Hanisch, room by room, as he had the means to pay for them and as the need for additional space arose.

Some of these rooms form a wing towards the back, the first of which was a small bedroom, the next one was the family dining room and then the kitchen.

The back room behind the kitchen is the rock addition which extends along the back and is elevated above the floor level of the other rooms, giving the impression of being over a basement or cellar, however, there is none below it. This was used as a storeroom.

There are no windows or any opening in the entire west wall, however all the rooms have doors and windows opening to the inner courtyard or patio. A bedroom and bath were added to the original four rooms at the southeast corner along South Orange Street.

Accounting for the unusual shape of the house is the fact that for many years a little rock house built by Gentemann stood in what is now the inner yard area. It faced South Orange Street, and was used by the Hanisches for various purposes until they tore it down.

The son, Frank, was graduated from the School of Pharmacy branch of Baylor University in Dallas in 1905 and returned to Fredericksburg to join his father. After his father died, Frank Hanisch formed a partnership with J. D. Payne and the two operated a pharmacy in the building now occupied by Arthur Stehling at 218 W. Main Street. After Mr. Payne moved away from Fredericksburg, Mr. Hanisch continued to operate the drug store there, but in the mid-1940's moved it back into the Hanisch home, utilizing the large front room at the west side for this purpose. Mr. Hanisch died, November 21, 1963, and his sister, Elsbeth, resided here with her companion, Miss Cora Kramer.

Miss Elsbeth kept up with current events by reading the Fredericksburg Standard, listening to radio and watching television, and had a very keen and perceptive mind. She died at the age of 95 on July 23, 1976, having spent the last few months in a nursing home. All the rest of her life was spent in this house with the exception of the time she was in college in what is now Southwest Texas State University and while teaching for several years at Victoria.

In her will, she left her home to Zion Lutheran Church.

The church sold the property to Thomas E. Alt and wife, Alethia, on May 31, 1977.

BENDER-WEYRICH-MATHISEN HOME

Sometimes the smallest house has the biggest story woven into its history. Such is the case with the little house at 329 West Main Street. It is occupied by City Radiator Service, but its interesting story involves the owners of the house in the 1890's, Christian Mathisen and his father, Mathis Mathisen, who came to Fredericksburg from Denmark in the 1890's, bringing with them many of their customs.

The house bears little resemblance now to the structure the Mathisens lived in, as the frame part of it was torn down, and changes have even been made in the little stone structure in recent years. In its earliest days it was a blacksmith shop and later a home.

The house is built on Townlot 224 which the German Emigration Company granted to J. (John) Leyendecker. He sold it to Christian Kraus on February 10, 1854.

Kraus probably built the little stone house and other structures on it because when he sold Townlot 224 to Adolph Wahrmund August 14, 1873, he received $1350 in cash for it, a sizable sum for that day. When Wahrmund sold the east part of the lot to Wm. Weyrich on which Weyrich built his home he sold that portion for $400. The portion on which this house is built was traded by Ad. Wahrmund and his wife, Elise, to Mary Neal Brodie and her husband, S. L. Brodie for another townlot which he valued at $1100. In the deed the rights to use a passageway adjoining or a part of the plot were retained, which provisions

were included in succeeding deeds.

The Brodies owned this property for only a short time, having acquired it April 5, 1879. They sold it to Catharine Bender June 24, 1879, for $700.

Mrs. Bender died and her only child and sole heir, Emilie Bender, married William Weyrich, a blacksmith, who had his shop in the little stone building. They were married January 30, 1875, and two weeks later he bought the adjoining part of townlot (February 13, 1875) on which he built their home. This is the two-story building now owned by G. E. Howard.

Weyrich operated his blacksmith shop in this little stone house but on November 2, 1892, he sold it to Christian Mathisen and his father, Mathis Mathisen.

Christian, the oldest of the seven children of Mr. and Mrs. Mathis Mathisen, who lived in southern Denmark, had become intrigued with the thought of coming to Texas when young Soren Hoisager came back to Denmark for a visit after having settled in Texas near Stonewall. About this time, Christian had finished his apprenticeship as a blacksmith, and as was customary in Denmark in those days, he was ready to take up his trade.

His father was an expert wheelwright and he had gained experience in his shop, so he finished the customary four-year apprenticeship in three years. He was planning to "take to the road" in Denmark and other

61

European countries, plying his trade, when he changed his mind and came to Texas with young Hoisager.

Hoisager's sister also accompanied them, and they made the trip from Hamburg, Germany, to New York in nine days abroad the biggest German liner of that day. From New York to Galveston took them another nine days, and then they came to Fredericksburg, arriving here November 14, 1890.

Christian's first Christmas in this new country away from his family was spent with fellow Danes, the Jens Hansen family (who were later to own this house). They had settled on a farm near Stonewall about four or five years before that.

The next year, young Mathisen's parents and the other children, Christine, Marius, Julia, Annie and Walter came to Fredericksburg. The oldest daughter, Andrea, remained in Denmark for a short while, coming here later to join her family.

The Mathis Mathisen family lived in a house adjoining this little stone house, however, it has since been torn down. Christian Mathisen practiced his trade of blacksmithing and his father that of a wheelwright at this location. In those days they were kept very busy as they shod horses, repaired plows and machinery, and the elder of the two made wheels, wagons, hacks and plows.

When Christian Mathisen married Emily Striegler in 1897, they renovated the blacksmith shop, converting it into a residence and moved in. They added floors and ceilings to make it more livable. In the rock part of the building which is that still standing today and used as the radiator shop, they had their bedroom in the front room and behind this their combination kitchen, dining room and sitting room. In the back at the time there was an open porch and a two-story addition. The oldest of their children, now Mrs. Louise Ergas, was born here.

The Christian Mathisens lived in this house for over two years leaving there to move to their farm in the Rocky Hill Community where they lived until their deaths. Mrs. Mathisen died April 7, 1975, at the age of 100. The rest of their children, Fred Mathisen; Myrtle, Mrs. W. C. Westerfeldt; and Ruth, Mrs. Arno Basse, were born on their farm.

While the Mathisens lived in town, they introduced many of their Danish customs. When this home was covered in the original series in the December 21, 1955, edition of the

Standard, Mr. and Mrs. Mathisen recalled for this writer some of these customs and Christmas traditions.

Their main Christmas in Denmark was on Christmas Eve, the 24th, when each family had its own tree and gifts at home. But first there was the big Christmas meal, being served that evening instead of on the 25th as is traditional in America.

One of the traditional dishes was a roast hog's head, as in the cold Danish climate pork was good eating, however, here they gradually gave up eating so much fatty pork, as the warmer climate here did not lend itself to eating such heavy food.

Another Danish custom Mr. Mathisen recalled sounds almost like American "trick or treat" on Halloween. On New Year's Eve, the children would go from house to house and throw bits of broken crockery against the front door, after which the occupants would let them in and give them such treats as cookies or sweets.

Since most of their toys, with the exception of dolls, were handmade, the children in the Mathisen family were quite fortunate. Back in the old country, as well as here in Texas, Mathisen was quite an expert at making wagons and wheel toys for the children.

He even made the Danish type "go-cart" for the babies in the family. This was a small two-wheeled cart with a handle in front for pushing or pulling it. The baby was bundled up amidst pillows, so when they went out in the wintertime they were snug and warm.

Another tradition observed in the Mathisen household during the Christmas week was the exclusive serving of white wheat bread. This was a contrast from the rye bread which they ate every other week in the year. It was supposed to be a treat, but Mr. Mathisen recalled that the whole family was sick of it before the week was up, and they were glad to return to their rye.

A touch of Danish hospitality for guests who came to call during the holidays was the serving of "coffee punch." This was a concoction of coffee, sweetening such as sugar, and brandy or whisky. He also recalled that hazelnuts were traditional for Christmas and they gathered them in the hedges and forests in Denmark.

Christian Mathisen sold his interest in this town property to his father on December 8, 1900, and Mathis Mathisen sold it to Jens Hansen (the man with whom Christian stayed when he first came to Texas) on December 2, 1911.

The title remained in the Hansen family for 59 years. Amalia Striegler, Ernst C. Hansen, Waldemar Hansen and Arthur Hansen, heirs of Jens and Agathe Hansen, both deceased, conveyed their interest in this house to their sister, Marie Hansen on September 13, 1938.

For many years the Jens Hansen family, and later the Waldemar Hansen family, used this house as their "Sunday house," as recalled by Kurt Hansen, a son of the Waldemar Hansens. It was a convenient place to stay when they came into town to shop and to attend services at Bethany Lutheran Church.

Through the years, the building has been used for many different purposes of such diverse nature as an upholstery shop and a "beer joint", but through it all it has retained much of its original charm. Marie Hansen sold it to Oliver and Evelyn Schaetter on September 24, 1970. The Schaetters sold it to Melton M. Keller, Jamie Keller, Mary Keller and Mignon Keller Feller on April 22, 1976.

What's left of the original building with its later alterations remains as a reminder of the varied cultural backgrounds that combined through the years to give Fredericksburg its distinctive heritage.

Mr. and Mrs. Gerald Howard, Owners

WEYRICH-HOWARD BUILDING

A building that has undergone many structural changes and seen many widely different uses is the two-story structure now owned by Gerald Howard near the corner of East Main and South Washington Streets.

Now there are seven apartments on the second floor, and the street floor is occupied by the business known as "Das Handwerk Haus" managed by the owner's daughter, Sharon Howard Grona.

Its other uses have been as divergent as a millinery store, rooming house, garage, and auto repair shop.

In giving it the face-lifting following Howard's acquisition of the property on September 15, 1970, the building even had touches of HemisFair 1968 put into use. These are the metal posts and porch railings used in the front and back that graced the entrances to the HemisFair grounds which were sold as surplus following dismantling of some of the property.

The building is located on parts of two Townlots -- Nos. 224 and 223. No. 223 is the corner lot, on the east side of which the present Exxon Station is located. It was granted to Gottfried Heymann (Heimann) by the German Emigration Company. He sold it to Louis Hasper on June 27, 1849, and following Hasper's death, his heirs, Louis Hasper, a son, and William Jordan, guardian of Hasper's grandchildren, Arminda, Edward, Felix, Bertha, Eugene, Hubert and Lina Jordan, by deed dated August 19, 1889, sold it to L. H. Wall. On the same date L. H. Wall (of Blanco County) sold the west 26 feet of Townlots 223 and 330 to Wm. Weyrich. The latter fronts on San Antonio Street.

Weyrich had owned the adjoining part of Townlot 224 since February 13, 1875, having bought it from Ad. Wahrmund. This is the same townlot on the western edge where Weyrich first had his blacksmith shop. Wahrmund bought that lot from Chr. Kraus August 14, 1873. On July 31, 1873, Wahrmund had also bought Fritz Stoffers' saddler business and shop which was located in what is now known as the Basse Building located on Townlot 224. Chr. Kraus had bought Townlot 224 from the original grantee, John Leyendecker on February 10, 1854.

William Weyrich was the son of a pioneer locksmith, Charles (Carl) Weyrich. He married Emilie Bender on January 30, 1875, the daughter of Catharine Bender who at the time of her death owned the house in which Weyrich had his blacksmith shop.

The Weyrichs built the house, now the Howard building, and at the time its story was told in the original old home series which appeared in the Standard November 28, 1956, Mrs. Robert G. (Selma) Striegler, a daughter of the William Weyrichs, was living and recalled many interesting facts about the house and its history.

Her parents modeled their home after the two-story part of the van der Stucken home next to Bethany Lutheran Church which the Alfred Hennigs now own. They even used the same door, window and porch arrangements, but unfortunately later owners made changes, additions and alterations, taking away some of the pioneer characteristics it had 100 years ago. Mr. Howard is trying now to conform it to a more historic aspect as near as is possible by complying with building codes. He plans to do additional exterior remodeling, including the tearing down of the frame "shack" at the west side and extending the porch around the west side of the building.

The original porch was torn down by one of the owners after it was sold by the Weyrichs

and the fieldstone front was added.

The west half of the building is the oldest part of the structure and it was this that served as the Weyrich home. Mrs. Weyrich had her millinery shop in the large front room. The kitchen and dining room were back of that. Now Mrs. Grona has her needlework shop in the front, and she and her husband, Billy, have their dining room, kitchen, bedroom and bath behind it. Their living room is very attractively arranged in the basement -- once the cellar of the Weyrich home.

Upstairs in the Weyrich home were two bedrooms, a large room that we would now call a family room, and in the front was the living room which was the biggest room over the store.

In 1886, the Weyrichs added on three bedrooms in a row and a large porch. Now they used the entire downstairs area for the millinery and dressmaking business. Mrs. Striegler in 1956 recalled vividly when this work was done because John Gentemann, who was also a fine musician, taught her to play little tunes like "Kommt Ein Vogel Geflogen" on the little piano she received as a Christmas gift while he was working on the addition.

When the new addition was finished, a complete line of dry goods was added, however, Mrs. Weyrich continued to make dresses and millinery. The well-dressed lady of that day had to go to a lot more trouble to acquire an ensemble than the shopper of today does.

Mrs. Weyrich would buy hat wire forms and then trim them according to the taste of her customers. Some were made of lace, net, satin, velvet and similar materials. All the elaborate embellishments the hats of this day had were added by the milliner. Mrs. Striegler assisted her mother in this work when she was old enough to help.

Mrs. Weyrich's first venture into dressmaking was typical of the resourcefulness of that era.

A lady requested Mrs. Weyrich to sew her satin wedding dress, and she accepted, although before she had done only plain sewing. When her mother, Mrs. Bender, who was living with them at the time and helping take care of the children, chided her about this difficult task, Mrs. Weyrich said she had ordered a dress-making chart and with its help would make the dress. And so she did.

She had no patterns to go by in those days,

and used the customers' measurements and the chart to draft her own patterns.

She also used dress forms which she could adjust to conform to the customer's measurements, eliminating many trips for fittings, because transportation at that time did not lend itself to getting back and forth as often or as easily as now.

Mrs. Striegler also recalled the rush she and her mother had when Fredericksburg was to celebrate its 50th anniversary, the golden jubilee of its founding. Everyone wanted a new hat and they were busy until late hours every night. In the end they used up all their forms, all their basic and trimming materials, and even had to get out some of their obsolete models which they redesigned for this festive occasion.

Life in the Weyrich home was not all work, however, as there was time for relaxation, too. Music filled their home, as Mrs. Striegler played the piano, and two of her brothers, Alfred and Edgar, could play almost any instrument, however their specialty was playing first and second violins for the family concerts. Mr. Weyrich played the flute and clarinet. Edgar was also a slide trombonist for the town band. Felix Weyrich was her other brother who also joined in the family concerts.

Guests at the Nimitz Hotel would often sit on the porch and listen to the music as it drifted down into the quiet street from the Weyrichs' living room in the evenings.

Mr. and Mrs. Weyrich celebrated their silver wedding anniversary in this home, and the Robert G. Strieglers were also married here. They built their own home diagonally across the street in the same block.

The Weyrichs had their store and home here until they sold the place to Max Wahrmund May 18, 1907, who kept it longer than most of the later owners. He sold it to Louis Klaerner January 5, 1914, who then sold it to Doc Rust August 6, 1920. Subsequent owners were Mary Wolff Schwinn, Anna Holland and husband, H. A. Franz, L. Lohrberg, Estella Lohrberg, Alfons Walter, Dora Maurer, Otto Kolmeier and Mrs. Louise Kusenberger Behrends, Edwin A. and Rubin Schumann, with ownership passing to Max E. Schneider and R.B. Reissig on January 1, 1946.

While all these changes in ownership were occurring, changes in use of the building were going on, too.

Most of the second floor was used as a rooming house, but the rooms were mighty small, Mr. Howard pointed out. He utilized some of the thick rock walls in planning the apartments he has made upstairs now, and tearing out the frame partitions in other areas. There are now seven apartments, some of which have one, and others, two bedrooms, baths, kitchens, dinettes and living rooms. They also have year-round air conditioning.

For many years there was a succession of garages, auto repair shops and auto parts store on the ground floor of the building. Now Das Handwerk Haus occupies the ground floor, with all its attractive merchandise, and the new addition of stock, a complete line of outdoor pottery imported from Mexico which Mrs. Grona features in the area where fruit was once sold in the summer months.

Alma Basse Herbort, Owner

STOFFERS-BASSE BUILDING

An old rock home built in 1855 on Fredericksburg's Main Street is still home today for its owner, Alma Basse Herbort, and her husband, Elgin Herbort. There are few old-timers left who recall its being known as "the Stoffers place" but there are many who will remember the building as the home of Basse Produce and later Basse Express.

Mrs. Herbort, then Alma A. Basse, bought this house and part of Townlot 226 on which it stands, from Fritz Stoffers heirs on May 28, 1938. Her first husband, the late Robert (Bob) Basse, founded Basse Express which operated out of this building for many years. In 1970 she sold the business and it became Southwest Motor Transport and the headquarters were moved away from here.

Before that, Bob Basse's father, Leon Basse, operated a produce business out of this building. He would go about the county, buying eggs, poultry, sausage and produce which he retailed and wholesaled from this location.

At one time there was a package store, here, too, at which time the front was altered, with one of the small windows enlarged to form a showcase for the liquor and wine bottles.

Once there was a partial second story on it, too, with the steps leading out of the front room, but this was torn off when Leon Basse remodeled it.

The history of the place goes back to its being granted by the German Emigration Company to J. Christian Doebner. The company executed a deed to "Joh. Geo. Chr. Doebner" on January 23, 1850, for Townlot No. 226 which adjoined No. 225 that was allotted to "Christian Doebner." Listed on the 1850 census for Gillespie County are two "Christian Doebners," one of them 68 years old and a farmer, and the other, 40 years old, a surveyor, in the same household.

Title to both lots, however, passes out of only one J. Christian Doebner, then of Galveston County, who executed a deed to Anton and Edward Maier on September 11, 1857, to "two house lots, Nos. 225 and 226, and all improvements thereon, and also an 8-acre Outlot." The sale price was $300.

Earlier Chr. Doebner had made a contract with Anton Maier to lease the house and lot to him on condition that Maier would make some improvements on the house. He agreed to make such improvements as: "four windows with frames and facings, inside and outside at $10 a piece; 1 panel door in front and one plain door in rear for $20; two side doors, $10; a plank floor in middle room, $14; plastering and white washing, $12; making in all $96." This contract was dated October 2, 1855.

Edward Maier conveyed his interest to Anton Maier August 23, 1860, and he in turn sold it to Johann Kallenberg on March 30, 1866.

He did not keep it long, however, as Kallenberg and his wife, Margarethe, made an agreement December 24, 1867, to sell the N.W. one-half of this Townlot 226 and 327 (which is behind it fronting on San Antonio Street) to Friedrich Stoffers. The warranty deed was made on July 6, 1870, in accordance with the agreement. The sale price was $200.

The 1860 census lists Fritz Stoffers, 20, a saddler; and Franz Stoffers, 63, also a saddler with Christian Stoffers, 19, a member of the latter's household.

Fritz Stoffers, as Friedrich was best known, had his saddler shop in this building. On July 31, 1873, he made a contract with Adolph Wahrmund to sell to him for $700 "all tools, apparatus, merchandise, work already completed, belonging to my saddler's business now lying and being in my house on Lot 226 on San Saba Street." Wahrmund was also to install him as manager of the business for at least one year, for a monthly wage and also to pay rent for his house.

What transpired after this is not of record, but evidently the arrangement was not satisfactory for either or both. In 1873 Wahrmund bought the little house farther east in the same block (the Hansen house). Stoffers also moved his saddler shop out of this building to a location a little farther up town where he also had a barroom.

As they had several children, this house was no longer big enough for the shop and as a home, so the family used it as their residence and Mr. and Mrs. Stoffers lived here until after their death.

Their children were Henry Stoffers; Lina, who married Henry Schaefer; Minna, who married Otto Braeutigam; Anna, who married Emil Braeutigam; and Bertha, who died in 1892. Mrs. Stoffers died in 1913 and he in 1915. Various transactions among the heirs took place, and at the time Mrs. Herbort bought it the house belonged to Lina and Henry Schaefer and Otto Braeutigam and his wife.

Now, after a useful life, this little house built in 1855 and added to in the rear as more space was needed by later owners, still serves a useful purpose as a home for the Herborts. Now plaster covers the old rock walls, but its sturdy pioneer lines add a distinctive touch along Main Street.

SCHAETTER BUILDING—NOW ANTIQUE STORE

In a block filled with several historic structures, there is one that has seen many different uses, but the oldest part of it started out as a home for a family, just as so many others along the city's Main Street.

Carl Green, owner of Hill Country Antiques, rents the building at 327 East Main Street from the Hilmar Schaetter estate, and has his antique store in it. Many will, however, remember it as Schaetter Furniture Store -- and those who are old enough, can recall, too, when it was Schaetter Funeral Home.

Long before that, however, the oldest part in the back was a home for the Heinrich Schaetter family. The first Schaetter in Fredericksburg was the great-grandfather of the present owner of the funeral home, Oliver Schaetter.

The building is located on part of Townlot 225, originally granted to Christian Doebner on the original list of allottments and conveyed to Joh. Geo. Chr. Doebner by the German Emigration Company by deed dated January 23, 1850. "Christian Doebner" leased this townlot and other property to Anton Maier October 2, 1855, and on September 11, 1857, J. Christian Doebner (then residing in Galveston) made a deed to Anton and Edward Maier, conveying for $300 two "house lots" (Nos. 225 and 226) and an 8-acre Outlot. Edward Maier sold his interest to his brother, Anton Maier, August 23, 1860.

Anton Maier sold these two lots and three behind them which fronted on San Antonio Street to Johann Kallenberg on March 30, 1866.

Kallenberg contracted to sell 34½ by 400 feet of Townlot 225 and No. 328 (which was behind No. 225 facing on San Antonio Street) to Chas. Schwarz on February 11, 1868, for $250 of which $50 was due on "Easter 1868" and $100 on January 1 of 1869 and 1870.

Estate of Hilmar Schaetter, Deceased, Owner

Schwarz either defaulted on payment or was not interested in the property any longer, for he joined Kallenberg in a deed to Heinrich Schaetter January 15, 1869. Schaetter paid $200 for it in installments of $50 each, due in 6, 12, 18 and 24 months, with 10 percent interest. Kallenberg and Schaetter agreed to joint use of a well on Kallenberg's land. Schaetter was granted the undisturbed right of using a trail or pathway over Kallenberg's land to the well and to get water for "domestic and usual household" use. Schaetter was to contribute in the future one-half of the expense necessary to "the conservation of the well." On October 14, 1872, Schaetter gave up the right to go over Kallenberg's land to get to the well.

Schaetter had come to Fredericksburg from Germany where he was born in 1835 in the town of Luenen, in the Kingdom of Prussia. He landed at the port of Galveston December 20, 1867, and became a naturalized American citizen at the age of 40 on February 18, 1875.

He and his wife, Lisetta, lived here in the old rock part at the back of the present building. He also conducted his business here. At first he made saddle trees out of wood and furniture. Soon, as some other cabinet makers or woodworkers of that day did, he turned to making coffins.

In those days when someone died, the family gave the deceased person's measurements and approximate weight to the coffinmaker, who then made the coffin. The body was left at home until the undertaker arrived with the completed coffin or someone went to town and called for it in a wagon or hack.

At first carts, wagons or hacks were used to transport the body to the cemetery or burial place, and by 1882 Schaetter found himself in the "undertaking" business. He saw the need for a hearse and in 1885 provided Fredericksburg with its first one. It was a "fancy" vehicle for its day. It had two smaller wheels in front and two larger ones in back. The driver was seated up high in front behind the dashboard. The "cab" in back was painted black and had scrolls decorating the sides. Along the top were six "feather trees," fluffy black plumes. On each side of the hearse was a large oval plate glass window and another like it was in the back door. When Mr. Schaetter conducted a funeral he would don his black formal coat and hitch up his two black horses, Nick and Prince. When the body was to be taken for a greater distance, he used a four-horse team.

Heinrich Schaetter, later known as H. Schaetter or Henry Schaetter, carried on his business in this location on East Main Street until his death on November 5, 1904, at the age of 69 years.

Additions were made to the oldest part of the house, using similar building stone for the walls, and adding the fancy tin front above the porch. This is practically the same today, with the exception of having the small top embellishment removed, and several years

68

ago the building front was painted with the dark rust-red it is now.

Lisetta Schaetter continued to make her home here until she died March 28, 1926, at the age of 91 years.

One of Heinrich Schaetter's sons, Joe Schaetter, who had been living in Kerrville with his family doing carpenter work and contracting, moved back to Fredericksburg upon his father's death in 1904 and carried on the family's undertaking business and a furniture store in this same location.

The undertaking business was carried on in back of the furniture store, later on taking over for the business that part used by the first Schaetters as their living quarters.

In 1920 Arthur Schaetter joined his father, Joe Schaetter, in the funeral home business, under the firm name of "Schaetter and Son." They built the first funeral home in 1928 behind this building on East San Antonio Street, later moving across the street to their present location at 301 East San Antonio Street, a building that has been enlarged and remodeled several times in the years since it was completed in June 1934. Now Arthur Schaetter's son, Oliver Schaetter, carries on the tradition begun on Main Street by his great-grandfather and carried on by Joe and Arthur Schaetter before their deaths.

Hilmar Schaetter joined his father, Joe Schaetter, in the furniture business, and the old building on Main Street passed into his name after Joe Schaetter died December 15, 1947. It now belongs to the Hilmar Schaetter Estate, and has been rented for the past few years by antique dealers.

Mr. Green has many mementoes of days long gone by for sale in his antique store now, and fortunately the old building also remains as evidence of Fredericksburg's interesting architectural heritage.

WAHRMUND STORE-BAKERY BUILDING— NOW FIRST FEDERAL OFFICE

One of Fredericksburg's most picturesque buildings had in recent years almost received the distinction of being its most dilapidated. Now, thanks to the face-lifting given it by First Federal Savings and Loan Association of Austin since they bought it August 25, 1975, it has been restored and remodeled for use as their branch office at 312 East Main Street.

Known at different periods in its history as "Mrs. Geo. Wahrmund's Millinery and Dressmaking Store," and in more recent decades as "Moellendorf's Bakery" and "Dietz Bakery" before the latter moved to its present location, this old house had caught the eye of many who passed by.

Vestiges of the fancy mansard roof, one of the few in town, were still visible at the sides and in back. In the early days, the shingles had been painted in a decorative design as shown in an old photograph. It was recalled for the writer at the time of the 1956 story on the house that the roof was patterned along the upper lines of the old Nimitz Hotel at the eastern end of this block.

The German Emigration Company granted Townlot 183 on which this house was later built to Ph. (Philipp) Meckel. His deed from the company is dated June 12, 1851, (courthouse records burned in 1850, so substitute deeds were made). A few days later, on June 25, 1851, he sold the entire lot to Johann Dietz for $60. Dietz did not keep it long, either, for he sold it to Wm. Marschall March 29, 1852, for $65. Less than three months later, on June 5, 1852, Marschall sold it for $90 to Wilke. The given name is missing in the deed, but it was Heinrich (Henry) Wilke.

Heinrich Wilke, a wheelwright, had his homestead on this townlot, and at first probably built the small one-story house to the east of it shown in the old photo.

In an 1857 mortgage transaction, he refers to it as his "homestead lot." Heinrich Wilke and his wife, Henrietta, are listed on the 1860 census as being 39 and 29 years old, respectively, and having five children, who were 8, 6, 4, 2 years and six months old. They were divorced later, however, for in the deed to the Northwest part of this lot to George Wahrmund on March 3, 1876, reference is made to Henrietta Wilke being "the divorced wife of Heinrich Wilke, deceased."

It is possible that the house had been under construction when Wahrmund bought it

First Federal Savings and Loan Association of Austin, Owner

because he paid $1100 for the Northwest 40 feet on which this house is located. That was almost 100 years ago, and a lot of changes have come about in that time.

Wahrmund in later years also acquired the Southeast portion of the lot. Henrietta Wilke married a man named Schneider, and on February 1, 1881, she sold the Southeast 60 feet to C.F. and Louis Priess of the firm of C.F. Priess and Bro. for $733. The deed states that this was formerly the property of her divorced and now deceased husband. When C.F. Priess made a deed to George Wahrmund dated November 6, 1893, the deed states that it carries out an agreement to convey it made on February 1, 1881, the same date the Priesses acquired it. Louis Priess sold his interest to a later owner.

Mrs. George Wahrmund had a millinery and dressmaking store in part of the first floor of this building and the family lived in the rest of the house. Their three daughters were Louise, who married George E. Wright; Edna, who married William Clark; and Ollie, Mrs. Herpel of San Antonio. The Wrights lived in the small house that once stood to the east of this, as George Wahrmund and his wife sold it to them October 1, 1896.

The George Wahrmund family was socially and culturally inclined, for when the Casino Club was organized in 1886 with 30 members, a member of the first committee named was George Wahrmund.

It would be interesting to know who helped design the original building as shown in the old photo. There was a large double door with five-paned transom in center front flanked with a window in the larger east room and a large single door with three-paned transom at the west side.

The porch was very distinctive and completely different from most Fredericksburg front porches of that day. It did not extend across the entire front -- its outside edges being about three feet in from each of the side walls. There was no roof above the second story porch, but the top was enclosed with gingerbread railing, and the large sign "Mrs. Geo. Wahrmund Millinary & Dressmaking" in center front. (Note the spelling of millinery in the painted sign.)

The second floor had a single door in front and was flanked by a window at each side with decorative modified V-shaped window frames at the top. Due to the mansard roof lines, each of the side windows were also built along the same lines with the side extending away from the gently sloping-upward walls.

There was more gingerbread along the front porch below the second story floor of the porch and the four posts that supported the second story were not the usual turned ones, but these were decorative with more gingerbread and carving. It's too bad that in the 1920's the

70

desire to "modernize" buildings here led to the removal of this attractive front, however the recessed lines of the porch were retained.

George Wahrmund and his wife, Elise, sold this property for $2,040 to James T. Clark on October 21, 1901, who also acquired Louis Priess' interest in the other part of the lot on October 28, 1901.

Mr. Clark died not too long after this, and his wife and some of their daughters conducted a boarding house here.

On August 13, 1913, the daughters conveyed their interest in this place to their mother. They were Ernestine Clark of San Antonio; Wilhelmine, wife of R.C. Bogusch of San Antonio; Ella, wife of Albert Walter of Gillespie County; Josephine, wife of Rev. I.J. Haag of Louisiana. On September 3, 1913, Mrs. Clark sold it to George M. Clifton, and on November 12, 1913, Clifton sold it to J.M. Montgomery. Montgomery, however, deeded it back to Clifton January 12, 1922, in cancellation of the debt against it.

Martin Schult, a bachelor who came with his mother and others in his family from Germany, bought it February 4, 1924, from Clifton and converted the house into a bakery. He "modernized" the front by adding the glass show windows, and built the large oven at the back of the building. He installed his brother, Werner Schult, as baker. Martin Schult owned and lived in the large two-story Darroch house which is now the home of Dr. and Mrs. Lorence Feller.

A few years later, Harold Kissel operated the bakery, and his family lived upstairs until the place was sold to William Moellendorf by Schult March 15, 1929.

Moellendorf had long experience as a baker at Gonzales, Luling and San Antonio before coming here. His family also made their home here, however, a few years later he added the frame bungalow at the east side of the building and lived in that. This has been moved away.

In 1939, Theo. Dietz, a brother-in-law of William Moellendorf, moved here and took over the operation of Moellendorf's Bakery, continuing to use that name.

In April 1954 his son, Edgar Dietz, who had been a flour salesman, came here from Harlingen to operate the bakery. Having grown up in his father's bake shop, the trade was not completely new to him. Before long, he changed the name to "Dietz Bakery," but that was the only change he made.

Ownership of the property passed from William Moellendorf to his son Walter Moellendorf, who was joined by his wife, Elenora, and their son, William (Billy) and his wife, Karen, in selling it to Wade Bazemore January 8, 1966.

Bazemore had grandiose plans for development of this and other property he owned in this block adjoining the Admiral Nimitz Museum, but his plans ended in bankruptcy. Arthur Stehling, who acquired it after this, sold it to First Federal Savings and Loan Association of Austin August 25, 1975.

Now that the building has passed into its present ownership, happy days are ahead for this charming old building.

The interior has been well adapted to use as a savings and loan institution. The tellers' counter is a reproduction of an old-time counter made out of walnut; the embossed tin ceiling has old-time light fixtures and antique ceiling fans; the limestone rock walls have been stripped of plaster; and the floor is carpeted in a floral design typical of early day floor coverings.

Even the door to the vault blends in with the old-time decor. It has a false front made of wood attached to the steel resembling in appearance old oven doors. In the kitchen area behind the manager's office, even the doors to the bakery oven were left intact, with one door opening into a small reconstructed replica of a part of the oven interior.

Beaded woodwork enhances the reception area in the front room, the manager's office, the downstairs kitchen and restrooms and upstairs in the large meeting room. The entire second floor had been made into one large meeting room with a kitchenette and restrooms in back.

A new tinner's roof that looks old is in place on the building and the new shingles that replaced those that had rotted in the mansard roof blend in well with the old. The front porch was reconstructed with its gingerbread trim, ornate posts and the balcony above it with its decorative wooden railing just as it was in the days when the Wahrmunds had their business and lived here.

An old photo, combined with the expertise of Tyrus Cox, local restoration expert, and Roy White, Austin architect, helped to bring the old building to its present state of beauty once more and made it a distinct addition to the city's Main Street.

———————

MORITZ BAKERY BUILDING

In the 200 block of West Main Street is an inconspicuous little rock building that seldom gets noticed by passers-by. It is behind the red-front store that formerly housed Kiehne's Variety Store. Otto Kiehne and his wife, both now deceased, owned this place since 1924.

Now the store is yellow and houses "The Calico Cat," a fabric store.

It is built on Townlot 242 which, together with the adjoining Townlot 241, were granted by the German Emigration Company to "Shubbert." These were two of the choice lots of the original layout of the city, and unlike all others along Main Street, these faced towards the Public (now Courthouse) Square for 100 feet, and Townlot 242 and its three adjoining ones ran for 200 feet parallel to Main Street.

This "Shubbert" was probably the Dr. Schubert who was appointed administrator and physician for the colony in its early days after he was recommended to John O. Meusebach, the founder. It turned out, however, that he "conducted a miserable administration" and was soon replaced, so he probably traded his claim to them off to someone else.

Title turns up in the name of F. (Fred) H. Schlador, who as attorney in fact of Huck and Schlador, sold Townlots 242 and 241 to John Z. Leyendecker for $250 by deed dated March 22, 1853. Henry I. Huck of Calhoun County (where

Indianola was located) traded these lots to Schlador by deed dated December 5, 1853, (after he had sold them earlier that year to Leyendecker) for two lots Huck owned in Indianola.

John Z. Leyendecker sold Townlots 242 and 241 for $450 "in lawful money of the Confederate States of America" to Caroline Graf on December 24, 1862.

Mrs. Graf and her husband, Carl Graf, must have built some improvements on this lot for when they sold Townlot 242 (the corner lot) to Heinrich Ochs on March 25, 1868, the sale price was $800 cash. Graf was a wheelwright and this was a good place for his business.

Heinrich Ochs and his wife, Elisabeth, sold a strip at the far west end of their lot, with 45 feet frontage on San Saba Street to Anton Kraus for $500 on January 1, 1870. While the deed conveys 45 feet of frontage on Main Street, there is a condition that the east five feet of this strip that Kraus now owned and which adjoined the remainder of the Ochs property would be used "solely for doorway and passage between the parcel herein conveyed and H. Ochs until said parties agree to apply it to other purposes." Kraus was to bear the expense of providing a "door" to his property.

Anton Kraus was a stonemason who was born in Germany. After the death of his wife, he and his children sold this property to Franz Moritz on August 16, 1890. Joining him in the deed were his children: Peter Kraus, Christ. Kraus, Joseph Kraus of Gillespie County; Maria Eisenloh, formerly Kraus of Karnes County; and Margaret Eisenloh and husband, Peter Eisenloh of Bexar County; also Dina Ernst, daughter of Magdalena Ernst, deceased, formerly Kraus, whose interest was conveyed by her father, Carl Ernst of Gillespie County. The price was $400 cash and a balance of $600 due in four years. The Krauses had added the frame addition at the west side of the little house.

While the Moritz family lived here they conducted a bakery in that building which is now occupied by Main Electronics, and prior to that by Heimann Jewelers.

The little rock house originally had only two rooms, one downstairs and another upstairs. The room on the ground floor was the kitchen and every-day dining room. It has only a door in the north or front wall, and one window in each the east and south walls.

Very steep, narrow steps lead up in the northwest corner of this house. Like others of that day, these had no bannister to hold onto.

The room on the second floor, which was used by their son, Carl Moritz, as his bedroom, is a pleasant room. There was once a very small window at the head of the stairs in the west wall (also something often found in old homes as this provided natural light on the steps). This window was closed up when the frame addition was added, and served later occupants as a small recessed shelf. There is a double, sliding window in the front or north wall and a good-sized window in each the south and east walls.

From this house, the Moritzes had easy access to their bakery. The oven was right behind the present electronics store building. The doors through which the oven was fired with cordwood were both on the inside of the building.

Mr. Moritz went to Galveston to learn the bakery trade. He learned how to make his own yeast, as it could not be bought prepared as the baker of today does.

At the time of the 1956 series, his daughter, Mrs. Joe P. Staudt, recalled how he mixed hops and other ingredients to make the yeast, then strained it into the dough mixture. He had to do this every time he baked, as there was no way of keeping it because there was no refrigeration as we know it today.

They baked white and rye bread. The white varied in size, one of which was a very high square in which the loaves were baked end-to-end and then broken apart. These loaves sold for five cents each.

Another size was broader in the middle and came to points at the end with a good crust all around. This sold for ten cents a loaf.

They also baked "zimmet kuchen," an early day variation of our coffee cake, plain rolls made out of the same dough with raisins, and also gingerbread.

At Christmas time they featured Christmas cookies which people bought to hang on their trees. For this Mr. Moritz used cookie cutters in all shapes and sizes which had been made by Lungkwitz, famed pioneer tinsmith, silversmith and locksmith.

Otto Kiehne, who in later years operated a variety store recalled that he bought 1400 of their cookies one year and sold them in his store during the pre-Christmas season for 15 cents a dozen.

Mr. Moritz was also a stonemason, so his wife assisted in running the bakery.

On September 25, 1916, Frank (Franz) Moritz and his wife, Katharina, sold this property to John Stehling, who in turn sold it to R.G. Striegler January 2, 1920. Otto R. Kiehne bought it September 3, 1924.

A fire had caused extensive damage in a cleaning-pressing shop in the building where the Moritzes had their bakery, so Mr. Kiehne tore off the second floor and erected his two-story combination store and residence immediately adjoining it. He conducted his variety store there from 1925 until he closed his business several years ago.

While the Kiehnes' son, the late Lee Kiehne, was in high school and college, he used the second floor of this rock building as a studio. Mr. Kiehne used the ground floor room as a beautifully equipped work and tool shop.

Mr. Kiehne died June 21, 1975, and his wife, Augusta, on March 10, 1976. They left as survivors two children, Flora, Mrs. Kenneth Hohmann and a son, Rudy Kiehne, with the later buying his sister's interest in this property.

The old building -- one that has seen many uses -- remains today as a reminder of the interesting past that has given Fredericksburg its distinctive heritage.

———

SCHANDUA HOUSE

Through a generous gift from Burt L. Joiner and his wife, Geneva, to the Gillespie County Historical Society, on September 19, 1963, the old Schandua house at 111 East Austin Street has been preserved as a classic example of a late Victorian period pioneer home of Texas.

It is one of the few local restorations made without the use of electricity or modern plumbing and visitors are taken back to the 1880's when they enter the little two-room house. It is furnished completely in the period of its early use, and as someone said, "It is a house that is always ready for company."

During the almost 100-year history of the building, it has been home to many families, and also served as a Sunday School house for Bethany Lutheran Church for many years.

Its history begins with the allotment by the German Emigration Company of Townlot 93 on which is built to "Schmidt II." Although no first name is given on the official list, the deed from the company dated December 9, 1852, (after fire destroyed the original records) is made to Adam Schmidt II. It is also of interest that the adjoining lot and another nearby were granted to other Schmidts.

After the formality of making the deed to Adam Schmidt II was taken care of, he sold his Townlot to Mathias Schmidt on February 16, 1853, for $40. Mathias Schmidt died in 1872, and the administrator of his estate, Adam Schmidt of Llano County, sold Townlots 92 and 93 to William Koennecke on October 4, 1876.

Koennecke did not keep it long, because he sold both Townlots to Peter Schmidt of Travis County for $500 cash on December 29, 1876. He didn't keep it long either, because his deed to E. T. Moore, also of Travis County, is dated January 6, 1877, with $500 cash the sale price, too.

Moore sold both lots to Daniel Ludwig October 11, 1883, for $400 cash, and a month later, on November 8, 1883, Ludwig sold Townlot 93 for $250 cash to John Schandua. At that time Ludwig lived behind his shoe shop to the south of this property which fronted on Main Street in the vicinity of the present-day Winn's.

Just who built the house is not certain, but probably one of the Schmidts, because it was on the property when the Schanduas bought it.

The house, as it stands today, has changed little structurally, except that when the Schanduas lived here they had a little kitchen and washhouse of frame construction behind it near the location of the old well. This was torn down years ago. At one time there was also a small, narrow wooden structure along its west side towards church, but this was also torn down many years ago.

When the Schandua family lived here, the small room in back was the children's bedroom and the front room was the combination sitting room and parents' bedroom.

John Schandua was one of the pioneer merchants of Fredericksburg. He and his family lived here until 1903 when they moved into the large new two-story building he had erected on Main Street which Gloria Hill and her late husband, George Hill, have so beautifully remodeled. The hardware store was conducted on the first floor and the family lived upstairs. After John Schandua died, his widow married his brother, Henry, who took over the operation of the store.

While the Schanduas continued their ownership of the little house on East Austin Street, after they moved away it was rented to numerous tenants, as it was such an ideal location in the middle ot town.

For many years, from sometime in the 1920's until 1947, this little house was also used by Bethany Lutheran Church (then located in the present Baptist Church) for Sunday School and confirmation classes.

While in its early days this property changed hands often, such was not to be the case in later years. The Schandua family owned it until June 9, 1921, when they sold Townlot 93 to Max and Fred (Fritz) Joseph for $2000. Long-time Dodge dealers, their firm, Joseph Bros., was located at the present site of Winn's.

Joining in the deed to the Josephs were John Schandua's widow, Bertha Schandua, then the wife of Henry Schandua, and Johna and Bertha's children, Olga Weirich and husband, Richard, of Bexar County; Alfred, Ella and Olinda Schandua of Gillespie County, and Emilie Leifeste and husband, Herman, of Mason County. In later years Ella married Wm. Jung and after his death, Felix Pehl; and Olinda married John Moehr. The John Schanduas had lost one son at birth, another at the age of one year, and a daughter, who died when she was five years old. The Henry Schanduas had one daughter, Bertha, who married John Goar.

Burt L. Joiner, a San Antonio business man, bought this little house and the property on which it is located at the same time he acquired the former Joseph Bros. Garage property on Main Street where Carl and Weimar Hein had succeeded them in the auto business. On March 4, 1963, Joiner and his wife bought this property from Fritz Joseph's widow and the Max Joseph estate.

Fortunately for Fredericksburg, Mr. and Mrs. Joiner recognized the value of the little house and when they made a big parking lot in back of Winn's, they made a gift of the little house to the Gillespie County Historical Society, deeding them the 40.8 feet by 48.3 feet on which it is located.

It took the Gillespie County Historical Society almost 10 years before they completed the restoration of the little house, but like so many good things that have to wait awhile, this is one project that turned out very well. Gloria Hill was one of the leaders for the society in its restoration and furnishing.

The large double doors in front are flanked by a window at each side. They lead into the large front room furnished in the style of a typical combination parlor and bedroom, just as it was used by the Schanduas.

The small room has a back door flanked by a window at each side, but no windows in the side walls. There is also no window in the west wall of the front room. The back room is now the kitchen and dining room. No effort was made to restore the wooden structures that were once on the property.

When restoration and furnishing were completed, the Historical Society had a beautiful and authentic old home of the 1880's to show on its tour of old homes and buildings, and one in which future generations can take special delight and pride.

WEYRICH-ARHELGER HOME—NOW ANTIQUE STORE

Sometimes an incident interwoven into the history of an old home almost makes an interesting story in itself. Such is the case with the Arhelger home at 420 East Main Street in which an antique shop is now located.

Built by Charles (Carl) Weyrich early in the 1850's, it rivaled in size the two-story rock house across the street built by Friedrich Kiehne. The house has been owned by only two families, the Weyrichs and Arhelgers. The present owners are the former Ellie Arhelger and her husband, Frank Thies, of Charlotte, N.C., who got title to it August 3, 1955, when her brother and sisters conveyed their interest in it to her in the name of Thies Realty and Mortgage Company.

The house is built on Townlot 192 which the German Emigration Company granted to C.F. Torczinsky. That he ever laid claim to it or used it is doubtful, for Carl Weyrich was the builder of the house, having acquired ownership of this lot and the unnumbered townlot behind it that extended to the creek now known as Town Creek, but referred to in an early deed as "Little Baron's Creek."

J. H. Herndon (to whom the survey on which this lot is situated was patented) quitclaimed any interest he might have in the lot by deed dated November 11, 1859, but which was not filed for record until 1871.

Carl Weyrich was born in Germany, August 3, 1819, and came to America late in 1845. His wife was Margarethe Heuser, who was born in Germany on March 21, 1822, and came to America in 1846. They were married in Fredericksburg on November 15, 1847, and lived together to celebrate their golden wedding, an event which was termed as "Eine Seltene Feier" (An Unusual Celebration) in the Fredericksburg Wochenblatt.

Carl Weyrich was a gunsmith and locksmith. He is best remembered for the many fine locks and keys he made, with the one on his own home one of the most ornate handmade ones in the county.

To supplement his income, he also made trips into West Texas to buy or barter buffalo hides from the Indians, and an interesting story is involved in one of these trips as revealed in a letter written in 1854. A tragedy that occurred on this trip prompted the writing of the letter, but its importance to the house is that the writer tells about the Carl Weyrichs having begun the building of their large stone house.

The letter was written by Elise Heuser, a sister of Mrs. Carl Weyrich, who was making her home with them. She later married Adolph Lungkwitz, a silversmith. It was written in German to a friend in Germany on August 1, 1854, to tell her about the tragic event that happened the year before. This letter was returned to Mrs. R. G. Striegler several Christmases before the original 1955 Old Homes feature on this house was written. She received it from a distant relative with whom she was corresponding who discovered it among some of the family's personal belongings.

The sad mission for writing the letter was to tell her friend about the tragic death of her brother. It had occurred on January 29, 1853, but she had put off writing the sad news. Her brother, August Heuser, had accompanied Carl Weyrich on a trip westward to get buffalo hides as they had done many times before. On their way home, the Llano River was on a rise. At the place they attempted to ford the river, the waters were flowing in three streams. They made it across the first and smaller one safely, but when they got to the second stream, it proved to be too deep and swift and the current swept their wagon over. Three soldiers who were coming to Fredericksburg with them sensed impending danger and jumped free of the wagon, swimming to safety on shore.

A man she did not identify in the letter, remained in the wagon, however, a roll of buffalo hides knocked her brother into the flood waters. He went under, so the man in the wagon said, and came up again about ten feet away, but could not get to the safety of the wagon and drowned.

Carl Weyrich was also thrown out of the wagon and started to swim to shore, however, his strength failed him, and he said he implored God's blessing upon his soul and upon his wife and children in Fredericksburg. Suddenly his strength was renewed, the letter states, and he was able to swim to shore safely.

The Carl Weyrich family was large, as ten children were born to the couple. They were Gustav, William, August, Carl, Adolph; Bertha, Mrs. Richard Braeutigam; Sophie, Mrs. Max Wahrmund; Mathilda, Mrs. Herman Feller; Teresa who died when she was about one year old, and another child who died in infancy.

After they had grown to young manhood, William and August Weyrich visited in Germany.

Of interest, too, is the fact that the two young boys shown in the famous sketch done by Lungkwitz in the 1850's of a scene overlooking the valley of Fredericksburg were none other than Gustav and William Weyrich. They were watching the family sheep which grazed on the Ten Acre Lot allotted to Carl Weyrich by the German Emigration Company southwest of Fredericksburg.

The house Carl Weyrich had begun building before August 1, 1854, has changed on the exterior only in that a later owner, F.W. (Willie) Arhelger added the two-story, arched concrete porch.

Originally the house had only a narrow two-story porch at center front over the double door entrance. Each room at the side of the front hall also had a doorway facing the street, and these remain.

The lock on the front entrance is probably the most distinctive one he made. It is of iron and has a five-pointed star at the top. In the lower part of the star is the hole in which the key is inserted. Right below that is a well-proportioned lyre. The key is large and heavy, over six inches long. The handles control one bar for opening and closing the door. A second bar for locking slips into place as the large key is turned three times to complete the locking operation.

There are several other interesting old iron locks and latches on some of the other doors in the house.

Since the house was home for the F.W. Arhelger family for so many years, a bit of reminiscing reveals their use of it. Now most of the building is used by the antique business.

The main, double front door leads into the hall. There is one large room at the west side which was the Arhelger dining room, and another room on the east side was their living room. A step down leads into what had been the Arhelger kitchen at the west corner in back, and another into the parents' bedroom at the east corner. Part of the back hall was converted into a bathroom.

Originally the stairs to the second floor ascended at this point, and then made an abrupt turn before reaching the hall upstairs. Later the stairway was changed to near the entrance in the front hall.

From the back hall, steps led down into the large cellar under what was the bedroom at the northeast corner of the house. Here the Weyrichs and the Arhelgers stored food and kept their wine barrels. Serving of good homemade wine was a mark of German hospitality.

Upstairs there is a hallway down the center, opening through double doors onto the second floor porch. On either side were two bedrooms, and behind these two smaller bedrooms.

From this area there is a stepdown just as

on the ground floor, into a small hall behind which is a bathroom. On either side were two more bedrooms.

The partitions are of frame construction. Originally, the front part of the second floor was one large area instead of being four bedrooms and large hall as it is now. This was the place that Carl Weyrich hung the tobacco to dry that he had grown in the lot behind the house and out of which he rolled his own cigars.

After his wife's death, Carl Weyrich lived here for a while by himself, and then moved out on the farm with his daughter's family, the Richard Braeutigams. In 1955 it was from their daughter, Mrs. L.E. Brodie, that much of the family history and personal recollections about the house were obtained, supplemented with clippings saved by her cousin, Mrs. R.G. Striegler.

Next to occupy the house were the William Weyrichs, parents of Mrs. Striegler. Her three brothers were Felix, Alfred and Edgar Weyrich. Their mother died in 1907, after the family had lived here for only a short time.

The father of Robert Penniger, early Wochenblatt and Standard editor, ran an upholstery shop at one time in the west front room.

William Weyrich sold the place to F.W. (Willie) Arhelger May 15, 1918. Mr. Arhelger had been in the wheelwright business with his father, William Arhelger. He retired from this business at this time, however, he continued to operate a ranch near Doss and farm near the city.

The six Arhelger children who grew up here were Laura, Mrs. Erwin Jordan; Dora, Mrs. Newell Kring; Ellie, Mrs. Frank Thies; Vera, Mrs. M.D. Puckett; Werner Arhelger; and Lillian Arhelger, who died in a tragic accident when she attempted to rescue a youngster caught in swift water at a summer camp in the east.

The house was generally filled with happiness and laughter, as all of them were a lively lot. Mr. Arhelger was a convivial host who "never knew a stranger" and Mrs. Arhelger was a sweet, quiet, gracious hostess.

Their daughter, Ellie, and her husband, the present owners, are deeply appreciative of anything that is steeped in tradition, and the present tenants, in carrying on their antique and collectibles business, are preserving another vestige of Fredericksburg's rich heritage.

RESSMANN-BOOS HOME

The old Boos home, immediately east of the Sunday House Motel at 511 East Main, is one where the earliest type of construction, fachwerk, is still visible in one of the front walls. Some old-timers will remember it as the Ressmann house, as it was in the Ressmann family from 1868 until June 26, 1946, when Christine Boos and her husband, Hilmar Boos, bought it from Bertha Ressmann.

The house is located on Townlot 214 granted by the German Emigration to an individual listed only as "Balmert" on the officially recorded list, but he never claimed it, or died, or assigned it without there being any record of it, and title turns up in the name of John M. Hunter, who was first county clerk and then sheriff of Gillespie County. He sold it for $150 to A.A. Lockwood of Bexar County August 11, 1852.

Two years later, Hunter, as sheriff, sold the townlot to satisfy a judgement in favor of W.J. Carey and others against C.J. Cook & Co. on

April 27, 1854. He executed the deed August 15, 1845, for the sale price of $85, selling it to "Hewitt and Newton" of Bexar County.

In the deed there is the statement that it covers "houses and two lots in Fredericksburg", one of which was 214 and the one adjoining it. The houses referred to are probably the oldest part of the present structure and the small one-room log house that stood immediately behind it which the Booses tore down after they bought the property.

I.L. Hewitt and S.G. Newton sold the property to Christian Althaus August 20, 1855, for $50, and about a year later on November 6, 1856, he sold it to John Petri for $60. John (Johannes) Petri and wife, Barbara, sold it to Mathias Schaefer December 28, 1858, for $130, of which $50 was cash, and the balance of $80 was paid by Geo. Weinheimer on his behalf.

The next transaction is an interesting one because Mathias Schaefer and his wife, Katharina, traded this townlot to Jacob

Zauner on July 25, 1860, for 160 acres preemption land on Grape Creek to which Mrs. Zauner, "born Julie Hahnzog" was entitled. The deed states they were to "swop" (swap) the property.

The Zauners did not keep it long, either, for they sold it to Heinrich Beckmann February 11, 1862, for $150. Heinrich Beckmann contracted to sell it to Chr. Ressmann June 20, 1866, for $250, of which $50 was cash and a note for $200 was due in installments of $100 in six and 12 months. The deed to Ressmann is dated March 31, 1868, and it states that part of the security for the purchase price was the townlot and "their iron ox-wagon."

It was to remain in the Ressmann family until 1946, the year of the city's Centennial.

The oldest part of the house includes the two original rooms of fachwerk and rock construction on the west side. The front room has a door and window next to it and a window in the west wall, both of which are the old-time casement-type found in the earliest homes.

Behind the front room is the kitchen which was built on a little lower level. The doorway between the two rooms is so low that an average-sized woman has to stoop to pass through. The original wide board doors are still in use. A small window in the side and another in the back wall next to the back door are also in the kitchen. The old loghouse stood right behind this kitchen, but this was torn down by Mr. and Mrs. Boos. For the 1956

feature on the house Mrs. Boos recalled the logs used in it were so heavy that it was impossible for the two of them to lift one of the logs.

The house was home to Christian Ressmann and his wife, Katharina. They had two sons, Christian Ressmann and John Ressmann and one daughter, Louise, who married William Feller. The elder Ressmann died while still a fairly young man, and his widow remarried -- a man by the name of Steneabach. They had a daughter, Anne, who married James Phillips.

During her last years, Mrs. Steneabach made her home with her son, Christian and his wife. The house was then occupied for a while by the John Ressmanns, however, in 1905, it was bought from the other heirs by the younger Christian Ressmann. His widow, Bertha Ressmann, rented it out until it was sold to the Booses in 1946.

During later years, a frame construction bedroom was added at the east side, and the interior of the fachwerk rooms was sheetrocked. They also covered the west side of the house with boards. Originally shingles had been placed on this wall by an early owner to protect the crude fachwerk which was exposed to the weather. That part under the porch was plastered, and a cement porch floor replaced the original one.

Now Mr. and Mrs. Boos are both deceased, and their son and his wife, Mr. and Mrs. Chester Boos, sold it to Lawrence W. Nebgen

November 23, 1973. Four days later, on November 27, 1973, he sold it to Kenneth Kothe and wife, JoAnn. It is now part of the Fredericksburg Enterprises properties, which include the Sunday House Motel and Restaurant.

Hopefully it will be preserved or restored befitting an old home of such interesting construction and one which typifies the pioneer homes of Fredericksburg.

Sauer Associates, Owners

WAHRMUND HOME—
NOW HILL COUNTRY SAVINGS AND LOAN OFFICE

An old home of Fredericksburg is now the new home of one of the city's newest businesses since Hill Country Savings and Loan Association of Kerrville opened a branch office in the old Wahrmund building at 214 West Main Street.

Now owned by Sauer Associates, Inc., this old rock building was renovated and remodeled by the association as their branch office.

This is one more instance of a modern business, with its eye on the future of Fredericksburg, retaining the architecture of the past to make the present day profitable for itself and at the same preserve an old pioneer building for posterity.

The story of this old home and its early owners is interwoven into the history of Fredericksburg and Gillespie County.

Its story begins in January 1846 when William Wahrmund, who was born in Wiesbaden, Germany, on April 21, 1824, came to Texas with his family. He and his brother,

Emil, stayed in New Braunfels for one year, and then William came to Fredericksburg.

The two corner townlots on West Main Street (then San Saba Street) which he acquired were to be long known as the William Wahrmund property. By coincidence, his brother, Emil, after he came to Fredericksburg, acquired the property on East Main across from the southeast corner of the Market Square where Sears Catalog Agency and the businesses adjoining it are now located.

This Market Square was also referred to as "The Public Plaza" in some early transactions.

Since the two townlots across from the southwest corner of the square were such strategically located ones it is natural that a good many transactions took place in the early years of the town's history.

The corner lot (No. 168) was originally granted to "Hch. Strackbein" by the German Emigration Company and sold by him on

80

October 19, 1853, to A.F. Wulff. The one next to it on which this house is located (No. 167) was granted to "Eckhardt," and H. Eckhard on August 20, 1853, sold it to Georg. Weinheimer, who in turn on the same date sold it to A.F. Wulff. Even in those days there were "middle men" (counterparts of modern real estate agents) in real estate transactions.

Mr. Wulff lived on the corner lot, as reference is made to that fact in the deed to him from Strackbein. He must also have had a store on these premises, because in Penniger's Fest Ausgabe (published 1896) reference is made to "Mr. Wolf's store" at an uptown site.

Wulff must have had extensive improvements on these two townlots because when he sold them to James R. Sweet of San Antonio on May 12, 1854, he got $2000 cash for them, a sizable sum for those days. While Wulff is listed as being from Gillespie County, he and his wife must have been living apart, because on April 8, 1857, "G. (Gonadeloupe) Paula Wulff, wife of A.F. Wulff" of Bexar County made a separate deed of her interest to Sweet.

On December 1, 1856, Sweet sold the two townlots "fronting on Public Plaza" to William Wahrmund for $1800, $500 of which was cash with a note for $1300 due in 12 months and bearing at 12 percent interest. Wahrmund paid off the note before it was due.

The two townlots were to remain in the Wahrmund name until May 10, 1924, when Otto Wahrmund, owner at that time, sold them to Emil H. Riley. The deed conveyed all of Townlots 168 and 167, with the exception of a strip four feet by 51 feet wide which Otto's father, William, had conveyed to Fritz Weihmueller (the owner then of the present-day Falstaff house facing the Market Square).

The house restored for use by Hill Country Savings and Loan was built in 1875. But the Wahrmund history goes back farther, because after William Wahrmund bought the two lots, he conducted a general store in the long-low building that stood right on the corner of what is now West Main and North Crockett Streets. The store was in the west half of the building and the William Wahrmund family lived in the east end.

William Wahrmund was also Chief Justice of Gillespie County, an office he was elected to in 1852 and held until 1862. In 1864 he was elected for another term, and in 1876 was elected County Judge, an office he held until

his death June 21, 1890.

William Wahrmund and his wife, Amalia, had six children, however, one daughter and one son died while they were children. Those who grew up in the old corner house were Henry Wahrmund; Clara, who married Eugene Staffel of San Antonio; Otto Wahrmund, who was one of the owners of Pearl Brewery in San Antonio; and William L. Wahrmund.

They were all musical, and the sounds of their Knabe grand piano and the violin played by Otto often echoed into the street and passersby would stop to listen as they strolled by. The family parlor was located right next to the sidewalk.

William L. Wahrmund and his wife, Elise, were the first to live in the rock house built in 1875 immediately west of his parents' home and store. Next to occupy it were another of the elder William's sons, Henry Wahrmund, and his wife, the former Meta Nimitz. Her sister, Sophie, married Henry's brother, Otto.

From Henry's daughter, Lorlie, Mrs. R. L. Kott, much of the family history was obtained in 1955 for the original series. The Henry Wahrmunds moved in into the 1875-built house after their marriage, and all of their children were born here. In addition to Mrs. Kott, the others were William Wahrmund; Henry Oscar Wahrmund; Margaret, Mrs. Myron F. Ward; and Ella, Mrs. William Lawson.

When Mrs. Kott was 16, her mother died, and two years later her father passed away. The children continued to live in this old house, with the family housekeeper taking care of them. Mrs. Kott married and made her home here, while the other children moved on to San Antonio as they finished school.

All of the Kott children were also born in this old house. They were Margaret, Mrs. J. H. Blackaller; Gertrude, Mrs. J. Peyton Barnes; R.L. Kott Jr.; and Mrs. Helen Kott Schuck.

Mrs. Kott recalled that originally the house had a large front porch with ornate trim and railing. The limestone rocks were covered with gray plaster and there were matching blinds at the windows. Climbing over the porch were vines of clematis, honeysuckle, and a Martha Washington rose, now extinct.

Entrance in front was through the large, recessed double wood doors with square paneling. The door led into the family parlor on the east side. Next to it in the front was a bedroom.

In back there was a bedroom behind the

living room with two windows in the east wall, however, one of them was made into a door by later owners. There was a back door to this room. Next to it was the family kitchen with a door in the west wall and a window to the north.

Some of the furnishings had been brought to this house from their parents' home at the corner by the Henry Wahrmunds when they lived here, and were still in Mrs. Kott's family in 1955.

Behind this house and the corner home and store was a large orchard planted with fruit trees and grape vines, also a vegetable garden. Here also was the washhouse, smokehouse and servants' quarters, as well as one small house with blinds or shutters for walls used chiefly for butchering.

The Wahrmunds had a lawn in front of this house, with flower beds and large cedar trees. Running along the sidewalk in front of the house to the porch of the other home and store was a rock fence several feet high. The children played behind it, and it was also a good perch to watch a parade pass by.

Among the parades that passed by were those commemorating the 50th, 75th, 100th and 125th anniversaries of the city, as well as numerous others during Saengerfests and on other auspicious occasions, such as Nimitz' triumphant return home.

From Emil H. Riley and his wife and

Central Power and Light Company who bought it from the Wahrmunds, title to the property passed to Walter Hollmig and his wife, Mary, March 15, 1934, and September 23, 1935, and the old home found many uses. It was a beauty shop for several years, then Mrs. Holmig conducted an antique store in it, and it was also used for storage.

Sauer Associates bought it from the Hollmigs November 1, 1972, and they have leased it to the Hill Country Savings and Loan Association.

With the expertise of Tyrus Cox, local restoration specialist, and old photos, the building has been well adapted to its present use. The front porch with its gingerbread trim, posts and railings were restored just as they were originally, and a low stone wall between the yard and the sidewalk, similar to the original one, was added.

On the interior the reception room and business offices have reminders of bygone days. There is a huge old iron safe, tellers' cages and counter from an old bank were added, and antique, as well as some modern pieces of furniture in period styling blend in well. There's even a kitchenette in a back room.

Now once more, an old building is serving a useful purpose in the community at the same time adding a distinctive architectural addition to Fredericksburg's Main Street.

DIETZ HOTEL—NOW STEHLING LAW OFFICE

The last Gillespie County Fair catalog published in the 1800's -- that for the Sept. 21-25, 1899, Fair -- had this advertisement:

"DIETZ HOTEL - Main Str., Above Post Office - Newly Furnished Throughout - The table a Specialty - Polite Attention - Special Rates made to Summer Guests - Louis Dietz, Proprietor."

That building at 218 West Main Street is now the home and law office of Arthur Stehling. It was also known as the Central Hotel with Mr. Dietz as proprietor; and before that was Schmidt's Hotel.

Completely renovated by the present owner, the old building has served many uses since its erection some time during the 1860's.

It is built on Townlot No. 166 which was granted by the German Emigration Company to Johan Schmidt, and deeded by the company

to his widow as assignee of her husband on October 5, 1852.

It is of interest that four adjoining townlots, from Nos. 163 at the west corner of the block through 166, were allotted by the company to Schmidts -- 163 to J. Schmidt, 164 to Lorenz Schmidt, 165 to Ludwig Schmidt and 166 to Johan Schmidt. Lorenz and Ludwig Schmidt were stonemasons.

In Penniger's 1896 Fest-Ausgabe he speaks of Johannes (John) Schmidt as the company's soldier who shot the large bear on the banks of the Pedernales River as the first train of colonists reached their destination and which provided their first meal here.

Lorenz Schmidt was with the first expedition that came to survey the site of Fredericksburg in December 1845. He also wanted to accompany the first train, but since his

brothers wanted to join it, too, he stayed behind to care for his mother, according to Penniger.

Elisabeth Schmidt, the widow of Johan (John), deeded Townlot 165 to her son, Ludwig, April 30, 1857, and he built the two story native stone building and operated it as Schmidt's Hotel for many years. Around 1892 the Schmidt family leased the property to Louis Dietz, who operated the hotel as "Central Hotel" and "Dietz Hotel." From his widow, who was 91 years old at the time the 1956 feature on this house was written, much of the information of its early appearance and use was obtained. She was making her home with her daughter, Mrs. Lawrence Krauskopf, at that time.

No structural changes have been made in the exterior of the old building, but over the years many have been made inside.

At the time the Dietzes ran the hotel and operated its dining room, they lived in a one-story house to the east of this building where the Schwarz Building now stands. This housed the large hotel dining room, kitchen and three bedrooms.

The hotel had a front entrance through the large double doors which remain today. Flanking them were two large windows, with the same arrangement on the upper floor. Above the double doors were attractive opaque glass transoms with decorative metalwork. All the windows were shuttered.

Originally the ground floor had a partition dividing the east two-thirds of the building into a lobby and office. Along the west side there was an office at the front where Dr. Glasser, an optician had his office, and another small office-room was behind this. Dr. L.K. Tainter (who built the home the Henry Josephs now own) also had his office here at one time.

The steps went up at the southeast corner of the building. On the second floor were the hotel bedrooms. There were two larger rooms along the west side; a hall down the middle from the double front doors to the double back doors; and four smaller bedrooms along the east side, with a narrow hall dividing the front two and back two. The hall led from the stairs to the large middle hall.

To the rear of the hotel was a large barn where Mr. Dietz kept his horses, and there was also a campyard where farmers could leave their teams and wagons when they shopped for provisions in town. A large sign between the hotel and the dining room proclaimed "Stabling and Feed."

When the Dietzes ran the hotel, the shutters and woodwork were painted brown while the porch railing and gingerbread trim were in yellow and brown. Between the hotel and the dining room was a tall carriage lamp post and a big square stone which was used by riders in dismounting their horses and onto which people stepped in getting into or out of coaches. Brass hitching posts topped with miniature horse heads lined the sidewalk.

The Louis Dietzes later moved into their new Dietz Hotel, a three-story structure that Louis Dietz built across the street, later known as Ostrow Hotel, then LaMesa Hotel, and now no longer standing.

On March 20, 1899, Maria Katharina Schmidt, surviving wife of Ludwig Schmidt, deceased, was joined by their children, Alvine Ochs and her husband, Herman; Ida Hotopp and her husband, Charles; Albert E. Schmidt, all of Gillespie County; Theodore, Louis, Herman, Benno and James Schmidt of Mason County; Henry Schmidt of Tom Green County, in selling this property to Charles Schwarz for $3,000, $1,500 of which was cash and $1,500 payable to the widow twelve months later.

Charles Schwarz was a pioneer merchant who for many years operated Schwarz Store in the former Wahrmund store at the corner where Security's drive-in bank is now located. For several years he had his store in the hotel building, later building the newer structure next to it in 1907.

For a while a saloon was operated here, and then Frank Hanisch and J.D. Payne conducted their drug store business here. They had a soda fountain in connection with their pharmacy. Dr. Chisholm, a dentist, had his office on the second floor. In 1917 Payne sold his interest in the drug store to Hanisch, who continued to operate the business here until

the middle of the 1940's when he moved his business to the Hanisch residence at the corner of the next block.

Charles Schwarz died October 19, 1911, leaving his widow and the following children as his survivors: Harry, Else, Hans, Charles, Elise, Margarete, Arthur and Dora. His widow sold the property to H.H. Schwarz January 1, 1931, and he and his wife, Edith, sold it to Peter Knopp and John Metzger (of the firm of Knopp and Metzger) August 14, 1943.

Ownership passed from John W. Metzger and wife, Ida, Max A. Metzger and Ella Metzger to Main Enterprises (Arthur Stehling) April 17, 1957.

Stehling converted the old building into a home, and since May 1971 he has also had his office on the ground floor. A large fireplace was placed in the west wall were a living area and office space are located, with kitchenette in the middle and a bedroom and reception room at the east side.

The upper floor is rented out as a two-bedroom apartment, with access via the stairway at the northeast corner.

Fredericksburg's Main Street has been enhanced in appearance with the renovation of this old building and its useful purpose in 1976 carries on the tradition of preserving and saving the old buildings for posterity.

OCHS-MOSELEY HOUSES

Behind the unimposing facades of some of Fredericksburg's old buildings are often found interiors that belie their plain exteriors. Such is the case with the buildings located at 211-215 W. Main Street renovated in the 1960's by Mr. and Mrs. Milton Moseley.

Now the former Moseley Galerie at 211 W. Main is occupied by The Friendship Shop. This building was once a saddlery shop and in later years a beauty shop.

Next door, at 213-215 W. Main St., the Moseleys combined what had once been a barber shop and an old home into a residence that was a real showplace when they had it furnished with their antiques and collection of art and other valuables. The Moseleys moved back to Fort Worth, their former home about

two years ago, and until this summer the house was vacant, however, now Kenn Knopp, owner of The Friendship Shop, and his mother, Mrs. Minna Knopp, are residing there.

The buildings are located on part of Townlot No. 242, one of four which faced on the courthouse square. It had a frontage of 100 feet, running back for 200 feet along Main Street. No. 242 was allotted by the German Emigration Company to "Shubbert." As pointed out in the feature on the Moritz Bakery which is located on the same lot, Shubbert was one of the aliases used by the Dr. Schubert who was appointed administrator and physician for the colony in its early days. His record is such a poor one,

Mr. and Mrs. Milton M. Moseley, Owners

though, that he probably traded these choice lots off to someone else as title turns up in the name of F. (Fred) H. Schlador, who as at- torney-in-lact of Huck and Schlador, sold Townlots 242 and 241 to John Z. Leyendecker for $250 by deed dated March 22, 1853. Henry I. Huck of Calhoun County (where Indianola was located) traded these lots to Schlador by deed dated December 5, 1853, for two lots Huck owned in Indianola -- this after he had sold them earlier that year to Leyendecker!

An affidavit is of record dated April 1, 1875, in which John Leyendecker Sr. states that he transferred Townlots 242 and 241 to his son, John C. Leyendecker "a number of years ago".

Leyendecker sold the lots to Caroline Graf on December 24, 1862, for $450 in Confederate money. Mrs. Graf and her husband, Carl, a wheelwright, sold all of Townlot 242 to Heinrich Ochs on March 25, 1868, and that part of the lot on which the residence is located was to remain in the Ochs family for 61 years -- until 1929.

This Heinrich Ochs was the "Schullehrer Ochs" who was one of the first to teach in the Vereins Kirche, then in his office of County Clerk in the courthouse, and also as one of the four teachers who rotated among schools in different locations in the county. He was

County Clerk from 1859 to 1869.

The elder Ochs and his family lived at first in a little log cabin that stood behind this rock home which was built after he acquired title to the property.

Ochs came to Texas in 1851, from Coblenz, Germany, and he married Elizabeth Otto of Westfalen, Germany, after he came to Texas. They had six children, two boys and four girls, but the girls died before they reached maturity. The two sons were Herman C. Ochs and Heinrich Jacob (Henry J.) Ochs.

On July 24, 1909, the widow of Heinrich Ochs Sr., Elizabeth Ochs, and the two sons, Herman and Henry J., signed a partition deed, stating that it carried out a mutual agreement and conveyance made between Mrs. Ochs and the two sons on November 26, 1894. Henry J. Ochs received the part of Lot 242 on which the Moseley buildings are now located. Herman Ochs received the Buckhorn Saloon property at the corner where Security State Bank & Trust is now located.

The Herman Ochs family lived in this residence until Henry J. Ochs married. Then he and his family made their home here. He was a saddler and conducted his trade in the building that is now occupied by The Friend- ship Shop and prior to that by Mrs. Christine Knopp when she operated a beauty shop here.

85

She bought that part from Henry J. Ochs and his wife March 25, 1929, and sold it to the Moseleys February 23, 1965.

Henry J. Ochs and his wife, the former Elise Schoenewolf, sold their house to Max W. Staudt March 25, 1929. He operated a jewelry store two doors west of here and lived in this house. Before the Max Staudts and later his parents, the Joe P. Staudts, made their home here, this building was used by Edmund Saenger who had a grocery store in it.

When the Staudts bought the property, they made some changes in it, including the removal of the front porch, adding a stoop over the front door and a railing around the front edge. They also made some changes in the interior, but it was the Moseleys who made the extensive renovations and additions to the building. They bought the Staudt property November 8, 1962.

The Moseleys enclosed the area that had been the porch, using old doors and lumber so the stuccoed walls would blend with the rest of the house. Behind the entry area this provided, they made the rooms along the west side into bedrooms and bath, with the kitchen at the southeast corner of the original house. The back porch became their raised level dining room, and the small building that adjoined what had been the Staudt house where a barber shop was located became Mr.

Moseley's office. He was a semi-retired architect and she was an interior decorator.

They enclosed the entire area behind the original rock house, providing on a lower level a spacious living area, with huge fireplace and book-lined walls. Behind that, at the southeast corner they created a garden room with fountain, and next to it a utility and storage area.

The passageway between the larger building and the former saddlery shop and beauty shop was paved with brick, a door was added in front and closed in back, providing privacy. From here the occupants have access to the galerie or shop, which also has a main entrance for use by the public from Main Street.

The little frame shop building was also stuccoed to blend into one harmonious whole with the old Ochs home.

The front of the house bears a Recorded Texas Historic Landmark erected by the Moseleys in 1965. It reads: "Little Rock House. Constructed shortly after Civil War on Townlot Grant of German Emigration Company. Bought 1868 by Heinrich Ochs, pioneer school teacher, owned by family 61 years.

"Has been home and store with floor plan virtually unchanged since erection."

RANSLEBEN-MOELLERING HOME

"C.L. RANSLEBEN - Wagon and Carriage Manufacturer" was the name of the business carried on in the old rock building that is now a home at 417 East Main Street. Built in 1880, this building was constructed to house the wheelwright and blacksmith business Mr. Ransleben conducted there for many years. In later years, one of his grandsons, Louis Moellering Jr., converted it into a residence.

His advertisement in the 1899 Gillespie County Fair catalog read: "C.L. RANSLEBEN - Wagon and Carriage Manufacturer. Fredericksburg, Texas - Agent for the Deering Harvester Co.'s Binders and Mowers, the Moline Plows and Cultivators, and the celebrated Hawkeye Grub and Stump Machine. Always on hand the Latest and Best Improved Agricultural Implements. A cordial invitation to all parties visiting our Fair to

come and see my stock and my exhibit on Fair Grounds."

For a blacksmith shop to become a home is typical of the multiple uses that the old buildings along Fredericksburg's Main Street have seen over the past hundred and more years.

It is built on part of Townlot 218 which was allotted to L. v. Donop by the German Emigration Company and deeded by them to Louis von Donop on December 20, 1949. Donop sold it to Friedrich Kiehne for $26 on June 16, 1851.

Fr. Kiehne Sr., joined by H.F. and W. Kiehne, in a conditional deed dated November 22, 1879, contracted to sell the entire townlot and the unnumbered lot between it and Barons Creek to Carl Ransleben for $200, due in five years, however, he must have paid it off a lot

sooner, for the warranty deed from Kiehne to Ransleben is dated January 24, 1882.

At the time the 1955 feature on this house was written, Ransleben's daughter, Valeska, Mrs. Louis Moellering Sr., was still living and could recall many interesting details about this place.

Carl Ludwig Ransleben was born in Comfort, and went to Austin as a youth to learn the trade of wheelwright. He learned how to make wheels, axles and entire wagons, and was also a blacksmith.

He and his brother, Oscar, first had their blacksmith shop in what had been Julius Hollmig's shop which faced Nimitz Hotel (now Zenner's Texaco). After he finished this building in 1880, they moved their business into it. The Carl Ransleben family moved into the Lehne house which faces on South Elk, southeast of this property.

In 1887, Carl Ransleben built the rock house next to the shop on East Main Street and the family moved in here.

This rock building was used as a blacksmith shop on the east side of the building, and the west end was where the wheelwright trade was carried on. They ordered most of the material they used from a firm in Austin. In the upper half-story they stored wood and iron. It was reached by a stairway on the inside of the shop, however, there was also an opening in the middle of the floor through which heavy objects could be raised or lowered by means of a crude elevator.

In later years when farm implements were manufactured and became more plentiful, Mr. Ransleben added this line to his business. Among the brands were the Avery plows and the Moline line. In greatest demand were the self-binders, cultivators, plows and planters.

Mr. Ransleben also made most of the furniture he and his family used in their home at first.

In those days when people came in for repairs or supplies, they often camped to the rear of the shop, and Mrs. Ransleben would frequently have to furnish lodging to some of them for the night. This took some doing, as there were nine children in the family.

They included Valeska, Mrs. Louis Moellering Sr.; Ella, Mrs. Hubert Kott; Bertha, Mrs. Herman Staudt; Max Ransleben; Bianca, Mrs. August Langerhans; Octavia, Mrs. Jasper Nixon; Carl Ransleben; Louise, Mrs. Bob Lee; and Cornelia, Mrs. Fred Langerhans.

The Carl (C.L.) Ransleben heirs deeded their interest in the two lots to Mrs. Moellering and her husband by deed dated February 1, 1926. On Oct. 9, 1939, the Moellerings deeded the part on which this house is located to their son, Louis Jr., and he and his family made their home here for many years after renovating it. The upper half story of the shop was torn down. The large double wooden doors of the shop were replaced with a conventional house door under the arched entrance flanked by four glass panes at each side. The house has a living room, kitchen, bath, small hallway and two bedrooms.

The elder Moellerings lived in a small frame house at the rear of this building.

In later years, the owners moved into the rock house adjoining this one, and the old building that had once been a blacksmith and wheelwright shop was rented out to tenants. Mr. Moellering is no longer living, but his widow continues to live next door and carries on a business of selling vegetable and flower plants from the location.

Mrs. Enid Collins, Owner
Mr. and Mrs. Hector Pedregon, Shop Owners
Mrs. Walter Pfeil, Owner

BONN HOMES—ONE IS NOW THE PEACH TREE

Two old homes of Fredericksburg, while not on Main Street, are located on one of the city's busiest thoroughfares and one of them probably draws as many out of town visitors as any place in the city. This is the former Adolph Bonn residence at 210 South Adams now owned by Enid Collins and the location of "The Peach Tree," Fredericksburg's distinctive gift shop owned and managed by her daughter and son-in-law, Cynthia and Hector Pedregon.

The older of the two homes is the one immediately north of it at 206 South Adams. This was the Peter Bonn residence since post-Civil

War days, and is now owned by Mrs. Walter Pfeil who makes her home there when she is not with her son, Clarence Pfeil, in Sinton.

The story of the "Haengerbande," the infamous gang that roamed Gillespie County after the Civil War, terrorizing citizens, looting, and committing other crimes, is interwoven into the story of Peter Bonn who owned the entire townlot on which the two houses are built and who lived in the oldest house.

Townlot No. 432, which faces for 200 feet on South Adams Street, (the Kerrville Road), has a depth of 100 feet fronting on East Creek

Street. It was originally allotted to "A. Hch. Heymann" by the German Emigration Company. Ownership shows up in Carl Weyrich, who sold the lot to Ernst Schaper September 13, 1865, for $30.

Schaper made improvements, and built the small rock house, for when he sold this lot to Peter Bonn on February 9, 1869, the deed stated it conveyed Townlot 432 "together with the improvements thereon" for $1,200 due in three installments, the first before April 1, 1869, the second one December 25, 1869, and the final one by August 1, 1870, with no interest due if paid on time.

The house was built at the north end of the lot, and near it was the "Kalkbrennerei" or lime kiln where he burned the lime used in building the house, according to Mrs. Pfeil.

Peter Bonn was a farmer, having his farm south of here, part of which was at the site of the old Fair Grounds on South Adams. He was born in Hanover, Germany, and came here at age 11 with his parents, the Mathias Bonns. His wife was Caroline Lochte, who came from Berlin with her parents at the age of 7.

Having left strife and unrest behind, he thought, when the family left Germany, he wanted only peace and a chance to make a good living here in Texas, so his sympathies as a young man of 25 did not lie with the Union or Confederate cause during the Civil War. As a consequence, after the Civil War he was on the "wanted" list of the infamous "Haengerbande" (band of hangmen) that took delight in taking a man out and hanging him for no other reason than the fact that he "minded his own business" during the Civil War.

Mrs. Pfeil recalled the story her grandparents told of how he hid under the family featherbeds in his wife's cedar chest in this house when the band of outlaws rode up one time looking for him. They searched the house and did not find him, but this did not deter them from keeping a lookout for him.

When he went to work in the fields and suspected the Haengerbande was in the area, he would often don his wife's long dress and big sunbonnet, so they did not molest him. It was not at all unusual for women to work in their fields in those days.

The rock fence that encloses part of The Peach Tree lot once extended along the entire front of the property, and was higher in places than it is now. At the far corner of the lot, now The Peach Tree lawn and garden, Mrs. Peter

Bonn would milk her cow with a feeling of personal safety.

The Peter Bonn residence and the little building behind it have changed little since the days when they were first built, but the Walter Pfeils, who bought it from the Peter Bonn heirs June 13, 1918, did make some alterations, such as providing a bathroom, enclosing the "durch gang" (counterpart of modern breezeway) between the two with frame construction.

Behind the front room is the kitchen. The little rock building behind the kitchen was used for the smokehouse and storage, a typical "Rumpelkammer" -- a catch-all room for odds and ends. From the frame enclosure a door leads to the front and foot of the steps that lead up the north side of the building to the bedroom on the second floor. In addition to the doorway at the top of the stairs, there are two large casement windows in the south-wall.

The Peter Bonns had nine children, a mighty big family to rear in such a small house, but this was typical of many families of those days. Their children were Heinrich, Albert, Adolph, Richard, Willie and Louis Bonn; Bertha, Mrs. Ed. Ruegner; Minna, Mrs. Alfons Walter; and Lina, Mrs. Emil Schellhase.

Mr. and Mrs. Peter Bonn conveyed the lower 100 by 122 feet of their Townlot to their son, Adolph Bonn, April 8, 1905, and he built the house that is now The Peach Tree. Originally it was an L-shaped building with only the three front rooms, two on the south side and a hall and another room extending towards the Peter Bonn residence. These rooms were built of limestone, some of the stones of very large size. Later on, behind this a concrete block addition was added, making an additional bedroom at the south side and a frame kitchen behind the front room in the wing of the "L."

The Adolph Bonns lived here during their life, with their daughter, Edna, marrying Walter Pfeil. They also had a son, Leroy Bonn, who with his wife joined the Pfeils in selling the Adolph Bonn home to Frieda Moellendorf October 28, 1949. She married Sam Schneider who joined her in the conveyance to her son, Walter Moellendorf, and his wife June 23, 1967, and they lived here for 14 years. The Walter Moellendorfs then sold it to Pedernales Finance Corporation, owned by W.L. Hahn and others, on October 10, 1971. Not long after that the corporation sold it to Enid Collins on February 10, 1972.

The Pedregons took out some walls between rooms, made one front door into a showcase window, and gave the wall treatment a look compatible with Fredericksburg of yesteryear, at the same time providing an ideal background to display their giftwares.

The trim over their counter in the front room is gingerbread saved from the old St. Mary's Rectory by Schatzie Crouch. The trim over a gift display alcove is a reproduction of gingerbread on a neighbor's house, and the corner pieces are copies of those used on the Schandua house restored about the same time on East Austin Street.

One large salesroom has been covered with rough cedar which Pedregon finished with white paint to resemble the "whitewashed" look of old. The walls of what had been the kitchen are rough unfinished cedar, also ideal for displaying the merchandise.

Life at this corner has changed greatly from that following the years immediately after the Civil War. Now in the corner where Mrs. Peter Bonn milked her cow, there is a pretty lawn and garden where the Peach Tree owners often hold art exhibits. Inside their building they sell many contemporary gifts, but also others with a nostalgic air, reminiscent of yesteryear, drawing a clientele from not only this immediate area, but from throughout a wide area of Texas.

Helen Stieler Crouch, Owner

SCHUMACHER-LEYENDECKER HOUSE— NOW RUMPELKAMMER

An old home, a tailor shop, a boarding house, a vineyard and winery, headquarters for a well-drilling firm -- all these fit into the history of the "Rumpelkammer" at 104 East Austin Street and the rest of the 100 block between North Llano, North Adams and Town Creek.

Almost as diverse use of the old Schumacher buildings is now being made of them in 1976. The large rock building is now known as the "Rumpelkammer," a German word used to denote a room or chamber filled with odds and ends. In this case, the house is filled with antique furniture, some of it restored, some in a dilapidated state waiting to be refinished, or to be sold "as is."

In connection with this business, there is a large concrete block building behind it where the owner of the property, Schatzie (few know her real name is Helen) Crouch, has a fur-

90

niture refinishing and restoring plant in partnership with Bob Borchers. To the rear of that, and fronting on North Adams, they have moved the wooden structure that formerly housed Gentemann Furniture Store on West Main Street, and use it, together with an annex to the concrete block building, as a place where they restore vintage and classic automobiles.

The story of this block, so near to Main Street in the busiest part of town, goes back to the very beginning of the city.

Friedrich Wilhelm Schumacher, a tailor, was one of the earliest settlers, and the German Emigration Company allotted him Townlot 67 on which he built his two houses. His deed from them is dated December 17, 1849, and he also acquired the other lots in this block between Austin Street and Town Creek.

Coming here as a young man with his wife and two children, his first concern was to provide a home, and part of this house is still standing today. In recent years, Mrs. Crouch has placed a new shingle roof over the house and made some efforts to stabilize the walls of one room, but no further restoration of it has been undertaken.

It provides a graphic picture of the methods used in building the first houses from the material that was available close at hand to the first settlers.

If the big oak trees at the back of the lot that line the south bank of Town Creek are indicative of the trees that grew in the rest of the block, he did not have to go far to get the logs used in building his house.

The first room Schumacher built utilized the fachwerk mode of construction, with vertical, horizontal and slanting logs or beams. These were not nailed together, but instead pegs were used which can still be seen. Slender willow sticks, probably gathered on the creek banks, were woven in a loose manner and then filled in with a mixture of red clay and grass. There is a red clay bluff on the creek right behind this property. These sections were wedged in between slightly thicker tree limbs used as crosspieces between the logs. The marks of the ax used to trim the bark off the logs are still there, as they had no time for fine finishing when they were trying to get a roof over their heads for shelter.

This front room had a wide board floor and a step led up into the room adjoining it which was added later. For this room, rocks and crude mortar and plaster were used instead of clay, sticks and grass in sections of the walls.

Little remains of the back part, originally two rooms, however, there was a dirt floor and the walls were made of limestone rock, with a combination oven and cooking fireplace in the room that was the kitchen.

At the time of the 1955 feature on this house, A.C. Klein, whose wife was a granddaughter of Schumacher, recalled stories he had heard about family life here in the early days.

He told how Mrs. Schumacher had finished baking bread one day and placed her loaves near the window to cool. Suddenly she looked up and saw an Indian standing there, holding a knife and motioning to her to cut some of it for him. She did, and he soon left, causing no disturbance or harm.

Mr. Schumacher planted a dense bois d'arc hedge along the northwestern edge of his property -- now North Adams Street. Left to grow as it pleases, bois d'arc (commonly known as osage orange) forms a thick, thorny, impenetrable hedge, and he felt this would be a deterrent to Indians sneaking up on his place from that direction. Though the hedge has been completely removed, it is almost impossible to eradicate it, and small plants are still coming up in the backyard of the adjoining lot now owned by the Herbert Grahams.

The larger two-story house Schumacher built later had no windows in the west wall, and only doors in the east wall, with windows in front and back.

How Mr. Schumacher did his tailoring in this house during the dark winter days is hard to comprehend. The front room he used for his shop has only two windows, one on each side of the large, paneled double door. The back room, their kitchen, has two windows in the back and a door in its east wall.

From the kitchen, steps lead to the second floor which also has only one window on each side of the front door and two windows in the back room under the eaves.

F.W. Schumacher and his wife, Anna Marie Elizabeth, had two children, a son, Gottlieb, and a daughter, Bertha, who married Carl Leyendecker. After the death of their parents sometime prior to 1899, Gottlieb, then of Bexar County, on April 5, 1899, conveyed his interest to his sister in this townlot and all the rest of the lots facing on Austin Street in this block, as well as in the ten-acre Outlot Schumacher had received for his farm.

The Carl Leyendeckers and their children

lived in this house and had a vineyard planted with many grape vines in the eastern end of the block towards the Llano Road. They made wine for sale, using a huge cellar to store their hundreds of gallons as they aged. The cellar, storehouse and smokehouse were to the east of the older of the two houses.

The town boys stole grapes so often that finally Mr. Leyendecker moved his vineyard to his ten-acre lot in what is now northeast Fredericksburg.

When children came to town to attend confirmation classes, then held for five or six days a week for approximately three or four months before Palm Sunday, Mrs. Leyendecker would board some of them in this house.

After the death of the Carl Leyendeckers, their children sold their interest in the two corner lots and the unnumbered lots behind them to their brother, Chas. J. Leyendecker, on November 26, 1915. They included Louise, Mrs. Ferdinand Knetsch; Mrs. Caroline Broetzman; Annie, Mrs. A.C. Klein; Mary,

Mrs. Joseph Keller; William Leyendecker; and Emma, Mrs. Albert J. Schmidt.

Chas. J. Leyendecker operated a well-drilling outfit and lived in the two-story rock house, using the lot to the north and west as parking area for his equipment when not in use. Leyendecker sold the lot with the two houses to A.C. Klein and wife on December 19, 1945, and their heirs, Laura Halbadier, Hilmar Klein, Walter F. Klein, Myrtle and Irwin Hubbard and Arnold Klein sold it to the Gillespie County Historical Society March 3, 1961.

John R. Crouch and his wife, Helen Stieler Crouch, bought it from the Society on January 13, 1969, and not long after that restoration efforts were begun here. Since August 20, 1973, it is the sole property of Mrs. Crouch.

Now furnishings of bygone days find their way here, as the owners bring them in for refinishing, or Mrs. Crouch buys them for resale or to restore to their original use and beauty.

PETER WALTER HOME—NOW EPISCOPAL CHAPEL

When Peter Walter built the little house on the townlot allotted to him by the German Emigration Company after he arrived here with the first settlers of Fredericksburg, he could never in his wildest dreams have foreseen that someday the President of the United States would attend worship services in it.

But that's just what Lyndon Baines Johnson, the 36th President of the United States, did when he would come to Texas to spend time at his ranch on the Pedernales. In the mid-1950's the Walter home became the first church home for the newly-organized congregation of St. Barnabas Episcopal Church.

Shortly after Peter Walter arrived in Fredericksburg, he began work on this little house on West Creek Street, near the corner of South Bowie. He used the material at hand, finding most of it in the immediate neighborhood.

For the walls of the front two rooms he used the fachwerk-type of construction he was familiar with in Germany, using rough hewn logs, mortar, rocks and plaster. The back

room was of solid rock construction with small logs above the windows. It even had a rock floor. The beams in the ceiling were whitewashed and the space in between them was filled with what was described at the time of the 1954 series by his granddaughter as "lehm-boden." It was a mixture of lime, black dirt and grasses that grew along Baron's Creek which flows southwest of the lot. When the Episcopaleans bought this house in 1954, some of this filler was still to be seen in the ceiling.

His granddaughter, Mrs. Minna Lang, at that time recalled hearing about how he had cut his beams and logs for the house and the adjoining barn he built later from the trees that grew nearby. He even sawed his own planks or boards, using them horizontally above the front two rooms for the attic.

Originally the kitchen was a few feet to the rear of this house. This was often the case, as fires were constantly burning in the stove for cooking, and if a fire were to get out of control, then the entire house would not burn down. The kitchen had a small fireplace with raised

St. Barnabas Episcopal Church, Owner

hearth for cooking. In 1954 Mrs. Lang still had the black iron pot they used to bake bread, heaping additional coals on its lid as it sat on the bed of coals in the fireplace.

Next to the kitchen they had their grape arbor planted with the grape stock Peter Walter brought from Germany and which still flourishes today.

Peter Walter, a "wagoner", had oxen he used for hauling freight and farming his surrounding acreage, having bought 10 adjoining lots from other grantees. Later his son, William, used mules for hauling freight from San Antonio to Fredericksburg, and then from here to Loyal Valley and Fort McKavett. The large barn which stood west of the house was used to store feed for the animals.

The Peter Walters had six children. After his death, his widow, Anna Margaret, was joined by John and Louis Walter; Mina Walter, the wife of Henry Walter, deceased; Margarethe Welgehausen and her husband, Conrad; and Catharine Bratherich and her husband, H. Bratherich, in conveying the property to her son and their brother, William Walter, on July 3, 1877. A condition of the deed was that she be permitted to live here and that her son would support her. The deed covered this and nine other lots, plus "a tract of land adjoining said lots in the Southwest known as the Old Mill Place numbered No. 614."

The tall pecan trees growing around this house and the church grew from nuts planted by Mrs. William Walter.

The William Walters made their home here. They had only one child, Minna, who was born here and later married Henry P. Lang. In later years the Langs lived in a new house they built at the west end of the block. Mrs. Lang, after the death of her husband, sold on June 12, 1954, to the Trustees of the St. Barnabas Episcopal Church the townlot on which this house was built, as well as the corner lot and the one immediately west of the house.

The interior of the little house was converted into a chapel by removing the wall between the front two rooms, taking out the dirt ceiling and exposing the beams under the roof. Almost symbolically at one end these supports formed a cross. A new shingle roof and other restorations were made.

There is an official Texas State Historical marker on the little chapel now, but there's a mistake in the wording. As Rev. Dean Pratt pointed out, it states that the building was consecrated on St. Barnabas Day, December 16, 1954, but that day is not St. St. Barnabas Day. It is, however, the date of the Saint's ordination, and that fact was brought out at the time Bishop Everett H. Jones consecrated the little mission.

This little chapel was selected as the site for their wedding by the eminent Texas historian, Walter Prescott Webb, and Terrell Maverick, the widow of Maury Maverick, in December 1961, with Bishop Jones as the officiant.

The trustees bought the additional land so they would have room to build a church as the congregation grew. This they did, and in 1964 the new building was finished. In one of its walls is a stone sent by the Bishop of St. Barnabas from that church-monastery on the island of Cyprus to Mrs. Lyndon B. Johnson as a gift for St. Barnabas in Fredericksburg. Present for the "stone laying" ceremony in 1963 were then - Vice President and Mrs. Johnson.

With the building of the new church edifice, the little chapel that was Peter Walter's house was no longer used for regular worship services, the congregation having long outgrown its meager space.

But few old homes ever received as much statewide, national and international attention as Peter Walter's little house on West Creek Street. An Episcopalian, Mrs. Johnson would be accompanied by her husband, first as Vice President and then as President, and the inevitable entourage of press, television, radio representatives and Secret Service detail when they attended worship services in St. Barnabas. Often, too, they would bring their distinguished guests who visited them at the ranch to worship in or just to see the little chapel.

The tall stately LBJ would have to stoop to enter and stoop to leave the low front door and even lower porch in front of it. But proud he was, and seemed to take special delight in letting the rest of the world know that he worshipped his God in this humble little cottage built by a German immigrant who found a new home on the frontier of Texas.

PETER-SCHMIDT-TREIBS-LANGEHENNIG HOUSE

As one passes by some of the old homes along Fredericksburg's Main Street, one wonders sometimes what happiness and sadness its residents experienced while living there.

Some of these homes that were the scene for near-tragedies fortunately saw times turn out happier for later owners, and such is the case with the old Peter-Schmidt-Treibs-Langehennig home at the corner of West Main and North Acorn Streets now owned by Abel and Ruth Pierce of Houston.

Built on Townlot 139, the west wall of the back of it is just about on the property line, as you can see by the slight offset. The lot is one originally allotted to Fredrich Metzger by the German Emigration Company and was deeded by the company to him on December 22, 1849. Metzger and his wife, Katharina, sold the lot to Johan Peter September 12, 1853, for $65. A year later, Johan Peter sold it for the same price to his son, Georg Peter.

The elder Peter was a stonemason and the oldest part of the house was built sometime in the mid-1850's. Originally there was one large front room and behind that the kitchen with sleeping quarters upstairs. A steep narrow stairway leads up from the kitchen to the upper room. There is a trapdoor above the stairway. The floor of the area above the front room is much higher than that of the area above the original kitchen, now used as a dining room.

Behind this was a small structure which enclosed the water well -- often referred to as the "brunnen haus," or "well room."

Now there is a floor over the old well, and buried in its depths lies, in all probability, the cause for much of the unhappiness that some of the residents experienced. This room is now the kitchen.

While the Peter family lived here, several members died of typhoid fever, and as the family circle was broken up, those who were spared, left home and moved elsewhere. For many years it was rented to various tenants. Among them was the Fritz Schmidt family.

Mr. Schmidt had been injured when he fell off a hay wagon at the age of 31 years. Within two years he was blind, and after some persuasion went to Austin where he learned the trade of making brooms and mattresses at the Institute for the Blind. He came back to Fredericksburg and followed that trade in the back two rooms that were added behind the "well room", however, ten years after his accident he died on April 20, 1901. His widow, Bertha Schmidt, bought the house on January 10, 1903, from G.F. Peter and wife, Celia, of Bell County, Clara Evers and husband,

94

Adolph Evers, and Lina Peter, sole heirs and legatees of George Peter and wife, both deceased.

In the meantime, typhoid struck again. This time, Mrs. Schmidt, her son Henry, and one daughter, Nellie, Mrs. Gus Klingelhoefer, became seriously ill, but by that time, better medicine was available, and doctors were able to help them and they all recovered. The other daughter, Adela, Mrs. Ben Kneese, did not become ill.

By now they figured the typhoid could be caused by the drinking water from the old well in the house. At the time of the 1954 series on old homes, Mrs. Schmidt was still living, and recalled how it was not uncommon to find some of the most fiendish-looking scorpions in the water that they drew out of the well. She said one was almost a foot long. Mrs. Schmidt's brush with typhoid did not keep her from living a long life, for she died at age 97 in 1957.

The Schmidt family had the well closed and a floor and floor covering have obliterated all sign of one being there. There is another well east of the house, but this is no longer used.

Mrs. Schmidt and her children sold the house and lot to Jacob Treibs January 17, 1920. Mr. Treibs died November 11, 1926, and on December 27, 1945, his widow, Emilie Treibs, and William E. Thiele, his executor and one of his stepchildren, conveyed it to Regina Langehennig, Mrs. Treibs' daughter and Mr. Thiele's sister.

Mrs. Langehennig and her husband, Albert Langehennig, had lived here for many years before that date, as they sold their farm and moved to town to help look after her mother. The Langehennigs and their five sons lived here, and Mr. Langehennig was a barber before his death.

His widow and the five sons, Andrew Harvey, Victor Wesley, Walton Albert, Oliver Lee and Kermit William Langehennig, sold it to Abel Pierce and his wife, Ruth, of Houston on Aug. 29, 1968.

Mr. Pierce is a retired architect. They have a home in Houston, and are now restoring their Victorian family place in Blessing. They come up here often on weekends, and members of their family and friends often are here, too, to use the house. They have made some necessary repairs, but have not gotten into any major restoration work.

That's in store, though, for this old rock home on busy Main Street -- and hopefully, the happiness that later owners of it found there will continue for all who call this house "home."

Mrs. Else Schneider, Owner

FRANK VAN DER STUCKEN BIRTHPLACE

A musician, composer and conductor who gained fame in Europe and America after studying in Europe under Edvard Grieg, Carl Reinecke and others, was a friend of such musical "greats" as Verdi and Massinet, was born October 15, 1858, in a house at 123-125 East Main Street in Fredericksburg that is still standing today.

Frank Valentin van der Stucken was his name, and now there's a red granite marker and an official Texas Historical Survey medallion telling passersby of that fact.

He was the son of Frank van der Stucken, a native of Antwerp, Belgium, who came to Texas at age 15 in the company of Henri Castro, French colonizer. His mother, Sophie Schoenewolf, was a native of Mainingen, Germany. Her parents were August and Anna Schoenewolf, however, after Mr. Schoenewolf's death, Anna married Valentin Hopf.

The composer's parents were married December 23, 1852, by the Rev. B. Dangers and the same pastor baptized young Frank, their son, December 25, 1859, in the Vereins Kirche.

Townlot 238 on which the house is built was allotted to August Nette, however, the original deed from the German Emigration Company, dated March 29, 1848, was to Emil Kriewitz de Czepry. For practical purposes he used only the name Emil Kriewetz while working with the early settlers. He organized a surveying company, lived with the Indians a while to learn their ways, helped establish the colonies of Castell, Leiningen and Bettina, and served in many other capacities for the colony here, according to his reminiscences in 1896 for Penniger's Fest Ausgabe.

October 21, 1850, while at Comanche Springs, he contracted to sell this townlot to Henry Basse for $60 cash to be paid eight days after that date. On November 13, 1850, he signed the deed to Basse for it, but it was not acknowledged until November 5, 1852, by one of the witnesses to Kriewetz's signature.

On June 24, 1856, Henry Basse sold this townlot to Frank van der Stucken who already owned the adjoining Townlot 237. He was a merchant in Fredericksburg, helped build forts under government contracts, and, at the beginning of the Civil War, was in a partnership which held government freight contracts. He was also the Captain of Company E of the First Texas Cavalry attached to the 31st Brigade of the Confederate Army.

Frank van der Stucken had been elected Chief Justice of Gillespie County in 1864, but in the spring of 1865 he resigned the office and Theo Buchholz was named as his successor.

Van der Stucken made preparations to return to his native Belgium, including the deeding on January 31, 1865, of these two adjoining townlots and "all improvements, house, store and stables" to his wife's step-father, Valentin Hopf, with the consideration being "valuable services rendered" by Hopf. He had a large cache of money hidden under the floor of his home which he used to finance the trip back to Belguim where the family was in the flour-milling business and he amassed a large fortune.

One of the reasons the van der Stucken family returned to Belgium was the musical training that young Frank could get there which began with the study of the violin in Brussels at the age of eight years.

His training continued in Europe and he gained fame as a composer and conductor in many of the major European cities, and later returned to the U.S. where he was the director of a large chorus in New York and later the conductor of the Cincinnati Symphony and dean of the Cincinnati College of Music. He made repeated trips back to Europe as guest conductor there, as well as in such places as Chicago, New York and Boston. He died August 18, 1929, in Hamburg, Germany.

While the native-born Texan was making a name for himself in musical circles, life was going on back home at the house where he was born on Main Street.

Valentin Hopf had a number of trades, being listed on the 1850 census as a shinglemaker, in 1860 as a farmer, and in 1870 as a shoemaker. He also acquired extensive landholdings in the county.

When Valentin Hopf married the widow, Anna Schoenewolf, she had two other children in addition to Sophie, who had married Frank van der Stucken. They were August Schoenewolf and Christine, who married Felix van der Stucken, a brother to Frank. Christine died in 1880, leaving as her survivors a son, Alfred; and three daughters, Constance, who married Gustav Mueller; Marie (Mary) who married Frank Lungkwitz; Olga, who married Henry Rodermund; and Louise, who married Mrs. W.J. Moore.

After marrying Hopf, the couple had two children of their own, Emil C. Hopf and a daughter, Elise, who married Frank Morgan.

Valentin and Anna Hopf died, and on various dates, beginning in the spring of 1899, all of their heirs conveyed their interest in this house to Elise Morgan, who then on November 3, 1899, sold it to her brother, Emil C. Hopf. The Emil Hopfs conducted a general merchandise and millinery business here.

Hopf sold it to Richard Bonn February 18, 1907, and he ran a general merchandise business in it for many years. Bonn moved to his ranch and sold this building to William Schneider July 14, 1920. Mr. Schneider was a cotton and grain buyer and had his office in the little white frame building adjoining the two-story house.

The Schneiders added the front two large rooms which are now occupied by Freda's Gift Shop and Hill Country Medical Products, as well as the porch in front of them. Originally there were only two large rooms with a wide hall dividing them upstairs and downstairs with a large two-story porch in front. Below these rooms is a large cellar with its entrance on the east end.

A wing was added during Hopf ownership. This L-shaped wing of matching limestone is in line with the rest of the building at the west side and has a two-story porch in back facing east with the same iron railing and decorative posts as those in front. This wing has two bedrooms in it now, with the original two rooms upstairs serving Mrs. Schneider as a large kitchen and equally large bedroom.

Above the two stores, Mrs. Schneider has a large dining room and a living room. Mr. Schneider died, but his widow continued to make her home here. They had two sons, Oliver, who is now deceased, and William (Bill), who lives in Austin. She has six grandchildren.

Now, as life goes on in 1976 in the home where a boy was born who gained international fame in musical circles, it's nice to reflect about modernized facades that hide the ageless limestone rocks that were used for the walls which sheltered all to whom the house was home and a place to earn a livelihood.

———

FELIX VAN DER STUCKEN HOME

The old rock home at 114 West Austin overlooking the north side of the Market Square has been a familiar part of the local scene since sometime after the end of the Civil War when the oldest part of the house was built. Though its architectural design is similar to other old German homes, its builder and first owner was a native of Antwerp, Belgium. It is now owned by Mr. and Mrs. Alfred Hennig.

The van der Stucken family was engaged in the milling business in Belgium, so it was natural for them to turn to that trade when they came to Texas.

Felix van der Stucken and his family engaged in the milling business that was carried on for many years by them and their predecessors in the present-day location of Bethany Lutheran Church and its parsonage.

The old home is built on the west one-half of Townlot 62 which was originally granted by the German Emigration Company to Henry Minkel. He sold this lot to Felix van der Stucken for $200 on October 29, 1864. Minkel owned much of the land to the west of this lot. Many years ago the route taken by Town Creek was much farther south than it is now. Before it was re-routed to provide the proper right-of-way for the 100 and 200 blocks of West Austin Street, it wound near to the present-day Hermann Sons Hall with much of the street in the "creek area."

Felix's brother, Frank van der Stucken, William Wahrmund and Frederick Wrede bought five lots, Nos. 29, 30, 63, 64 and 65, to the east and northeast of this house from Heinrich Otte and his wife, Louise, for $160 on October 28, 1859. The deed states that this is "the same lots formerly occupied by me (Otte) as a residence."

When Frank van der Stucken, who also had other business interests here, decided to go back to Belgium, he sold to his brother, Felix, his interest in the mill and the five lots on July 1, 1864. In the deed reference is made to "Fredericksburg Steam Mill" owned by the firm of "F. Wrede & Co." The conveyance included all "improvements, buildings and machinery." He paid $3200 cash for his interest.

Felix van der Stucken in 1858 had married Christine Schoenewolf, a sister to Frank's wife. After their marriage they moved to a ranch on the Llano River, an area still inhabited by Indians, but after the birth of two children, they decided to move back to town for safety.

Finally Felix van der Stucken acquired all of the interest in the mill, with F. Wrede selling to him and Wahrmund his interest for

$2800 on March 29, 1865. The "steam mill" was then known as "Wrede & Co." On January 21, 1872, van der Stucken became the sole owner of the steam mill then operated by the firm known as "Wahrmund & Stucken" with $4,650 the sale price.

In the years following, the nature of the business changed somewhat, and it was known in its last years as Reliance Roller Mills before Bethany bought the property, razed it and built the church and parsonage there.

The Felix van der Stucken heirs owned the house until August 30, 1928. The first Mrs. Felix van der Stucken had died October 13, 1878, and several years later he married Dora Mueller of New Braunfels. Mr. van der Stucken died December 4, 1912. The children of Felix and Christine van der Stucken conveyed their interest to his estate on January 13, 1913. They were Alfred van der Stucken; Constance, Mrs. Gustave Mueller; Marie, Mrs. Frank Lungkwitz; Olga, Mrs. Henry Rodermund; and Louise, Mrs. W.J. Moore.

The second Mrs. van der Stucken died in 1925, and on August 30, 1928, the heirs sold this house and other lots to Ben Hagel. Mr. and Mrs. Hagel sold it to the Hennigs July 11, 1940, and it has been their home ever since.

The oldest building on the place is the little one-room fachwerk building atop a cellar well-ventilated with six windows. This was used by the van der Stucken as a maid's room, and is located behind the big house.

The big house is unique in that one side is one-storied and the other side two stories high. The two rooms in the one-story part at the east side were built first, and even these were built at different times as noted by the difference in rock work. The back room was the van der Stuckens' kitchen, and the front room their dining room and every-day living room.

The two-story part was built later, with a wide hallway separating the two older rooms from the two rooms at the west side. The front room on the west was the van der Stuckens' parlor and is now the Hennigs' living room. The room behind it which is now the Hennigs' dining room was Mr. van der Stucken's office when he had his desk, safe and a daybed.

Upstairs above these are two bedrooms, with hallway and a bath at the end of it.

A frame addition was added later in back. The Hennig kitchen at the back was utilized by the van der Stuckens as a dressing room. A bath and screened porch are included in this later addition.

Adding charm to the place is the long porch in front of the house, and a distinctive touch is the front door. It has a big oval glass pane with scrollwork, and is flanked by similar panes in the two side panels.

Reminiscent of the "elegant" homes of yesteryear, the van der Stucken-Hennig home facing the public square is a pleasant reminder of the city's historic past.

PRIESS BUILDING—NOW KEIDEL CLINIC

Through the years, the townlots along Main Street and the buildings on them have been used in many ways by many people. There's one that was first referred to on county records in 1852 as the German Emigration Company's "old school house lot."

Later a tailor owned it, then a wheelwright, then a big limestone rock building was erected on the corner part of the lot, and it became both a home and store, still later a boarding house, and finally a hospital and doctor's offices.

This is just a bit of the history interwoven into Townlot 180 located at the corner of East Main and North Lincoln Streets, originally known as San Saba and Garten Streets. It now belongs to Dr. J. Hardin Perry, who has his office there, and his wife, the former Victoria (Nooky) Perry, whose father, the late Dr. Victor Keidel, remodeled the building into a hospital in 1937-38. It is no longer used as a hospital since Hill Country Memorial Hospital opened here in 1971.

Townlot 180 was originally granted to M.A. Dooley, an early-day promoter, but he never exercised title to it. On September 7, 1852, Geo. Freeman, Gillespie County sheriff, sold it for $76 to satisfy a judgment against the German Emigration Company in favor of C.J. Cook & Co., with title passing to A.A. Lockwood of Bexar County. It is in this deed that reference is made to its being "known as the

Dr. and Mrs. J. Hardin Perry, Owners

old school house lot late the property of the German Emigration Co."

June 18, 1854, a judgement was issued against Albert A. Lockwood, and John M. Hunter, then Gillespie County sheriff, sold it for a pittance, $11, to G.H. Giddings. George H. Giddings sold this lot and other property to D.C. Giddings January 6, 1855.

Title to the lot next turns up in the name of R.W. Cecil, who was Gillespie County's first Tax-Assessor Collector, so he probably acquired them when absentee owners failed to pay their taxes. John H. Herndon, to whom the survey was patented on which it is situated, quitclaimed his interest in it to Cecil October 9, 1858.

Cecil sold the lot to Vinzent Wahl, a tailor, July 3, 1860, but Wahl did not keep it long and contracted to sell it to Jacob Fenske, September 20, 1861, giving him full title on February 24, 1863. From Fenske title passed to Heinrich Wilke, a wheelwright, on April 4, 1867. Wilke had his "homestead" in the 1850's in the block east of this one, the site of old Dietz Bakery, now owned by First Federal Savings, but he also owned property in this block, part of it being the adjoining lot where the Keidel residence now stands. Heinrich Wilke and his wife, Henriette were divorced, but he continued his business at the corner lot site.

Wilke sold a 25-foot strip to Adolph Lungkwitz July 8, 1867, along the western edge of the

lot, leaving the eastern 75 by 200 feet of it intact for his use.

He made a will date February 19, 1876, and must have died soon thereafter, for in March, 1876, probate proceedings were taken out on his estate. In the inventory reference is made to numerous items, such as tools and equipment, which indicated he was still following his trade at that time. Reference is made to several "ambulances," but the word as used in those days referred to large hacks or buggy-type vehicles and not ones used for transporting the sick as we now know the word's use today. He also made furniture.

This townlot was sold at public sale on November 11, 1878, by the executor of his will, Friedrich Kneese, for $725 to Charles F. Priess.

Priess began construction of this building for use as a combination of home on the second floor and a business on the ground floor. He used limestone quarried in the Louis Lehne pasture off the Bear Mountain Road which was hauled to the building site by Conrad Bolinger. There is a huge cellar, or basement, under the house which Sylvester Kleck excavated. Lime used for the construction was slaked on the sidewalk of what is now North Lincoln Street, and later a hackberry tree was planted in the hole that was left.

At the time of the Keidel Hospital dedication in 1938, some of Mr. Priess' records on the building which were preserved by some of his children, reflected that he quarried the stone at a cost of 60 cents per foot. In 1938 stonemasons estimated it cost $5 a foot at that time.

The building was completed July 24, 1883.

The Priesses had a general merchandise and hardware store on the ground floor and the family lived upstairs. Since he was also the agent for Lone Star Beer Company of San Antonio he used part of the basement to store his beer. He had an ice factory uptown and would bring surplus ice down here to store it in the basement and also to cool the beer. He continued his business here until the late 1890's.

Other firms which succeeded him in this location were R.M. Burrier & Co., Burrier & Maier, Rossenwasser & Levy, and others. Various tenants rented it over the years, and it was often vacant. At one time Mrs. Lina Zimmermann had a boarding house in the building.

Priess died May 24, 1900, but his heirs continued ownership of it until February 9, 1917. On that date his widow, Dina, and the children Bertha Priess; Alma and husband, Harry W. Kusenberger; Ella and husband, Felix W. Maier; Dora and husband, Herman Usener, all of Gillespie County; and Hulda and husband, E.J.P. Patton of Falls County sold a one-third interest to Ernst Herbort and a two-thirds interest to R.M. Insall. Two years later, Insall and his wife, Ida, sold his interest to Alfred Petsch on March 6, 1919.

Dr. Victor Keidel on July 26, 1919, bought this property from Herbort and Petsch and the Keidel family made their home on the second floor for several years. On October 22, 1923, the Keidels sold it to Katharina Kleck, wife of Peter Kleck.

When Dr. Keidel was looking for a site for a new hospital, since he felt the one he had on South Heights was no longer adequate, he bought this property back from the Klecks on September 10, 1937, with the idea of using the corner location. His son, Albert Keidel, then already interested in preserving and restoring old buildings, convinced his parents that the stately old building could be utilized and expanded as an efficient hospital. The one-story warehouse was torn down and a matching two-story wing took its place.

With Edward Stein as consulting architect, the plan Albert had for the building was carried out and it was dedicated July 31, 1938, followed by a day-long open house.

Dr. Keidel's offices were downstairs, as were those of the doctors who were associated with him and his successor, his son-in-law, Dr. J. Hardin Perry.

Dr. Keidel died November 19, 1952, as the result of of injuries received in an automobile accident, and his wife, Clara, died the following year. Dr. and Mrs. Perry had owned a half-interest in the property since February 27, 1950, and on March 18, 1960, acquired the other half-interest from her brother Albert, and sisters, Ruth Givigliano and Emily (Mrs. Henry J.) Schmidt.

Now the stately old building, with its decorative wrought iron trim, plantings of shrubs and native plants in the patio area, are admired by all who pass by, and stand as a reminder of generations past who contributed much to the history, heritage and well being of this city and its citizens.

LUNGKWITZ HOME

The north side of the 200 block of East Main Street seems to have more than its share of historic buildings, several of which have been covered earlier in this series, with more to follow soon. The previous story covered the Keidel Clinic at the corner which was built in 1882-83, and this feature is on the Lungkwitz home which adjoins it.

The early history of the lot on which both are built is identical.

Townlot 180 on which both are built is referred to in an 1852 transaction as "the old school house lot and represented on the map of said town as Lot No. 180, late the property of the German Emigration Company." On the list of Townlot allottments, Townlot 180 has the name of M.A. Dooley written behind the number, but a line is drawn through his name, so he probably never claimed it.

In an 1855 deed, reference is made to the lot as being located on "Garten Street." This is now North Lincoln, and was called Garten Street then because its southern end led to what had been set aside originally as the "Company Gardens" for use by the first settlers. It covered the blocks adjoining South Lincoln between East San Antonio Street and Barons Creek where the Webb Millers, Arnold

Klinksieks and others now live and where National Grocery warehouse is located.

Heinrich Wilke, who then owned the entire 100 by 200-foot townlot, sold 25 feet of frontage by 50 feet along its west side to Adolph Lungkwitz on July 8, 1867. This condition was made in the deed: "...provided that said Adolph Lungkwitz is held to build a house on the herein parcel of land within the next nine months, and provided further that the said Adolph Lungkwitz shall not sell again the herein conveyed premises within the first five years to any other person than myself, the said Heinrich Wilke, if he is willing to sell the same at all, and if he chooses to do so afterwards, I, the said H. Wilke shall also have a preemption in buying, thus, that I may get it to any price offered by any other person if so wanted by me."

Lungkwitz must have gotten started on his building right away, because less than a year later, on March 9, 1868, Wilke sold him the other 25 by 150 feet behind the front 25 by 50-foot plot, and this time no such conditions were made in the deed.

Adolph Lungkwitz, the builder of this combination home and business place was by trade a silversmith, goldsmith and tinsmith, being listed on the 1860 census as a "tin man" and on the 1870 census as a "tinner." When the 1870 census was taken he was living in this house, as it shows Heinrich Wilke was his neighbor.

With Engelbert Krauskopf he cooperated by using his skill as a tinsmith perfecting guncaps during the Civil War. They were made in the guncap factory and house Krauskopf owned where now the western edge of Community Savings and Loan is built.

Lungkwitz also made jewelry for people out of gold pieces. At the time of the 1955 series of old homes, several people recalled that he made jewelry out of five-dollar gold pieces, among them Irene Riley Osbourn and Mrs. August L.C. (Bertha) Weber who both had some gold earrings he made. The Webers lived across the street from the Lungkwitzes at the present site of Weidenfeller's Service Station, and their daughter, Elise Kowert, the author of these articles, is named for Mrs. Lungkwitz and her daughter, both of whom were named Elise.

He also made flat silver on special order, and in 1955 Mrs. W. H. Schaefer had some spoons made by him.

His handiwork can still be seen in the artistic bow and arrow transom above the front door of this house, as well as in the hardware he made for the front and back doors. The transom is the most distinctive in Fredericksburg, and catches the eye of almost as many passersby as does the white elephant on the saloon building three doors west of this house.

Mr. Lungkwitz carried on his trade in the front, one-story protion of the building. After his death, his daughters, Elise and Martha, carried on a dressmaking business in that part of the building. They also had a millinery store here and sold fancy laces and trimmings.

While their father was still living and before they went into business for themselves, the girls would go to homes to help with sewing. Mrs. Schaefer in 1955 recalled how they would come to the Nauwald home (now part of the Nimitz Center complex) and help her mother with sewing for the children in the family.

The one story front has a porch which is flush with the sidewalk. The double front doors with handmade iron locks are flanked by a window at each side.

Behind the "store" part, the two-story part of the building begins. The first room was used by them as a bedroom with the stairs ascending out of it to the upper floor. Behind it was the family dining room, and behind that the large kitchen. Each room has one window in the east wall, with no opening at all in the west wall. The wide cypress boards used in the floor are still in place.

Entrance to the rear of the building is gained through the back door which also has on it a large wrought iron lock similar to that in front.

Upstairs there is one large room which the Lungkwitz family used as a bedroom. It was ideal for that as there are two windows in each the south and east wall, and one in the north wall. An interesting Bavarian railing encases the stairway.

After the death of their parents, the brother and sisters deeded the house on November 4, 1915, to their sister, Antonia, the second oldest, and wife of C.H. Nimitz. They were Frank Lungkwitz, the oldest; Cornelia, the third child, who married Alfred van der Stucken; Elise, who never married; and Martha, the youngest, who married W.R. Burrier. The Burriers at one time had a store in the building that is now Keidel Clinic.

The Nimitzes never lived here, and on April 9, 1920, sold this place to Dr. Felix Keidel, a dentist, who made his home here before building another home elsewhere, and also conducted his dentistry practice in the front part of the building.

In later years, Dr. Victor Keidel also conducted his medical practice in the old building, and still later a beauty shop was operated in it for several years.

Ownership of it passed on September 24, 1938, to Kurt Keidel, who owns and lives in the old Keidel home which adjoins it on the west. The Lungkwitz house now belongs to Alberta Bonnell, wife of Dr. Albert Bonnell, a dentist, of Muskogee, Okla., who acquired it from her parents, the Kurt Keidels, on September 4, 1969.

Although the house has been vacant for many years, it presents a real potential for restoration as a combination home and business, the use for which it was originally built, or for any number of other uses.

Dr. Bonnell died May 14, 1977.

103

KEIDEL HOME AND KEIDEL DRUG STORE

Dr. Albert Keidel's name is still on the iron gate to the house that in the 1880's became his home and doctor's office. Located at 252 East Main Street, it is home now, too, for his son, Kurt Keidel, a retired pharmacist. Mr. Keidel and his wife, Margaret Pfeiffer of Selma, Alabama, live here with two of their daughters, Mathilde (Tillie) and Margaret Keidel.

Keidel Drug Store is located next door to the house in Gillespie County's first medical building which was built by Dr. Albert Keidel in 1909.

The Keidel home and the drug store are built on Townlot 179, originally granted by the German Emigration Company to August Nette. His deed from the company is dated April 9, 1850. On February 27, 1854, Nette, then of Bexar County, sold it to John Kleck for $90. John Kleck was a blacksmith, and had his business here. He sold the lot on December 21, 1858, for $135 to Heinrich Wilke, a wheelwright, who later owned the corner lot where Keidel Clinic now stands.

Two years later, for the same sum, Heinrich Wilke sold Townlot 179 to Frederick Wilke, a blacksmith, on December 31, 1860. According to the 1860 census Heinrich was 38 years old and Frederick was 31 years, so they were probably brothers. The 1870 census gives their respective ages as 46 and 41, and the order of visitation by the census-taker shows that the

Adolph Lungkwitz family lived between the two Wilke families. The blacksmith shop was located at the present site of the drug store.

On July 11, 1862, Frederick Wilke executed an instrument stating it was his "last will and testament," giving the following to his wife, Amalia: "Townlot 179 with all improvements thereon; household stuff, furniture and tools; outstanding debts as to see in a proper business-book to which reference is hereby made; 1 wagon; cattle branded V5; and 2 horses." Ad. Lungkwitz, a neighbor, was a witness.

He did not die then, however, and joined his wife on April 25, 1881, in deeding it to Carl Koennecke. Wilke, however, also joined Koennecke in the deed to Dr. Albert Keidel on May 21, 1881, with $1800 listed as the purchase price.

The Keidel family name goes back to the county's founding. Dr. William Keidel, born March 1, 1825, in Germany, was among the first settlers and when Gillespie County was organized he was elected as the first Chief Justice (County Judge). He practiced medicine here from 1846 until his death January 9, 1870. He also farmed in the Pedernales community.

His son, Albert, was born in Gillespie County July 1, 1852, and at the age of 14, was sent to Germany to be educated there. He first obtained a degree in pharmacy from the

"Gymnacium" at Goettingen. and in 1878 was graduated with honors as a medical doctor from Georg Augusts University, with a major in internal medicine, surgery and obstetrics. When he left Germany to return to Texas to take up his medical practice, his fiancee, Mathilde Eisfeldt, promised to follow him to Texas.

He met her when she arrived in Texas at Galveston in company with Helene Siedschlag, the fiancee of Paul Hanisch, a German-born Fredericksburg druggist, and they were married December 18, 1878, in the coastal city. Their firstborn, William, died in infancy in 1880. Their other four sons, of whom Kurt is the only survivor, were educated in medicine, dentistry and pharmacy. Dr. Victor Keidel was associated with his father in the practice of medicine. Dr. Werner Keidel and Dr. Felix Keidel practiced dentistry in Fredericksburg.

After Dr. Albert Keidel bought the lot and the house, he made extensive renovations in it. Originally it was only a story and a half high. The oldest part of the present house is the first story behind the "L" which he added at the west side. He raised the roof, adding a complete second story and the large porch.

An English architect and craftsman named Thompson was in charge of the main renovations done in 1888. The addition to the front of the "L" became the family parlor, while the room next to it, which was part of the old house, became the "stube" or dining room, and was often referred to by the boys as "piano room."

When the Kurt Keidels made extensive renovations in the house in 1936, they took out the dividing wall, making a large living room out of it, adding a fireplace at the northwest corner. The large windows are shuttered and add privacy for the occupants from the busy, noisy Main Street.

The front room of the east wing is the Kurt Keidels' dining room, but it was here that originally Dr. Albert Keidel had his office. This room has double doors leading out of the east wall to the veranda.

In the center of the house is the hallway with beautiful old stairway. A Mexican-Italian woodcraftsman named Cruz, of Fredericksburg, carved the posts and railings. All are of solid mahogany, except the newel post which has inlays of light-colored wood, probably sandalwood.

Also of interest are the old front doors which have a baroque design in the panels while the interior side is paneled in the conventional manner. The window lights at the sides of the door and the transom above each have sandblasted glass panes. The same type of door treatment is repeated on the second floor.

When the Albert Keidels lived here, the back rooms were used as sleeping quarters for the man who cared for the doctor's horses and the other servants. Now there is a breakfast room with glass brick wall partially separating this area from the den. Part of the rock wall was taken out to tie the den in with the terrace and the garden beyond that.

Back here, too, is the kitchen which has cabinets built out of large cypress planks taken out of the ceiling in the adjoining room during the house's 1936 renovation.

A bedroom with sunny bay window and bath were also added on the ground floor in the back.

While the remodeling was underway, the stonemasons who tore down part of the old wall found Indian arrowheads embedded in some of the mortar.

Upstairs there are three bedrooms and bath, with the east bedroom having the advantage of a balcony over the ground floor veranda.

One of the many distinctive features of the house, however, is the cellar that runs along the entire length of the large front room that was Dr. Keidel's office. The old hermit, Peter Burg, is credited with having constructed it, and how he went about it is interesting in these days of "fast work."

First, the area was excavated, then the four thick stone walls were built. These have slants at shoulder-heighth for the fresh air vents. There were two vents in the front, but when the porch was added, these were closed. There is one to the east and one in the north wall that makes a turn under the house to the east end.

After the straight side walls were built, the entire area was filled with sand, with more added from time to time as the domed ceiling rocks were put in place. After the ceiling had "cured" the sand was laboriously removed, bucket by bucket. Stone steps lead to the cellar and were originally covered by a trapdoor, but there is now a wrought iron railing at the head of the steps, part of which was once the old iron gate between the house fence and the drug store.

From his home and office here on Main Street, Dr. Keidel treated many patients, and he would also travel throughout the country-side by buggy, alleviating the illnesses and delivering the babies of Gillespians. Mrs. Keidel died March 12, 1902, and after her death, Mrs. Fritz Knust, the former Mariechen Gessler, came here to help take care of the family. After Dr. Keidel's death December 21, 1914, she continued to live here for a while. Later the house was rented to a Mr. Glied, who had a photography studio in it.

Complete title passed to Kurt Keidel January 1, 1920, when he bought the one-half interest his brother, Werner, had in it. The four brothers had each inherited a one-fourth interest from their father. Felix sold his fourth to Werner and Victor his fourth to Kurt on June 22, 1917.

In 1909 Dr. Albert Keidel had built the two-story rock Keidel Medical Building on the west side of his home. With its distinctive moulded tin facade and wrought iron railing, it provided medical offices upstairs for his son, Dr. Victor Keidel, and dental offices for the other two sons, Doctors Felix and Werner. The ground floor was where Kurt opened his

drug store which is still in business today. He was graduated from the University of Texas School of Pharmacy, Galveston, in 1906. After working briefly in Seguin and for Striegler's in Fredericksburg, he opened his own drug store.

Born May 2, 1885, Kurt Keidel was 91 in the Bicentennial year, and while he is no longer active in the business, life goes on in the stately old home and the medical building adjoining it. Their "middle" daughter, Alberta, is married to Dr. Albert Bonnell of Muskogee, Okla., and one of her daughters, Bonnie, is a medical doctor. The couple's only son, Dr. Robert Keidel, was a dentist practicing in Kerrville at the time of his death several years ago.

Mr. and Mrs. Keidel will have been married for 67 years in 1976 -- for more than half of the 130 years that have passed since the founding of the city. The two old buildings which they have owned for over 56 years have close ties to Fredericksburg's early history, and are not only still serving useful purposes, but also enhance the beauty of the city's Main Street.

WHITE ELEPHANT SALOON

Next to the octagon-shaped Vereinskirche, the building that attracts the most attention in Fredericksburg is the White Elephant Saloon at 246 East Main Street. Despite the fact that it is not occupied and has not been restored, the old building has so much charisma (if buildings can be said to have this) that it catches the eye and imagination of almost everyone who sees it.

What's even more remarkable is that here is one townlot on Fredericksburg's Main Street that has been in only two families since the city was laid out, the Kleck and the Keidel families.

The building takes its name from the white stone elephant on the front of the building put there when it was built as a saloon in 1888. As eye-catching as the white elephant is the beautiful ornamental wrought iron trim along the roofline at the front of the building. These are embellishments rare in early buildings here.

The saloon was built on part of Townlot 178 which the German Emigration Company allotted to Heinrich Stalp, but deeded to his

assignee, H. Kleck, on November 14, 1850. The acknowledgment on the deed, however, is dated Feb. 13, 1852, and the "Mr. H. Kleck" referred to in the deed should have been John Kleck, for a quitclaim deed to John Kleck was executed May 20, 1859.

John Kleck and his wife, Victoria, lived in a house on the west side of what is now the White Elephant, where he had a blacksmith shop. John's widow, Victoria, deeded 36 by 200 feet to her son, John W. Kleck, September 20, 1888. He built the saloon that year, and engraved "1888" in the cornerstone of the building. He also engraved the name "J.W. Kleck" above the front door.

The John Kleck family lived in a frame house behind the saloon which in later years was moved to the middle of the north side of the 200 block of East Austin Street in which the Jung family lived in 1956 and which was torn down in the mid-1960's to make room for the Frantzen Insurance Building.

The saloon was built of rough-finished limestone rocks, however, those at the front of the building were more artistically-shaped.

Margaret Keidel et al, Owners

Three double doors provided the front entrance to the building. There is no opening of any kind along the entire west side of the building, and it was against this wall that the bar was placed. It was traditional in appearance, complete with brass railing. Along the wall in the back was a large beautiful mirror and below this in neat open shelves were arranged the glasses. The brandy and liquor bottles were also placed here "for show" and to appeal to the tastebuds of the customers.

At the back end was the huge ice chest used mainly to keep the keg beer cold. The kegs were rolled in and the ice was kept in a compartment above this. There is a large cistern under the floor near the front of the building.

When it was first built, the saloon was equipped with carbide lights, but these were replaced with electricity when it became available from Pfeil's power plant.

At the rear of the rock building was a small, two-story frame addition, the upper room of which was used for gambling games involving higher stakes than those smaller games carried on around the tables in the main

saloon. Excitement ran high at times around there, but there was never any of the "shoot 'em up stuff" associated with the saloons of the 1890's in the western movies.

John W. Kleck ran the saloon for about five years, and also added a saddlery shop which Otto Evers ran for him.

Of interest is the lease agreement Kleck negotiated with John Klaerner and Henry Langerhans in 1893. For $1400 ($400 cash and a note for $1000) he sold the saloon contents, including the liquors, cigars, one pool table, one oil tank and stove to them. The $1400 did not include the price of the glassware as the price of this was to be determined separately.

They were also to pay $25 a month rent, but there was the provision that Kleck could terminate the lease if a railroad were completed to a point within one mile of Fredericksburg. He foresaw the possibilities of good business if this were to happen and he wanted to run the saloon himself again under such favorable conditions. Business must have been good for they paid off their note within one year.

Others who ran the White Elephant Saloon were Ad. Reichenau and Richard Arhelger

107

who formed a partnership.

Another proprietor of the Saloon was Frank Schaper, during whose ownership the Sunday laws were enacted. These made it unlawful for a saloon to be open for business on Sunday, however, before long the practice was to leave the front doors locked, but the back doors were always open for thirsty customers.

Weekdays the saloon was open from early in the morning until midnight, however if an exciting "game" was going on or business was good, only the front doors were locked at that hour and the back remained open.

The Klein brothers, Joe and George, followed Schaper in business here. From George Klein, who was still living in 1956 many of the recollections of life in the saloon business were obtained. The Kleins ran the White Elephant during the years 1908 through 1910. Their ad in the 1910 Gillespie County Fair catalog invited visitors to their place during the fair and stressed they had "nice ice cold beer, wines and liquors. A full line of choice cigars always kept on hand." When the Kleins ran the White Elephant, Henry Schaefer also had a barbershop in it.

The White Elephant around that time was in the middle of the "beer war" which took place between Lone Star and Pearl, with the San Antonio Brewing Co., brewers of Pearl, having the White Elephant under lease, so only their brand could be sold there.

Dr. Albert Keidel had bought the building and land on March 23, 1905, from Kleck who had moved to San Antonio with his family. Dr. Keidel rented the building to the saloon keepers. He at one time also used a part of the rear of the old building as a place where people could stay after he performed emergency operations.

The saloon business must have been discontinued before prohibition went into effect January 29, 1919, because August Stahl operated a grocery store in it, which he sold to Max T. Henke in 1917. About six months later, Henke moved his store business to 308 N. Llano St., where he and later his son, Sidney, operated it for many years.

During the late 1920's Max T. Henke, Louis and Eddie Kott formed the Kott-Henke Motor Company which handled the Hudson-Essex dealership in the White Elephant. For many years Scahefer Tractor and Implement Company rented the building. Other tenants have rented it for storage and other purposes over the intervening years.

In the years after Dr. Albert Keidel bought the property, different ones of his sons owned it, with the only son now surviving, Kurt Keidel, the last owner. Mr. and Mrs. Kurt Keidel deeded the property to their children, Margaret and Mathilda Keidel, Alberta Keidel Bonnell and Dr. Robert Keidel, September 26, 1961, however, the son is now deceased.

From Margaret Keidel comes one of the explanations of "why" a White Elephant was used on the building. She believes it stems from a custom found frequently in Germany, where often the white elephant is a crest or symbol of an eating and drinking establishment. It is thought the custom had its origin with the white pygmy elephant that was said to have been the pet of Hannibal when he set out to cross the Alps with 60,000 foot soldiers, 9,000 horses and some elephants.

Whatever it was that prompted Kleck to put the white elephant on the front of his building and to add the beautiful wrought iron work on the top of it, Fredericksburgers can be glad he did. He provided Main Street with one of its most distinctive buildings.

Mr. and Mrs. Oliver C.W. Kowert, Owners

BANK OF FREDERICKSBURG BUILDING

The global influence on the history of some of Fredericksburg's old buildings is found in a stately structure in the middle of the 100 block of East Main Street.

Situated on a townlot granted to a German immigrant, it later became the property of a gentleman-banker born in Virginia who came to Fredericksburg to open a private bank in 1887. The building was designed by one of Texas' leading architects who was born in London, England, and it now belongs to the grandson of a Lutheran missionary who sailed around the world from Germany in the 1880's to bring the Lutheran faith to the Maori tribes of New Zealand, where the father of the present owner was born.

Peter Schandua was the first owner of record of Townlot 171 on which Temple D. Smith commissioned Alfred Giles to build the Bank of Fredericksburg building which is now owned by Oliver C. W. Kowert.

Although Temple D. Smith, the man who built the historic structure has been dead for almost 50 years, there are many who still remember him vividly, while others recall his role in the early-day banking history of the county. There's even a community named after him, "Bankersmith," in the southern end of the county, which was once a stop on the railroad that came to Fredericksburg. He was generally referred to as "Banker Smith" in conversation, hence the naming of the stop. He had played a prominent role in bringing the railroad to this city in 1913.

The history of this lot begins with its being assigned to Peter Schandua on the original allotment list by the German Emigration Company. Peter Schandua and his wife, Margaretha, sold it to Henry I. Huck of Calhoun County (where Indianola was located) and Frederick H. Schlador of Comal County on March 24, 1848, for the sum of $520 -- a handsome sum for that day.

There's also a deed dated February 23, 1850, from the German Emigration Company to Huck and Schlador, as assignees of Gottlieb Fischer, stated in the deed to be the original grantee, however, the official allotment lists Peter Schandua.

Huck and Schlador must have been "speculators" because they acquired two other well-located townlots, Nos. 241 and 242, where Security State Bank and Trust and the Moseley Buildings are located. Huck traded his interest in the three lots, 241, 242 and 171 to Schlador on December 5, 1853, for three lots they owned jointly in Indianola.

Later that month, on December 31, 1853, Schlador, then of Bexar County, sold Townlot 171 to Heinrich Beckmann for $90. Title next turns up in the name of Conrad and Louise Wehmeyer, who once had a bakery, store and millinery shop in the middle of this block. They sold the northwest one-half of Townlot 171 to Jacob Zauner on December 26, 1871, for $600. This was the strip, 50 by 200 feet, on which the bank building and the annex built later are now located.

Zauner sold the 25 by 200-foot strip on which the bank building is located to Ferdinand

Doebbler October 6, 1874, for $300. His surviving wife, Auguste Doebbler, sold it for $450 to John Walter January 12, 1891. Walter apparently served as the "agent" for Smith who wanted to locate his bank here, because he conveys it for the same sum to Temple D. Smith two days later on January 14, 1891.

Smith was born in Hannover County, near Richmond, Virginia, August 22, 1846. When he was 15, his family moved to Indianapolis, and in 1884 he came to Anson, Jones County, Texas, where he went into the banking and mercantile business.

In 1887, Smith came to Fredericksburg and opened the Bank of Fredericksburg in the building now occupied by the Main Book Store.

Smith began to make plans for a new bank building. He commissioned Alfred Giles, an architect and a native of London, England, who was at that time one of the leading architects in Texas and Mexico. He was born May 23, 1853, near London at Hillingdon, in Middlesex, a county bordering London. He came to America in 1873 and later that year to San Antonio. Hillingdon Ranch, near Comfort, where he died August 13, 1920, is named for the ancestral home in England.

His office announced that they would receive bids on April 24, 1897, for a bank building to be erected for Temple D. Smith in Fredericksburg, according to the San Antonio Daily Express of April 17, 1897.

Mary Carolyn Hollers Jutson has put together a beautiful book on Giles, and in it touches on his architectural works in Fredericksburg which include the bank; the McDermott Building which was Gillespie's second courthouse; and the William Bierschwale home. In it she says of Giles' work: "Although most of Giles' commercial patrons preferred the Italianate style, the architect's partiality for the Richardsonian Romanesque throughout the last decade of the nineteenth century was reflected in his design for the Bank of Fredericksburg."

She also quotes from the San Antonio Daily Express of April 18, 1898: "One of the most notable signs of the era of improvement which has been inaugurated in Southwest Texas during the past year is evidenced in the fine business and residence structures which are being erected in many prosperous towns throughout this section. In the substantial, conservative old town of Fredericksburg, the Bank of Fredericksburg just completed and occupied commodious new quarters. The owner is Temple D. Smith.

"The building is of the most modern design. Its walls are native cream-colored, hard limestone from quarries nearby, quarry-faced, finely pointed and laid in courses, the front being ornamented with very fine carving out of the rough rock.

"The building is two stories in height, the first floor being devoted exclusively to Mr. Smith's bank office. The second story is devoted entirely to Mr. Smith's residence, which is arranged and fitted up with every convenience of a modern city house."

Mrs. Smith was the former Mary Alice Francis of Lawrenceburg, Indiana. They had one daughter, Estelle, who was educated at Wellesley. She never married. They also had extensive landholdings in several counties in New York state, and would spend several months each year up north.

Next to the bank building was a 25 by 200 foot strip which had been sold by Jacob Zauner to Mary A. Shardein December 1, 1882, for $250. She and her husband, Philip Shardein of Bexar County, sold it to Temple D. Smith January 11, 1899, for $500. This gave Smith a little open space between the bank and what is now Central Drug Store.

On May 6, 1903, Smith and his wife deeded to the Bank of Fredericksburg the 50 by 200-foot strip of land and the bank building on it, with the consideration listed being $9,000. (This was the same price Kowert paid to the bank receiver for the two parcels which he bought in 1937 and 1943).

In the spring of 1901 Smith had been joined in his banking business by Fred Walter and Adolph Gold, and later Albert Koennecke became a partner.

Smith died April 24, 1926, and his widow became bank vice president. She and her daughter continued to make their home upstairs. His funeral services were held in the Bank of Fredericksburg and he was buried in the City Cemetery. Later, after his wife and daughter moved away from here, his body was disinterred and buried in Brownwood where they moved after leaving here.

One of the most traumatic events in Gillespie County history involves this old building. The Fredericksburg Standard, in its Friday, February 19, 1932, edition inserted this small last-minute piece of news on its front page:

"LOCAL BANKS CLOSED

"Friday morning of this week (February 19), the local banks closed, posting the following notice, 'Closed for Reorganization.' We could not obtain any details, but are positive that our bankers are pursuing the wisest course possible under the circumstances."

In the next week's paper (February 26) there were two news items. One was a published statement by the two banks issued after a meeting of the depositors of the Citizens Bank Wednesday afternoon and the depositors of the Bank of Fredericksburg Thursday afternoon.

The other item concerned the meeting that the Chamber of Commerce directors had called immediately after the banks closed for the following Saturday night (February 20) at the Hotel Nimitz which was attended by 150 businessmen and residents of Fredericksburg.

John W. Metzger, CofC president, appointed two committees -- one to take charge of plans for the liquidation of the two banks, and the other to have the responsibility of organizing a new bank.

Alex Grosse of Mason was appointed by the District Judge as the first receiver, a post later filled by D.J. Hoerster, as the assets of the two banks were liquidated.

Meanwhile, a new bank was organized. It was the Fredericksburg National Bank and it opened for business April 6, 1932, in the old Bank of Fredericksburg building. They leased it at a cost of $65 per month.

This old building served the new bank until October 13, 1936, when they moved into the new building that had been erected on property they bought across the street, a site now occupied by Showcase Antiques.

On May 31, 1937, Oliver C. W. Kowert bought the bank building and the strip of land on which it stands, 23 feet and 10 inches by 200 feet, for $7000 from the Receiver. On October 5, 1943, he bought from the Receiver the ad-joining strip with frontage of 26 feet and two inches by 200 feet which had no improvements on it for the sum of $2000.

He built the one-story annex on this strip between the bank building and the drug store in 1948.

During his ownership of the building, Kowert used it in his business, first having a music store and appliance firm there, and now for many years it has been the office of Kowert Exchange, the real estate business he founded.

For many years, also, Mr. and Mrs. Kowert and their son, Oliver J. Kowert, lived on the second floor. Over the years they made extensive renovations and an addition in the back. Since early in 1974 the Kowerts have no longer made their home upstairs having moved elsewhere.

Fortunately much of the exterior appearance of the old building has not been altered, with the exception of the first floor front. Originally the front was straight, flush with the sidewalk. At the left the door opens to the stairs which lead to the second floor. The entrance to the bank was a recessed doorway at the extreme right. Between them was a large plate glass window with the bank's name on it. Part of the black and white tiled floor has been retained.

The two show windows and present recessed doorway were put there years ago when the one side was used for a dress shop, and the other a shoe store, however, now the Kowert real estate firm utilizes all of the building, including part of the annex next door.

The distinctive wrought iron balcony is still there in front of the large arched window arrangement in front, but the balcony at the east side front has been removed.

On a street that has many historic old homes and buildings, the Bank of Fredericksburg remains as an example of the distinctive architecture that has come to be one of the city's chief attractions.

A.L. PATTON BUILDING

Not all pioneer Fredericksburg business-men came from Germany.

The second of Fredericksburg's pioneer banks, Citizens Bank, was housed in a building erected by a man from Missouri, just as the first one was in a building erected by a Virginian who came to Texas by way of Indiana.

Albert Lee Patton built the two-story building in 1897 in which the bank was later located. He conducted all his business in the name of "A.L. Patton" and that's what he had carved into the upper front of the building. This two-story building shares a common wall with the one-story building to the west of it in which Patton had his general mercantile and hardware store.

But the story of the buildings he occupied goes back to the city's founding, and the early history ties in which some of the adjoining buildings.

Townlot 164 on which it is built was granted to Lorenz Schmidt, a stonemason, who was among the earliest settlers of Fredericksburg. His deed from the German Emigration Company is dated October 5, 1852. Four of the adjoining lots, 163 through 164, were granted to Schmidts. Schmidt Hotel was on one of

them and is the building now owned by Arthur Stehling in which he lives and has his law office.

Schmidt sold No. 164 to Frederick Lochte for $125 on July 5, 1859. Frederick (Friedrich) Lochte and his wife, Dorothea, died and their children partitioned their property, with Karolina (Caroline) Bonn, wife of Peter Bonn, getting title to Townlot 164 through a deed dated September 16, 1867, from the administrators of the estate. Her brothers and sister were Frederick and Henry Lochte and Dina, Mrs. C.F. Priess. The partition was confirmed by a later deed on August 6, 1883.

On January 8, 1878, the Bonns sold to Peter Schuch, a blacksmith, a 12 by 200-foot strip along the eastern edge of the lot. The remaining part (88 by 200-feet) was sold by the Bonns to August Wahrmund for $500 on May 29, 1879, and Wahrmund then sold it for $700 to A.L. Patton on July 17, 1882.

Patton was born June 9, 1851, in Independence, Missouri. In 1856 his family came to Texas, settling near San Antonio, but a year later decided to return to Missouri. On the way home his father became ill and after his death, his widow and her family returned once more to Texas. Patton grew up in San Antonio

112

where he learned the trade of tinner. In 1871 he came to Fredericksburg, and after a brief stint in Austin, returned here in July 1872 to make his home.

At first he had his tin shop in one end of the building owned and shared by his friend, Paul Hanisch, a druggist. This is the Hanisch building at the corner of West Main and South Orange Streets.

Later he moved and expanded into other business, operating a general mercantile and hardware store in a rock building which now belongs to a San Antonio couple. He sold a complete line of clothing and shoes for men, women and children, glassware, dinner sets, lamps, bed linens, albums, hardware and many related goods in his store, according to the early ads which ran in the Fredericksburg Wochenblatt. Pieces of crockery are still around with his name on them. His firm was conducted under the name of "A.L. Patton and Son," which he sold out to his son in August 1906. In a Wochenblatt of September 12, 1906, his son E.J.P. (Emil) Patton began advertising, stating that he was adding farm produce. Andrew Moursund was a partner in this business at one time.

At first the Patton family lived in a log house at the corner of West Austin and North Orange Streets, and then he built the house south of it on North Orange that faces the Community Savings parking lot.

They built the two-story limestone rock building in 1897, as recalled by his daughter, Ruby Burgdorf. The Patton family then moved upstairs, using the entire second floor as their living quarters.

Mr. Patton had married Emma Auguste Wahrmund, a daughter of Mr. and Mrs. Emil Wahrmund Sr., on October 24, 1875. Their children were Emil; Henry; Elizabeth, whose husband was Judge Anton Moursund; Emma (Emmie) who married Albert Detjen; and Ruby, who married Otto Burgdorf.

Entrance to their living quarters was by way of a stairway inside the northwest corner of the building, with a second entry into this stairway from the inside at the back of the bank building.

Their living room was at the west front with two windows facing Main Street, and behind that was the bathroom and stairway. At the east side, the girls had their bedroom at the front, with two windows facing Main Street. These windows had interior French shutters for privacy, while the other windows at the

sides had shutters on the outside. The graceful arches above the windows added a decorative touch to the front. Behind the girls' bedroom was that of the parents, and to the rear of that the dining room and the kitchen.

They had a rose garden at the east side of the building, and one of the tall palm trees they planted is still standing.

When the building was erected the stones were brought in from the quarry near Fredericksburg and piled in the street in front where the workmen "dressed" them with their tools.

Mrs. Burgdorf recalled that her father operated a banking business on the first floor of the bank for a few years, and in 1899 organized a bank in Lott, Falls County, which was later managed by his son, Henry.

The exact date of the organization of the Citizens Bank could not be recalled, however, their first advertisement appeared in a Wochenblatt of May 3, 1905, stating that they were now open and welcomed transactions, large and small, and had facilities to take care of banking needs quickly and with dispatch.

Early advertisements show that Alfred van der Stucken was the president; Oscar Krauskopf, vice president; and William Bierschwale, cashier. After her husband's death, Mrs. van der Stucken continued to hold his interest, but later sold her one-third interest to the other two partners.

The Citizens Bank closed at the same time the Bank of Fredericksburg did February 19, 1932. Both banks were placed into receivership and their assets liquidated.

This building, however, belonged to the Patton estate, so it was not among the bank's assets.

Mrs. Patton died January 8, 1927, and he died March 18, 1934.

When the estate was partitioned March 4, 1938, Mrs. Burgdorf received the one-story building which she sold to Dr. and Mrs. John C. Meadows Jr. of San Antonio, August 9, 1972. Mrs. Moursund received the Citizens Bank building which she and her husband sold to Elton M. Hyder Jr. of Fort Worth March 1, 1965. Hyder and his wife sold it to the present owners, M.M. Moseley and his wife, Johnnie, March 7, 1972.

The bank building is now vacant. The Meadows have renovated the rear of their building into living quarters, and the Used Book Store occupies the front.

Vernon Penick et al, Owners
Mr. and Mrs. L.C. (Jack) Estes, Owners

MAIER BUILDINGS—
NOW MAIN BOOK STORE AND JACK'S EMPORIUM

Two buildings on one of Fredericksburg's busiest downtown street corners are built on the same Townlot and most of their history centers around the city's business life and members of the Maier family who owned them for almost 115 years.

Their use changed through the years, and now Main Book Store is in the two-story native limestone rock building on the corner of South Adams and East Main. L.C. (Jack) Estes has opened "Jack's Emporium" on the first floor of the two-story concrete block building next to it which he bought in 1975. The second floor has been made into a charming home for himself and his wife, with an enclosed patio behind the building.

Townlot 239 (the corner lot) and 240, both of which face on South Adams and the courthouse square for 100 feet each, run parallel to East Main for 200 feet, and were originally granted to Herman Wilke, who helped lay out the original city lots.

They were sold by George N. Stebbins to Chester B. Starks on October 1, 1850, for $1,000. On October 29, 1850, Starks and Joel Ankim, who owned lots 313 and 314 (where the Clinic now stands), made and recorded an agreement regarding a house on 240 "known as the Fandange house built by the firm of Stebbins and Company or Stebbins and Martin, or by George N. Stebbins or Lewis Martin" doing business "formerly in Fredericksburg in 1850, as merchants and grocers."

Starks was originally from New York and was a merchant in Fredericksburg in 1850. He later acquired Ankim's other two lots which faced the courthouse square and on November 1, 1858, sold all four to Adolph Assig for $1,310.

Edward Maier bought the four lots (239, 240, 313 and 314) from Assig on February 16, 1860, for $2,500, paying $210 cash and giving a note for $2,290, payable to Frank v.d. Stucken, his brother-in-law, who loaned him the balance of the purchase price. He paid off the note by the end of the next year. Part of the two lots on which these two buildings are located were to remain in the Maier family until 1973 and 1974 when Vernon E. Penick bought them.

Edward Maier was born August 7, 1831, in Fulda, Hessen, Germany. He came to Texas in 1854, landing at Galveston, and then came to Fredericksburg. A few months after he bought these four townlots, he married Adele van der Stucken on May 2, 1860. She was a native of Antwerp, Belgium, and the sister of a pioneer merchant, Frank v.d. Stucken, whose son by the same name became the famous American and European composer.

Here in the center of the little village, the Maiers made their home and he went into the mercantile business. He built a grist mill and a steam cotton gin in about the location of the present-day Showcase Antiques. He also acquired ranch lands in the Spring Creek community. According to the cornerstone, he built the two-story limestone building at the corner in 1874 and conducted his general store here.

Their home was in a one-story limestone building later expanded in front into the two-story structure that now is part of the Fredericksburg Clinic building.

Edward and Adele Maier had four sons and a daughter who lived to adulthood, Edward, Richard, Hilmar, Florent and Bertha, however, the latter was drowned in the Concho River while visiting with her brother, Edward, at San Angelo. One son died in infancy.

Adele Maier died February 21, 1874, and on December 14, 1877, Edward Maier married Sidonie Wehmeyer. Their three sons died in 1882, and their daughter, Meta, born in 1883, later married Louis Kott.

Edward Maier's busy life came to an unexpected end. He was fatally injured in the explosion of the boiler in his cotton gin October 1, 1884, and he died the next day. An administration was taken out immediately on his estate because of his involved business interests, and the inventory filed and found of record in the Probate Records offers an interesting sidelight on what his business assets and merchandise were. His widow later married August Sembritzky and they continued to make their home in this block.

A few years after Edward Maier's death, the corner building was occupied by Temple D. Smith, a Virginian who came to Texas by way of Indiana, and opened a bank in this building. The way the building looked then is shown by an old photo with the sign "Bank" visible on the side.

Fredericksburg's only bank robbery took place while Smith had his bank here. At 3 p.m. on July 2, 1888, two men burst into the bank, and while one of them held Mr. Smith and his assistant at gunpoint, the other took the money that was outside of the safe. They succeeded in making their getaway in spite of shots fired at them as they fled across the Public Square and were never apprehended.

Smith moved away from here when his Bank of Fredericksburg building was completed in 1898.

Two of Adele and Edward Maier's sons sold their undivided interest in Lots 239, 240, and 313 to A.W. Keller, Edward on May 4, 1891, and Hilmar on December 27, 1890. Their deeds noted that the conveyance included "all mill and other machinery standing on said lots."

A.W. Keller operated a livery stable and feed store, and on February 5, 1900, sold his interest in these three lots and "also the stables and sheds on one lot of which A.W. Keller is sole owner" to George Grobe. Later, in June, 1904, Grobe and the other Edward Maier heirs partitioned the estate, with Richard eventually becoming the sole owner of that part of the lots on which the two buildings facing on Main Street are standing.

Richard Maier had a saloon and feed store here, having added the one-story part at the back for the feed store.

After Smith moved away from here the business was known as the "Bank Saloon" according to an 1899 Fair catalog ad. When Estes was chipping away the plaster in the hallway, several letters of the painted sign could be seen against the east wall of the book store building.

When Prohibition came in 1920, Richard Maier had to discontinue his saloon. His son, Henry, had gone into the business known as "R. Maier & Son" with him. They decided to open a grocery store because they reasoned that farmers coming in to buy feed and supplies would also be in the market for groceries. Finally Henry took over the grocery store in his own name and after the death of his parents, he inherited the corner building. He operated the store later as a Piggly Wiggly store.

Vernon Penick bought the building from the Henry Maier heirs in 1974, and now rents it to Bob Gates, owner and manager of Main Book Store.

The old building during the 1900's was also used by the telephone company, the second floor was once the American Legion Hall, Scout troops met there, and many older residents will recall other uses it was put to during the 1900's.

After Richard and Olga Maier's deaths, their property was partitioned among their children, Henry, Felix, Max and Alex Maier; Adele, Mrs. Eugene C. Schmidt; Clara, Mrs. Max Willmann; and Emma, Mrs. William Petmecky. Felix's twin, Oscar, died at age 27. Mrs. Petmecky still owns the building in which Montgomery Ward's sales agency is located.

For many years Alex Maier operated a saddlery and leatherwork business in the concrete block building, and other tenants occupied parts of the building at various times.

The two-story concrete block building, erected in 1913, which Estes now owns belonged half to Max Maier and half to Clara Willmann. Maier bought his sister's half of the building later, and his widow sold it to Vernon Penick November 26, 1973. He conveyed a one-third interest to each of his two sons, Michael and Jimmy.

Estes bought the building from the Penicks September 29, 1975, and got to work renovating the two floors for use as his business on the ground floor and for his home on the second floor.

Estes added a two-story front porch in front of his building, complete with intricate gingerbread trim -- all painted white -- and later the Penicks added white gingerbread trim and painted it white, too. They also extended the porch along the Adams Street side of the book store.

"Jack's Emporium" which Mr. and Mrs. Estes operate in their building is filled with memorabilia and artifacts from the past -- many of the vintage of Maier's first store at this busy corner in downtown Fredericksburg.

Cordie Bierschwale, Owner

WILLIAM BIERSCHWALE HOME

"Aside from its charm, the old house at 110 North Bowie in Fredericksburg, Texas, the William Bierschwale residence, is notable for two reasons. It has remained in the hands of the same family since its construction in 1888, and the original working drawings and specifications prepared by Alfred Giles are extant, preserved by the present owner. As the architect had done in specifications for the Gillespie County Courthouse, he stated the following: 'The whole of the masonry where not otherwise described to be first class rustic rubble work (similar to Officers' Quarters at San Antonio) of rock from the best local quarries well laid in mortar'."

So reads the description accompanying photographs of the William Bierschwale home now owned and occupied by his daughter, "Cordie" Bierschwale, as found in the book, "Alfred Giles: An English Architect in Texas and Mexico," by Mary Carolyn Hollers Jutson.

The year "1889" is carved into the cornerstone of the house, and the above 1888

116

reference is to the year in which the plans were made and steps initiated for its construction.

The Bierschwale home is one of three buildings in Fredericksburg for which this noted architect, Alfred Giles, drew the plans. The fact that they have been preserved by the present owner is of special interest. Giles was born in England, near London, May 23, 1853, and came to America and Texas in 1873. He settled in San Antonio where he soon established an outstanding reputation as an architect.

The beautiful old two-story rock home faces on North Bowie at the corner of West Austin Street. It is built on Townlot No. 121 which was originally granted to "Seigman." The one next to it, No. 122, was granted to Christian Wicker and forms part of the property. The lots face for 100 feet each on West Austin Street and run back 200 feet parallel to North Bowie.

Title to both was in the name of Peter Schuch when he sold them to William Bierschwale on November 2, 1886. Schuch also owned other townlots in the same block facing on West Austin.

William Bierschwale served as Gillespie County Clerk from 1898 to 1906, following his father, H. Bierschwale, in that office. His father had served in that office from 1870 to 1898. William also served as a Representative in the state Legislature for 16 years, one of the few Republicans in the state during his tenure in office. He was also one of the founders of Citizens Bank.

His wife was the former Lina Jung, whom he married in 1884. At first they lived in the Jung family's house in town, but within a few years he made plans to build a home of their own. That he was concerned with getting a beautiful, and at the same time a well proportioned and built home is shown by the fact that he hired the well-known architect, Giles, to draw the design and specifications. That these plans have been preserved is not only interesting, but valuable from an architectural viewpoint.

There is a two-story porch in front of the "L" that faces North Bowie. The main entrance is the large door with two gracefully-shaped glass panels flanked by glass sidelights and topped with a transon. This door leads into the hall at the center of the house.

From this hall the stairs lead to the second floor, and there are doorways into the dining room on the north side of the "L" and to the sitting room on the south side of the "L." This sitting room is almost a miniature museum with its mellow parlor set, massive handmade secretary, and objects of art. One of the four fireplaces is in this room.

In front of the sitting room is the original "parlor" which has the second fireplace, back to back with the one in the sitting room. The owner has converted this room into a spare bedroom, and a door leads out of it onto the front porch.

There is a slanting offset in the wall from the original parlor to the sitting room, with a narrow window on each floor in this wall, giving additional light and ventilation.

The third fireplace on the ground floor is in the dining room. It is flanked at one side by a large window, and two windows are in the front wall. The large, elongated clock on the wall at one time belonged to A.O. Cooley, one of the first lawyers in the city, and a native of New York. Telling the time of the day is only one of the many things it does. Mr. Cooley was the first person buried in the Greenwood Cemetery.

Two large dining room "safes" are filled with fine pieces of china and silver. Behind the dining room is the kitchen, with a large built-in closet, something found in few old homes of that day.

Extending across the back is a frame addition in which there is a bathroom, a breezeway which connects with the laundry room and the tank house. There is a large cellar under this structure.

On the second floor are three large bedrooms, a hall and a large porch. The bedroom on the north side has the fourth fireplace in the home and was the boys' room. They had a big blackboard on the wall which they could use in doing their homework.

Across the hall was the parents' bedroom, and the room in front of that was the girls' room. These two bedrooms were heated by wood stoves.

Furnishings are in harmony with the period of the old home and even include the family cradle.

The William Bierschwales had nine children: Ernst, who died during the World War I flu epidemic; Max, Walter, Alfred, Henry; Annie, Mrs. Alex Maier, all of whom are deceased; Concordia (best known as "Cordie"); Laura, Mrs. J.J. Hanus, now of

Austin; and Julia, Mrs. Aram Krikorian, formerly of Holly, Michigan, who has now moved to Fredericksburg.

Mr. Bierschwale died in 1932 and his widow in 1944, after which their daughter, "Cordie," continued to reside here. Now their fine old home belongs to Cordie, who appreciates its architectural significance and its history. Even the swept yard, the two-seated yard swing, the iron and wire fence, and the flower garden at the side add nostalgic touches to this old home of 1888-89 that is still a "home" today to one of the same family.

San Antonio Catholic Archdiocese, Owner

H.B. MECKEL HOME—NOW CONVENT

The transition from a home for one of the city's wealthiest families, to a hospital, and then to a convent is the story of the two-story building at 307 West Main Street. First it was the Henry B. Meckel home, then the Hanus Hospital, and is now the residence of the Sisters of Divine Providence who teach in St. Mary's Catholic School.

Like so many old homes, the "stories behind the story" of ownership are involved and interesting.

Built on Townlot 248 which was granted by the German Emigration Company to Conrad Pluennecke, it was sold by him and his wife, Sophie, to John Schmidtzinsky. They entered into a sales contract on December 28, 1850, with the price being $50 cash and $50 to be paid by September 1, 1851. On that date Pluennecke and his wife signed the deed to Schmidtzinsky,

giving him full title.

Wilhelm Hardt turns up as the next owner on record, and Schmidtzinsky must have sold the lot to him because in 1915 his children and grandchildren quitclaim any interest they might have in it.

There is a deed from Wilhelm Hardt to Henry Winkel on December 9, 1851, stating the purchase price was $151. When Winkel sold it to Theodor Specht on March 9, 1852, the instrument states Winkel bought it at "auction of Mr. Hardt" and paid $150 for it by giving two horses and $70 cash to J. Dietz.

Specht was Fredericksburg's first postmaster and owned townlots and a store at the corner of South Milam and West Main. He sold Townlot 248 to Anton Kamp on July 26, 1852, for $60, and Kamp, then of Bexar County, sold it for $75 to Henry Kammlah on October 30,

1864. Kammlah had been granted the lot next to it by the German Emigration Company and established his home and later a store there at what is now Pioneer Museum, often referred to as the "Kammlah house."

Kammlah must have built a house on Townlot 248 for when he sold it to Charles Feller September 1, 1870, the price was $800. This deed states that title came to him through Pluennecke, Schmidtzinsky, Hardt, H. Winkel, Th. Specht and Kamp.

When Feller sold it to H.B. Meckel March 26, 1886, the price was only $725. Henry B. Meckel had married Mathilde Wahrmund, a daughter of Mr. and Mrs. Emil Wahrmund Sr., on December 1, 1878, and they built the two-story rock home. One of its most distinctive features was the two-story front porch which curved gracefully at the sides, had wide white columns and balustrades upstairs and downstairs.

Henry B. Meckel was a son of Conrad Meckel who married Henriette Luckenbach June 12, 1853. Conrad operated a store at the present-day Community Savings corner, but was killed in October 1866 by Indians near Loyal Valley while on a trip to take cattle to the Meckel ranch. Conrad Meckel also traded livestock. He was accompanied on this trip by his brother, Bernhard Meckel, and a Mr. Heinrich of Llano. They had planned to take Henry along, but when they were unable to find a horse for him, they left him behind in Fredericksburg.

About 12 miles from Fredericksburg, Bernhard Meckel left with a part of the herd for Squaw Creek. The other two delivered their herd and started back to Fredericksburg, bringing a cow along.

About a mile and a half from Loyal Valley on the Mason Road, between Loyal Valley and Cherry Spring, they halted for a midday rest and to allow the cow to graze. They probably fell asleep and were attacked and killed by Indians.

When their bodies were discovered, the group who gathered wanted to bury them at the scene, however, two of the men, Peter Crenwelge and Christ Kothe, recognized the men and their bodies were carried to Fredericksburg for burial.

The 1870 census lists his (Conrad's) widow as a merchant, with their oldest son, Henry, who was then 16, as a clerk in the store.

Henry Meckel and his cousin, Adolph Meckel, later ran a saddlery shop at that location, with their advertisement in the 1899 Fair catalog stating "H. & A. Meckel" were "Dealers and Manufacturers of saddles, harness, whips and spurs and everything that is carried in a First-Class Saddle and Harness Shop. Buggy Trimming a Specialty - Repairing of All Kinds Done."

Henry Meckel, who became one of the city's most prosperous businessmen in the late 1800's and early 1900's, died March 16, 1909, at the age of 54 years and 10 months.

He and his wife, Mathilde, had two children - - Alma, who married R. T. Gliddon in 1899, from whom she was later divorced. They had two children, Mathilde and Mae Gliddon. The Henry Meckels also had a son, Charles H. Meckel.

Mrs. Meckel died September 17, 1913, and her son was named the executor. In getting the estate affairs in shape, they must have discovered that there had never been a deed out of John Schmidtzinsky, the second owner of the townlot on which their home was built. A quitclaim deed to C.H. Meckel, executor of the estate of Mathilde Meckel, was made November 25, 1915, by the children and grandchildren of John Schmidtzinsky and his wife, Anna (Anny). Signers of the deed were the couple's living children: Anna Besier, a widow; Mathilda and her husband, John Metzger; Lina and her husband, Otto Weinheimer; John, Frank, Charles and Joseph Schmidtzinsky; and the children of their deceased sister, Catharina Kunz, and her husband, Jacob Kunz: John and Otto Kunz; Anna and husband, Joseph F. Jenschke; Lina and husband, George Jenschke; Bertha and husband, Willie Petsch; and Emma and husband, Christian Jenschke.

Felix Walch bought the house and lot on October 30, 1915, from Mrs. Meckel's estate. Walch at the time was a promoter and real estate developer, including the Walch Terrace Addition in the southwest section of the city. He deeded the Meckel house and lot, together with other tracts he owned, including many lots in the addition, to Albert Koennecke, "Trustee for Owners and Holders of Shares" on November 16, 1920.

Robert Blum, who was a holder of a 1-12 interest, bought out the other 11 shares held by Walch, F.J. Maier, Albert Koennecke as Trustee, Fritz Scharnhorst, Nellie Doebbler, Eddie Herbort and Louis Wehmeyer in the years 1921 to 1924. Blum had his store in the building that is now occupied by Schwettmann

Taxidermy and wanted some additional space at the west side of his store.

Since he was not interested in keeping the house because he had a nice home elsewhere, he sold the west 78 by 200 feet of it on which the house is built to Dr. J. J. Hanus September 8, 1927.

Dr. Hanus was married to the former Laura Bierschwale, a daughter of the William Bierschwales. He at first had his office in the Striegler Building, but after he bought this property he had his office here and remodeled the home into a hospital. The two-story porch was removed and the small one-story "stoop" was added in front. Other changes included adding x-ray, operating and patients' rooms, and they even had facilities in back for doing all their own laundry.

Dr. Hanus left here during World War II to serve in the Medical Corps and closed up the hospital, never reopening it. After he got out of the service, Dr. and Mrs. Hanus made their home in Austin. He took some special courses in psychology at Columbia and at first was on the medical staff of the State School, and later the State Hospital. He was in ill health for a number of years and died in 1966. The couple had two sons, E.J. and Jack.

Mrs. Hanus still lives in Austin, but visits here often with her sisters.

Dr. and Mrs. Hanus sold the hospital to Robert E. Lucey, Archbishop of San Antonio, May 31, 1949, for use by St. Mary's Catholic Church as a convent and home for the sisters who teach in the parochial school here. In 1976, the usefulness of the building continues and it adds to Main Street's architectural appeal.

Mr. and Mrs. Belton Muller, Owners

PFIESTER HOME—NOW MULLER GALLERY

When Belton and Virginia Muller of Nacogdoches decided to buy an old rock home in Fredericksburg after having visited here frequently with her parents, Dolly Nabinger, noted landscape artist, and her late husband, it was certainly this city's gain.

Not only have they done a beautiful job of restoring and enlarging the house they now call home at 205 South Orange, but they have opened Muller Gallery and Studio in it.

The Mullers bought the house and portions of Townlots 359 and 360 on which it stands and the adjoining 100-by-200-foot Townlot 421 from Chas. A. Howell of Jefferson County May 24, 1969. Mr. Muller was a building contractor in Nacogdoches at that time, but they began making plans to renovate the house and move here. She is an artist and loves the Hill

Country.

When the house was ready, they moved in, and became fulltime residents of Fredericksburg. With Mr. Muller's construction know-how and Mrs. Muller's artistic ability, they have created one of the most distinctive restoration jobs done in this area.

The German Emigration Company granted Townlot 360 to Franz von Wameln and Townlot 359 to Julius von Wameln. It is doubtful that either lived in Fredericksburg long, if at all. On April 27, 1854, Franz von Wameln of Austin County conveyed his Townlot 360 to Julius von Wameln of Bastrop County. Julius sold both lots for $120 to Georg P. Hofacker by deed dated March 8, 1854.

Mr. Hofacker died and his widow, Maria Anna, married Joseph Dengel. One of their daughters, Maria Anna, married Christian Kraus, and they joined her mother and stepfather in the deed of the two lots to Fritz Jordan October 3, 1865, although there must have been other children as Mrs. Hofacker stated in the will she was signing for the "minor heirs of Hofacker". Jordan paid $220 for the lots, $100 cash and gave a note for $120.

Friedrich (Fritz) Jordan and his wife, Catharine, sold that part of the two lots on which the Muller house stands to Johann Joseph Stein for $100 on October 11, 1870. John Joseph Stein, listed as a laborer on the 1870 census, and his wife, Catharine, sold this property to Franz Koehler for $250 on September 10, 1872.

Franz Koehler signed a title bond, agreeing to sell this part of two lots to Franz Stein Jr. on the same date, with the condition that he pay a $450 note by September 10; 1877. Koehler and his wife, Magdalena, in whose name he had put this property, along with other lots March 30, 1875, signed a warranty deed to Franz Stein dated July 14, 1876.

Living in Gillespie County and listed on the 1860 and 1870 census were a Franz Stein, teacher, and his wife, the former Anna Jenschke. Franz Stein, a cabinet maker, the founder of Stein Lumber Company also lived in Fredericksburg for a short time after he came to Texas from Germany, moving to Kendall County later, and then returning to Fredericksburg to found his lumber company. The record is not clear which Franz Stein this is, but it may have been the lumberman, because when the property was conveyed back to Magdalena Koehler September 10, 1879, the deed states the grantor to be "Franz

Stein of Kendall County."

Koehler and F. Winkel had gone surety for F.C. Radeleff, a local businessman and one-time ousted county official, against whom a judgement was rendered and some of Koehler's property was sold to satisfy the claim of Norton & Deutz. A.O. Cooley, a local lawyer and native of New York, bought it at Sheriff's sale for $100 on November 3, 1880, and on December 1, 1880, sold it to Edward Wahrmund for $125, making a little profit on the deal.

Since the two-story rock house that the Mullers bought was built in two different periods, Muller feels the one-story, two-room structure at the front was built during the 1870's. The walls are of solid limestone rock with a thin frame partition wall. The original front door with its old hardware is still in use, and it is flanked by a window at each side. A door led out the back and another door led out the south wall where the Mullers have now constructed a large fireplace.

The back two rooms and the second floor were added sometime in the 1880's, probably around 1887-1888, according to recollections of older citizens who were familiar with the old home. The walls of the addition and second floor were of matching limestone rock, and the partitions were also of thin frame construction, there being four tiny rooms on the second floor.

Edward Wahrmund married Anna Marschall January 19, 1879, so this was probably their first real home. They owned the house until August 22, 1905, when they sold it to William Pfiester for $2000. The conveyance included the 100 by 200 foot corner Townlot 421 which Muller also owns.

The William Pfiester family made their home here. He died September 19, 1928, and after their mother's death, the children, Minna and husband, Otto R. Stoffers, Richard, Chester and James Pfiester sold it to Chas. A. Howell May 29, 1951, from whom the Mullers bought it.

What the Mullers have done to the house has to be seen. They retained all of the old that was good and the new that was added has been "antiqued" so well that it blends in perfectly with the old.

The original two front rooms which are now one large room highlighted with the fireplace in the south end are the Mullers' living and dining room, however, they "double" as the gallery, as the walls are hung with beautiful framed paintings.

The original back two rooms are now their kitchen and office. Each of these rooms had outside doorways. The office had one in the south wall and another in the back and the kitchen had one in the back wall, too. The stairs to the second floor begin in the kitchen. Here the Mullers did some outstanding renovation, using the weathered rough boards of a barn that stood behind their house to finish the walls of one side of the kitchen and the stairway. The same boards are used for one of the walls in the breakfast room which they added back of the kitchen.

Next to it, at the southeastern corner of the house, they added a master bedroom. In this Mrs. Muller's artistic ability is evident in the antiqued smoky-blue finish with warm overtones she gave the yard-high panels along one side of the wall. Then she did their entire bedroom suite in the same finish to match. Gray-blue wallpaper and a shag carpeting add to the overall effect. Adjoining this bedroom is the master bathroom.

Upstairs they removed all the frame partitions, except one. There is a small bedroom they use as a guest room and a full bath. The guest bedroom comes in handy when their 23-year old CPA daughter, Normah, and her husband, Rob Atherton, come for a visit.

The rest of the area is devoted to an everyday living room for the couple, a studio where Mrs. Muller and her mother like to paint, an area where Mr. Muller can indulge in his "reloading" hobby, and shelves and closets are under the eaves along the entire front of the house.

There is a fireplace on the second floor, too, almost in line with the one downstairs, and a copper hearth adds interest, as well as serving a practical purpose. They left the original floor, had it sanded, and then Mrs. Muller gave it a warm antique finish, using bluish tones to blend it with the decor.

A solid stone privacy fence encloses their small backyard, complete with rock-paved walks and an old well topped with shingled roof. Instead of drawing out well water, however, Muller has fitted his barbecue pit into the well frame. This area will also be utilized when the Mullers hold art shows and exhibits at their gallery.

The work the Mullers have done on their old home has provided them with a livable home that easily doubles as a gallery and studio and is a distinctive addition to Fredericksburg's growing list of restored buildings.

LOEFFLER-WEBER HOME

One of Fredericksburg's "big" attractions is a "little" house at 508 West Main Street. It is the Loeffler-Weber house which George and Gloria Hill bought from the Weber heirs November 24, 1964, and lovingly and authentically restored.

The official Recorded Texas Landmark medallion and marker erected in 1971 gives its history in "capsule" form:

"Loeffler-Weber House

"Log room and loft were built by German emigrant Gerhard Rorig as his home in first winter of Fredericksburg's existence, 1846-47. Noted cabinet maker, Johann Martin Loeffler, added typical rock and half-timber rooms and cooking fireplace, 1867. His son-in-law, J. Charles Weber, in 1905, restored the southwest lean-to.

"For Loeffler-Weber family this was home or Sunday House for 90 years."

The house is built on the southeast one-half ot Townlot 149 which was originally granted by the German Emigration Company to Gerhard Rorig. He was one of the founders of Zion Lutheran Church, located nearby, and according to research done by the Hills, built the oldest part of the house.

Rorig sold Townlot 149 and whatever building was on it to John William Schupp for only $40 on May 26, 1851. When Schupp sold this property to John Martin Loeffler January 22, 1867, they used the reverse of the same piece of paper on which the Rorig-to-Schupp deed had been written. Also, the earlier deed, though dated in 1851, had never been acknowledged before a notary public or other official, so the acknowledgment on that deed bears the same 1867 date.

Loeffler's occupation is listed on the 1860 and 1870 U.S. censuses as "joiner." The

122

By April 11, 1859, the need for a new jail had been shown and a contract was let for $900 to Ludwig Schmidt to build the second jail at a location behind the first courthouse -- approximately where Nimitz Parkway now intersects with South Crockett Street. According to the Commissioners Court Minutes, the first one was badly built and several prisoners had broken out without an effort.

This second jail was to be 30 by 14 feet of "hard rocks with vaulted ceiling", with four rooms -- three above ground, and one "underground." This second jail proved to be inadequate, too, as the records show it lacked sanitation, was too damp and improperly ventillated -- especially in the summertime.

As early as 1870 plans were underway to build the third jail, but lack of funds and various controversies caused changes in plans and building was stopped. Finally on Aug. 10, 1874, a contract was awarded to Louis Doebbler for the sum of $1645 for a jail to be erected on the "South side" of the courthouse.

This third jail is the one that burned down 10 years later. About daybreak January 7, 1885, fire broke out and the prisoner, Wm. Allison, lost his life. He had been indicted for the murder of John Braeutigam November 17, 1884, and one source states he started a fire, hoping to burn his way out of jail, but it got out of control. According to "Fredericksburg, Texas...the First Fifty Years," Penniger states "The real cause of the fire was not known, but it was assumed that somehow while the prisoner was reading, the oil lamp caused the conflagration."

Gillespie County had built its second courthouse by that time in the middle of the square. This is the building that was beautifully restored as the McDermott Building in 1967 and now houses Pioneer Memorial Library. The contract for it was awarded in January 1882 at a cost of $23,000.

On March 23, 1885, a little more than two months after the jail fire, the county closed a contract with C. F. Priess and Bro. for the construction of a new county jail (the fourth) at a cost of $9,962. It was completed in December 1885 and is still standing.

The site chosen was on a part of Townlot No. 352 in the middle of the block directly south of the Courthouse Square. The Townlot was originally granted to Justuss Herber, and title passed to Ottocar Mueller, as assignee of Justus (also spelled "Julius" at one place) Herber by deed dated November 15, 1850.

County of Gillespie, Owner

On May 16, 1855, Mueller sold this Townlot to Wilhelm Leilich, a cabinet maker, and the County of Gillespie bought the South one-half of it from Leilich on February 10, 1885, for a price of $150 to be paid for in monthly installments of $10, without interest, the deed containing the condition that it was to be used "for the purpose of erecting a jail thereon."

The contract for the fourth jail stipulated that it was to be 25 feet wide, 35 feet deep and from 20 to 22 feet high, and to have two stories. The ground floor was to have four rooms, one to be used as a lockup, and the others for the jailer. On the second floor were to be the steel-clad cells or cages.

The contract also called for "waterclosets, privy, sinks, wash sinks, water tank," etc., and advertisements for bids were placed in the San Antonio Express, Austin Statesman and Friederichsburger Wochenblatt.

The bid of C. Priess and Bro. for $9,962 was accepted. When Priess completed the job he asked for more money, however, as he said he had to dig the foundation deeper due to heavy rains and on account of having to use more rocks. After some controversy he was allowed an additional $100.

John Kollett, pioneer well digger, had the contract for digging the well for the jail at the sum of $2.75 a foot. It was to be five feet across "well walled out" (gut ausgemauert) with all the material to be furnished by Kollett. After he had worked on it a while, he petitioned the court, stating that due to heavy rains it was unsafe and dangerous to continue the first well, so he was paid $20 for his trouble, was instructed to fill up the hole and dig another well according to the original contract.

N. Ankemann was hired by the county to superintend the building of the jail at a cost of $200, but was later given an additional $120 when work continued during September, October and November, three months longer than the original contract called for.

A few changes have been made over the years since the jail was finished in December 1885, but basically it remains the same, especially the second floor.

The jail had a heavy solid steel plate door and another one with bars as the front entrance. All the windows had bars, but the ones on the lower floor and the two front doors were removed after its use as a jail was discontinued in 1939 when this building became a home for the custodian of the new courthouse, William (Bill) Heimann, and his wife.

The room at the northeast corner on the ground floor was the original "lock-up," but was used in later years as the women's cell. The door between this and the other front room is a solid steel plate, with a heavy brass key used to work the massive lock.

The rooms in the back on the ground floor were those originally intended for the jailer. The door which led from the front room into the back was a heavy steel plate, with steel frame.

Each of the back rooms has a door leading outside, and there are two windows in the outside walls. (These never had bars.) For many years, the county used these rooms as quarters for indigent persons who were dependent upon the county for their upkeep.

Iron steps lead to the upper floor out of the west front room. Part of the ceiling in this room is open, with the rest of curved corrugated steel upon which concrete was poured on the second floor.

Upstairs the front room has an open space at the head of the stairs. Against the east wall are two steel cells, each with a crude iron lavatory and commode, and at one time there were steel cots riveted to the walls. The doors are of heavy flat crossbars, while the floors and ceiling are of solid steel plates.

Going through a solid steel door, with an opening resembling a bird cage through which food could be passed, one reached the back room.

Maximum security was provided in the back part of the second floor in the large cell and two cages in the center.

There is a "run-around" around the two cells where prisoners who were incarcerated for long periods of time could get their exercise.

The massive door leading into back room has several bars and locks. An ingenious device is the P. J. Pauly and Bro. Lever Lock which was used from the outside to open the doors of the cages into which the prisoners were to retreat, then the doors of the cages were closed again, and the officer or jailer could go in to leave food in the cell. Once he was outside of the cell door again and had barred it, he used the lever lock to open the cages and the prisoners went back into the larger cell where they ate and slept. The crude sanitation facilities were also in the larger cell.

The only heat for the upper floor was a wood heater in the corner of the back room in the "run around." When there were prisoners in the front part of the jail during bitter cold days in winter they would often have to be moved in with the others in the back cell, often crowding the quarters.

A high stone wall was built surrounding the jail, with iron pickets along the front part. The solid rock fence was topped with pieces of broken glass, designed to make escape over its walls painful. John Dietz had the contract to build the fence for $348 and Chas. Ahrens was paid $5.25 for the iron gate at the front.

When its use as a jail ceased with the dedication on August 10, 1939, of the new courthouse which contained the fifth jail, a new era opened for this old building. After it was no longer used as a residence by the Bill Heimanns, it was used for many purposes -- chiefly storage. At one time the Gillespie County Historical Society had custody of it.

Now the Fredericksburg Historic Federation is undertaking its renovation for use as a depository for historic county archives.

———

WEBER SUNDAY HOUSE

An old home that made its way mechanically to Fredericksburg's Main Street is the Weber Sunday House that now sits at the back of the Pioneer Museum Complex. Here it joins the Kammlah and Fassel homes and their outbuildings in giving visitors a glimpse into the interesting history of Fredericksburg, showing a bit of how the people in them lived, worked and played.

The Gillespie County Historical Society was the grateful recipient of this Sunday House for its museum complex when Mrs. Adelbert Weber, a native Gillespian who now lives in New Braunfels, donated it to the society and it was moved to the present site in 1972. It made its way to Main Street from its former location near the corner of West San Antonio and South Cherry Streets by means of a mechanical housemover and was shown to the public for the first time during the Founders Day celebration held at the Pioneer Museum Complex on May 1972.

It was built in 1904 by Mr. and Mrs. August Weber on a lot which Mrs. Weber inherited from her parents, Mr. and Mrs. Conrad Wehmeyer. Wehmeyer was among the first settlers in Fredericksburg and for years conducted the first bakery in town in the middle of the 100 block on the north side of East Main Street. Alwina was one of their nine children.

Mr. and Mrs. Weber had a farm about seven miles out the Kerrville Road where they made their home. They built this small frame house, with one room of dimensions approximately 16 by 20 feet, on this lot in town to use as their Sunday house.

Sunday houses were as much a part of early day Fredericksburg history as people's lake homes or country cabins are now. Those who lived in the country would build these tiny houses in town to use when they came to town to attend church services and Sunday School on Sundays and other church holidays. They were a place to eat and rest when they came to town to shop, to see the doctor or to visit for a brief time.

This was how the Webers used their house. They were members of Zion Lutheran Church, and that was not too far away. Also, they lived near enough to town so they could make the trip in and back the same day. They would come in for church services, and then eat a

Gillespie County Historical Society, Owner

leisurely dinner in the house, staying over in the afternoon for Sunday School and to visit with relatives and friends.

It is furnished in much the same style as it was when the Webers and their two children, Bertha and Adelbert, used it. They had a third son, who died as an infant.

They had no running water in the house and there was no well near it, so they brought their water to drink and to cook with from their home in the country in jugs.

There was no electricity, so lamps and candles were used, but the Webers usually did not stay overnight, as they departed for home before dark.

Mr. and Mrs. Weber died in 1929. The house belonged to their daughter, Bertha, for a while, and later Mr. and Mrs. Adelbert Weber bought it, but none of them ever lived in it.

After the deaths of Adelbert and his sister, Mrs. Weber decided it would be a nice gesture and tribute to the early pioneers who used this type of house to donate it to the Gillespie County Historical Society. Her offer was gratefully accepted. She sold some of the furnishings in the house, giving the money to the church, but several of the original pieces of furniture and some of the dishes used by the Webers went with her gift and are in the house now.

The little house has a small front porch supported by four turned posts. At center front above the porch is a wooden opening into the attic. There is only one door into the room,

11

flanked by a window at each side under the porch. Each side has one window with solid wooden shutters, but there is no opening in the back wall. Now unbleached domestic curtains with red print ruffles hang at the windows.

On the bare wooden floor in front of the small bed used by the Webers is a crocheted rug. The bed is covered with the original white coverlet used by the owners. The Webers' old kitchen "schrank" with its glass doors has crochet-edged shelf liners and here some of the Weber dishes are displayed.

Typical is the long wooden table along one wall with one bench against the wall and the second bench along the other side. The Webers always had a white oilcloth over it, and a similar one is on it now.

Other furnishings include a small child's high chair, one cane-bottom and one rawhide-bottom chair, a small table on which their drinking water bucket stood, and in one corner is a large black kitchen stove. It is not the one the Webers used, but is one the society provided that is similar to those used at that time.

An oil lamp on the wall, another on the table alongside a white candle in a tin candleholder, dishpans hung against the wall, and some large framed family pictures add to the furnishings of the house.

Now when the Sunday house is open to visitors, they have a chance to see what these looked like in the early days. Too many of them have been remodeled, enlarged or changed completely with the passage of years and when the need for them no longer existed once the automobile and paved road era got here.

Mrs. Weber's generous gift of the old home is something that all generations can now appreciate as they come here to look at one that is typical of Fredericksburg's Sunday Houses.

At the front of the Pioneer Museum Complex rock fence is an official Texas State Historical Marker which "capsules" their story. The inscription reads:

"Sunday Houses

"Small townhouses built by German settlers who lived in distant rural areas. Used over weekends by families while they traded or attended church.

"A typical early Sunday House had one room with a lean-to kitchen and a half-story above, which was reached by attic stairway or ladder. Built during 1890's-1920's, most Sunday Houses were frame, but some were rock.

"Houses found use during school sessions, periods of religious instructions or serious illness.

"Some of the larger ones made comfortable retirement homes for elderly German farmers. 1970."

OLD JAIL

Since Gillespie County was formally organized February 23, 1848, it has had six jails.

The oldest jail still in existence is the fourth jail, built in 1885. It stands across the street from the new Law Enforcement Building that houses the sixth jail. The fifth was on the third floor level of the present Gillespie County Courthouse.

Of the first three jails, one burned down and two were razed when better ones were needed.

At the July 1852 session of the Commissioners Court it was voted that a jail be built, to be 18 by 18 feet wide, with stone walls 8 feet high and 2 feet thick. On July 19, 1852, the contract was awarded to John Ruegner and John Walch for the sum of $413.50.

Ruegner was the stonemason who built the present home of Kneese Law Office and Walch built the home which now belongs to Oliver and Nell Betty Harrison at 402 E. Austin St.

John Kleck received the contract for the "necessary ironworks" at 37½ cents per pound. According to "Fredericksburg, Texas...the First Fifty Years," this jail "stood near the east corner of the fence around the old school building on the market place." That would place it near the present City Hall site.

At the January 31, 1853, session of the Commissioners Court, a contract was given to Christ. Durst for laying a stone floor in the county jail at a cost of $26.

So, Gillespie County had a jail before it had a courthouse, as its first courthouse was authorized October 3, 1854, when Jacob Arhelger was given a contract in the amount of $2200. This stood where the present post office is now located and was razed in 1940.

for Jacob Gold Sr., to whom he conveyed it that same month on February 28, 1902, for $1,150.

Jacob Gold was born in Coblenz, Germany, in 1842 and came to Texas in 1850. He was a Confederate soldier in Company E, First Texas Cavalry and was wounded during the Civil War. During the Reconstruction Days, he was a freighter hauling cargoes by ox team from Indianola west to beyond the Pecos and east to beyond the Brazos. He later joined the Trail Drivers and took cattle as far north as Illinois and Tennessee. In 1869 he married Elizabeth Habenicht and settled in eastern Gillespie County where he founded the community of Rheingold. In 1906 they moved to town.

The Golds made numerous changes in the home, chief of which was the adding of the second story rooms and porch. The house is built in the style of homes in Germany, with the front porch immediately adjacent to the sidewalk. Gingerbread trim and railing added a distinctive touch to the porches.

The front entrance is through a large double door over which is a gracefully curved glass transom. There are three panels in each door. Of special interest is the large old wrought iron lock on the door, with its heavy brass key.

There is one room on each side of the hallway. The room on the north has a fireplace in the north wall which the Golds closed up as it did not draw well. The wood closure and mantel give it the appearance of an old-fashioned folding bed so popular in olden days.

To the rear of these rooms and the hall was their kitchen in the one-story part of the house at the southwest corner, and a dressing room and bath were at the northwest corner. Upstairs there are two bedrooms separated by the hall into which the stairway from the first floor rises.

Jacob Gold Sr., though wounded in the Civil War, was an erect and striking figure as a young man. He was also a far-sighted pioneer businessman, erecting in 1909-10 the first office building in town still referred to by many as the "Gold Building." This is the two-story structure at 134 East Main, between Winn's Store and Stehling Bros.

Anna Gold, assisted by her sister, Alwina Gold, daughters of Jacob and Elizabeth Gold, owned and operated the fine ladies ready-to-wear business known as "The Vogue" in the northwest half of the Gold Building.

Their brothers and sisters were Ernst, Herman and August Gold; Emma, Mrs. Max H. Schoenewolf; Clara, Mrs. Henry Braeutigam; Bertha Gold; and Olga, Mrs. August Welgehausen.

Mr. Gold died September 12, 1930, at age 89, and his wife died September 28, 1940, at the age of 92.

From the Gold heirs Anna and Alwina acquired title to the house on July 25, 1941, and continued to make their home here, Anna Gold died November 4, 1958, and the Kruegers bought the house from her sister September 7, 1960. Rev. Krueger, a retired Lutheran pastor, did not get to enjoy it long, for he died July 2, 1962, however, his widow continues to live here.

Basically, she has made few changes in the home, but in adding her antique furniture she has kept the period look on the interior.

Mrs. Krueger died March 16, 1977, and her daughters are selling the house.

Minna Perry and Loreen Blount, Owners

SAUER-MOELLERING HOME

Around the corner from the Schmidt-Gold house now owned by Mrs. Elizabeth Krueger is the old Sauer-Moellering house at 216 East San Antonio Street. The early family histories of the two houses are interwoven.

The Moellering house has been in the same family ever since Townlot 323 on which it was built was granted by the German Emigration Company to Wilhelm Sauer when Fredericksburg was settled. The deed to Sauer is dated December 2, 1852, because the original probably burned up in the fire that destroyed county records in 1850.

Wilhelm Sauer died prior to 1850, and his widow, Louise, married Lorenz Schmidt, a stonemason. Wilhelm and Louise Sauer had a daughter, Louise, who was listed as being two years old and living in the household of Lorenz and Louise Schmidt on the 1850 U.S. census. When she grew up she married Henry Moellering (Sr.) on March 10, 1868. She inherited this house and lot.

As built originally, the house had a large front room, "a stube" that served as the bedroom, and behind that was the original kitchen out of which the steps led to the upper half-story which provided added sleeping quarters.

The front entrance is a double door -- used in many homes because it provided good ventillation, flanked by two small windows. Originally there was only one window in the east wall of each room, with a small one added halfway up to provide light on the stairway.

Although they never owned the house, some of the early occupants of it were the George Goehmanns. He was a "stellmacher" or wheelwright, and the wagons, buggies and wheels he made were as important to the people of his time as tractors, trucks, cars and tires are to people today.

The Carl Tatsches also lived in the house. She was one of the Lorenz Schmidt daughters.

Louise and Henry Moellering lived here for a number of years before moving to their farm in the Rocky Hill Community. When their son, Max R. Moellering, married Augusta (Gussie) Hahne June 27, 1910, they moved into this house and lived here until his death in 1958. Mrs. Moellering continued to live here until about five years ago when frail health made it necessary for her to move to Knopp Nursing Home.

The Max Moellerings bought the house from his parents October 28, 1920. They made a number of changes in it during the years that followed, including the addition of a kitchen in the back. They also took the stairway out of the original kitchen and put an outside stairway up at the west side of the house, enlarging the small window in the upper west wall to provide a doorway.

The original kitchen then became a bedroom and bath.

Now the house is owned by two of the Max Moellering daughters, Minna, Mrs. Robert E. Perry, and Loreen, Mrs. Benroe Blount. They acquired it July 30, 1975, from their mother. Their sister, Norma, Mrs. Thomas Howard, died several years ago.

Mr. and Mrs. Perry, both retired, live in a mobile home to the rear of the house, and Mrs. Blount's son, Don has been doing a lot of work on the old home. Don and his wife now live in Fredericksburg.

The walls of the native stone house were plastered and all this has been chipped away. Plans for its renovation and future use are underway.

Helen Stieler Crouch, Owner

CORDES HOME

The old Cordes home sits on the bank of Town Creek, overlooking the Market Square and waiting patiently for the restoration its present owner, Helen Stieler (Schatzie) Crouch, has in mind for it one of these days. She's put a new shingle roof on it to preserve the interior, and hopes to find time someday to fix it up the way she has visualized it.

Folks have often wondered why the original builder put it so close to the creek bank. He didn't -- the course of the creek bed was changed years ago when West Austin Street was graded, improved and paved. The creek bed used to be much farther south -- almost near the corner of the present-day Hermann Sons Hall and where the Girl Scout Cabin now stands.

The house is built on what was originally Townlot 61 which the German Emigration Company granted to Johan Alsenz II. Adam Alsenz I was granted Townlot 27 which adjoins it on the northeast. Who they were and what happened to them is not known.

Henry (Heinrich) Minkel got possession of Townlot 61, and finally acquired all eight townlots in the entire block bounded now by West Schubert, North Crockett, West Austin and North Orange Streets. They were Townlots 23b, 24, 25, 26, 27, 59, 60 and 61. Minkel and his wife, Anna Maria, sold these eight townlots to Heinrich Cordes on March 16, 1857, for $160, payable $100 on May 1, 1857, and $60 due December 25, 1857. In the deed reference is made to their being "all in one enclosure," probably meaning he had them all under fence.

That part of this block on which the old home is built was to remain in his descendants' possession until 1969.

Heinrich Cordes was a stonemason and carpenter and was also referred to as a "baumeister" (architect). He helped to build the Nimitz Hotel and old St. Mary's Catholic Church. He also built this home and although it has not been lived in for many years, it is still structurally sound and in good condition.

When he built this house, North Crockett Street was little more than a footpath, and the Cordes family had their hen house and pig pen on what is now the street.

Heinrich Cordes and his first wife had one girl, Sophie, who married William Dietz. In 1859 he married Minna Henke and they had four children, Charles Cordes; Heinrich Cordes Jr.; Minna, Mrs. Fred Koennecke; and Augusta, Mrs. Henry Evers Jr.

Heinrich Cordes Sr. died in 1875, and for a number of years Heinrich Jr. and his wife lived here with his mother. Their daughter, Olga, who married Hugo Kallenberg, was born in this house. After Heinrich Cordes Jr. built a home of his own not far away for his family, Mrs. Cordes Sr. went to live with the Fred Koenneckes at Cave Creek.

Ownership of the house passed to Minna and Fred Koennecke. On October 2, 1922, Fred Koennecke laid out the entire block as the Koennecke Addition. He built the frame house that stands at the corner, 201 Mistletoe, where Mrs. Crouch now lives. This is the street he created through the middle of the subdivision. Even after his wife's death Mr. Koennecke continued to make his home here, using the old house for storage, as a washhouse, and even used the porch as a garage for his automobile. He took good care of the old house, fortunately, even though he did take out part of the back wall of one room.

When the Koennecke estate was partitioned, the old and the new house were set aside for Alma Ottmers. She died, and her husband, Helmuth Ottmers, and the children, Guenther, Gilbert, James and Harold Ottmers, Minna Novian and Norma Campagna sold it to Mrs. Crouch and two of her friends, Dorothy Beckmann Leslie and Margaret Shafer, on May 12, 1969, thus passing out of Cordes heirship. Mrs. Leslie and her husband, Roy F. Leslie Jr., and Mrs. Shafer and her husband, W. Pressley Shafer Jr., sold their interest to Mrs. Crouch November 12, 1971. She now lives in the frame bungalow and like Mr. Koennecke, uses the old house for storage.

The oldest part of the house are the two rooms on the east side next to Crockett Street. The front room is built of logs chinked with rocks and mortar, which in later years were covered with shingles to "waterproof" the wall. The back room was the Cordes kitchen. It is built of native limestone and had a stone floor and cooking fireplace in the east wall. In later years, a hole was made above the fireplace into the flue, so a wood stove could be used. The beams are of wide, heavy, rough hewn lumber, with wide boards placed on them for the ceiling and as the floor of the attic. The windows are different from those in most old houses. Each half had three panes, one above the other, and the one half slides sideways over the other half.

The two rooms at the west side were added later and are of heavy limestone rock construction. These two rooms have conventional windows in them. There never was a stairway to the attic above the front two rooms -- to get there they used a ladder.

Mr. Koennecke took out part of the rear wall of the room on the northwest side. This room has a cistern in it and a washpot in the corner.

Mrs. Crouch has plans for restoration of the house, but is kept so busy restoring old furniture for others at her place of business, the Rumpelkammer, about a block away, that she just has not gotten around to it. "But I will, someday," she says. With her know-how and experience, you know it will be great when she does.

WILLIAM KLINGELHOEFER HOME

One of the few old homes along Fredericksburg's main thoroughfare that still sits by itself, surrounded by most of the acreage its builder owned is the William Klingelhoefer home located west of the intersection of US 290 West and US 87 North.

It's home now for his son, Armand F. Klingelhoefer, who has owned it since October 22, 1941, when he acquired it from the other Klingelhoefer heirs.

When William Klingelhoefer built this typical limestone house for his family it was completely surrounded with liveoak and postoak trees, and the highways that pass it now were little more than deeply-rutted wagon trails.

The property it is built on has been in the Klingelhoefer family ever since Fredericksburg was founded. It is located on part of Outlot 581, one of the ten-acre lots laid out by the German Emigration Company as "farm" lots for the early settlers. The original allotment shows Jacob Schneider as the one to whom it was allotted, but ownership was acquired by J. J. Klingelhoefer, who was also allotted nearby Outlot No. 583.

J. J. Klingelhoefer built his own home on his townlot nearer to the center of town which still stands today and is owned by his granddaughter, Lyne Klingelhoefer Lewis Harper. One of the sons of J.J. Klingelhoefer and Elisabeth Heiland Klingelhoefer was William, who was born in 1853. After the death of his parents (his mother in 1881 and his father in 1886), William inherited Outlot No. 581 and 582, receiving a deed to it October 5, 1896.

William married Maria (Mary) Eckert and they moved into this house which he built in 1879. In 1955, one of their children, Miss Alma Klingelhoefer, then a retired school teacher who was living here temporarily with her brother, Armand, recalled many details about their parents, their house and its surroundings.

William Klingelhoefer was a stonemason and built his own home. She also recalled that he spoke of working on many of the old stone churches in the city, and that he was especially proud of his work on the Bank of Fredericksburg building which was built for Temple D. Smith, banker, from plans and designs by noted architect, Alfred Giles.

When William built his own house, there were only two rooms on the ground floor with a half-story above them. Each room has a window and doorway facing the front, and a window in the east and west walls. The walls are over 18 inches thick and constructed of native limestone. Beautifully designed "gingerbread" trims the upper part of the front porch enclosed with a "gingerbread" railing.

The larger of the two rooms, at the east side, also had a doorway to the southwest. The smaller room was originally their kitchen and had a stairway in the corner which led upstairs. There was a small shelf built into the wall. where Mrs. Klingelhoefer kept her spices.

Later the kitchen was moved into the little rock house a few steps from the backside of the old house. Still later, when the two rooms were added at the back of the house, the kitchen was moved into the southwest room where it is still located.

The other back room is used as a bedroom, with a bath at one end. A door leads out of the east wall to the stairway which was added later to provide access to the upper story.

The upper story was where the boys in the family slept. There is a large window in the west wall, and before the two rooms were added in back, there were two little windows in the back wall. The window in the east wall was enlarged into a doorway when the outside stairway was added.

Along the back of the house is a large porch with cement floor, the back side of which is enclosed with a grape arbor. The grape vines at one time grew along an arbor that extended into the garden, but were transplanted along the porch to shade it.

The well in back is interesting. First there was only a deep "dug" well with an old iron water pump on it which still pumps water. A deeper well with casings was drilled in the middle of the dug well and a windmill put on top of it. Adjacent to it is a a large cement tank, providing an ample supply of water.

Next to the wells and tank is the little one-room stone house once used as the kitchen. At first entrance to the cellar below it was gained through the trap door in the floor, but later steps to the cellar were put outside.

Mrs. William Klingelhoefer always had many flowers in the yard and garden around her home, and some of the flowering shrubs and trees remain. One interesting shrub is the Kastanie (chestnut) that grew from seeds brought from Germany by August Zinckes and given to Mrs. Klingelhoefer. In Germany people make "Kastanie butter" out of these, similar to American peanut butter.

The Klingelhoefers always had a big vegetable garden in back, and the present owner, Armand, has kept it up. He has a good stand of corn and many varieties of vegetables growing in the same spot where his parents had their garden before him. A big, majestic liveoak tree shades the entire front of the house.

The Klingelhoefer children who grew up here were August W., Alfred G., Alma, Albert, Arthur, Adolph, Alvin and Armand F. One of their sisters, Asta Louise, died at the age of three months. Fortunately, Armand is very appreciative of his ancestral home and its surrounding property and has taken very good care of the place.

Just as all the children's names began with an "A", so does this old house rate an "A" for being such a well-preserved, typical old rock home that adds so much to the charm of Fredericksburg.

VEREINS KIRCHE

Of all the old homes and historic buildings in Fredericksburg none is more familiar than the Vereins Kirche. Through the years it has become the "hallmark" of the city -- almost an emblem or logo. Though the structure that now stands in the middle of the Market Square is not the original Vereins Kirche, it is a replica of the building that once stood in the middle of Main Street between the Courthouse and Market Square.

Reminiscent of the distinctive municipal buildings that often stood in the middle of the public squares in Germany and other European cities, the settlers of Fredericksburg must have had something of the same thing in mind when they built this octagonal structure. It was to serve them as a community church, a fort for protection against the Indians, a storehouse and a meeting place.

The replica was begun in 1934 and dedicated in a two-day celebration Saturday, May 11, and Sunday, May 12, 1935. While this was both a solemn and gala occasion, it missed some of the "local color" that the laying of the cornerstone of the original Vereins Kirche had.

The first year was spent by the settlers who arrived here May 8, 1846, in providing themselves at first with crude shelters, then with homes and with making peace with the hostile Indians that surrounded them. It was following this peace that John O. Meusebach brought about with his treaty negotiated

Gillespie County Historical Society, Owner

March 1-2, 1847, that brought the Indians who were to sign it to Fredericksburg May 9, 1847, a day and a year after the town was settled.

The treaty called for the Indians to come to Fredericksburg on the second full moon after the March date on which the treaty had been negotiated. On the day of the Vereins-Kirche cornerstone laying, the Comanches appeared, led by their chiefs, Ketemoczy and Santana, and some of their tribe arrived in the village. They were arrayed in beaded buckskin attire and feathered headdresses. The Indians brought with them tanned hides, bear fat, and deer skins filled with wild honey. They spent the day taking part in the festivities, their colorful attire a contrast to the folk costumes of the different provinces in Germany worn by the settlers.

In an account written by Dr. Schubert (Friedrich Armand Strubberg) he describes the procession up the street. It formed at the

"Vereins House" (probably referring to the original building erected by the surveyors on the east side of the 100 block of South Washington St.) They marched up the street to the place where the walls of the Vereins Kirche were being erected. First came the minister, the teacher and officers of the Adelsverein, followed by the Vereins soldiers on horseback and the small Vereins cannon drawn by four horses, with the citizens bringing up the end of the procession.

After much oration and ceremony, the large limestone cornerstone was laid in the opening left in the wall. In its niche was placed a document of the building of the Vereins Kirche, and then it was sealed. The director, the minister and the officers of the Verein took turns placing trowels of mortar upon the stone.

This same cornerstone was used when the replica was begun in 1934. After the original building was dismantled in 1897, it found use in a much more mundane way, being used as a chicken watering trough when it was reclaimed for the replica.

The original cornerstone-laying ceremony ended with a cannon shot, but that did not end the festivities. Then the fun began. The Indians staged ceremonial dances in the street, after which the German settlers drifted toward a dancing green that had been prepared under the trees. The ground had been cleared and stomped smooth.

Near it was a platform for the newly-organized orchestra and all around it were benches for the ladies. Just as the white settlers wondered in amazement at the Indian dances, so the Indians stood by in wonderment as the Germans swirled through their schottisches, waltzes and gallops.

When the second cornerstone was laid Saturday afternoon, January 6, 1934, there was one marked difference. At the first ceremony in 1846, there were mostly young couples, a few middle-aged people and children, but no old people. In 1934, there were many old people in the crowd -- many with grayed heads and bowed shoulders who, as infants and young children, had been baptized and confirmed in the old church.

In 1887 H. Ochs Sr. wrote an account that described the building of the Vereins Kirche in 1847, and Penniger, in his Fest Ausgabe published in 1896 for Fredericksburg's 50th anniversary quotes from it.

"When the site for the colony was surveyed

and laid out into streets and lots, a place for a church building was also designated, namely, in the middle of the main street on the market place square in the center of town. The building itself was planned by Schubert, an official of the Society.

"The structure formed a regular octagon, with sides eighteen feet long and about eighteen feet high. The incline of the roof was such that, after a rise of ten feet, a cupola of the same height and also ten feet wide was erected. This formed an eight-sided roof six to seven feet high which came to a point.

"A weather cock was placed on the tip, but it was knocked down by lightning in 1862 -- there was no fire damage -- and it was replaced by a cross.

"The entire structure was built of wood and the best trees in the area were selected for that purpose. On the inside of the church stood four strong pillars on which the cross timbers of the prism rested and from which the connecting timbers and rafters rose. (A fifth pillar was placed in the center a few years ago when the large church bell was installed). (Translater's note: This report was written in 1887.)

"At first the walls were made of plain boards and the floor of sand. It remained in that condition until the floor was covered with stone slabs and the walls lined with masonry.

"An ordinary table served as the altar and clumsy wooden benches as seats until a pulpit, better seats and a ceiling to cover the timbers could be provided. A very small bell had to serve the purpose until the larger one was installed. The congregational singing was led by a song leader until the year 1868 when a melodeon was added. The church was considered common property for all settlers in Gillespie County.

"Mr. Basse, who was also an immigrant and who came as pastor from the principality of Wittgenstein, was appointed pastor for the Protestants. He served three years after which he resigned and was followed by Pastor B. Dangers, an immigrant who was still in New Braunfels. The latter served at least twenty years, namely, until his death in 1869."

During those years Pastor Dangers preached for Sunday and festive services, baptized the babies, confirmed the young people, married and buried the adults.

It was no uncommon sight to see couples walk for miles from out in the country to be married in the Vereins Kirche. Sometimes they marched up the street in festive wedding procession, followed by relatives and friends, as was the custom in certain provinces in Germany. Sometimes he walked to their homes for the wedding ceremony. It was on his way home from a wedding he performed in the country in 1869 that he was caught in a shower, and the cold and pneumonia that followed this exposure brought on his death.

The original church had two doors, one facing southeast (downtown) and the other faced northwest (uptown), making it possible to walk straight through the church on the way up or down the street. The southeast door was for the men and the women entered on the northwest door. The men were seated on the right side of the aisle and the women at the left side of the aisle. This "segregated" seating carried over for many years in the other churches built later.

After it had been used for a number of years, the weatherboarding was torn down on the walls and replaced with limestone rock between the logs. The two doors were enclosed and one door was built facing the courthouse, as does the present door in the replica. The walls were plastered inside and out. The church had a ceiling added to eliminate the disturbance from swarms of bats that inhabited the belfry and would swoop down on the congregation.

The building in later years was used for school examinations when on the last day of school children would be assembled here to be examined by their teacher and interested school patrons.

The various congregations using the Vereins Kirche eventually built churches of their own and gradually the old church was forsaken and soon fell into a state of neglect and deterioration.

When Fredericksburg celebrated its 50th anniversary in 1896, the rock parts of the walls were removed and the building was used as a pavilion. Thus its final use was for a significant and festive event, for within a year a court decree ordered that the remainder of the old church be removed from the "heart of the town" so that San Saba Street (as Main Street was officially designated), and the road between San Antonio and Mason which followed the street, could be straightened.

In 1897 the building was completely demolished and all traces of it removed from the center of the town's main thoroughfare.

Memory of it remained alive, however, in

describing a very small house that was evidently located on the corner lot.

Philipp Klaerner was discharged as administrator June 28, 1852. Chester Schneider recalled that his grandmother, Catharina Schneider, had been reared by her uncle by the name of Klaerner.

He must have been a good business man, because when the original county records were destroyed by fire in 1850 he had duplicate deeds made from the German Emigration for these Townlots the Mahrs were entitled to as well as some he was entitled to, and filed them for record.

George Schneider and his wife, Catharina Mahr Schneider, sold this corner lot, No. 157, together with the three adjoining ones along Main Street, to F. Wrede, then County Clerk of Gillespie County, on June 2, 1856. This deed stated that she was the daughter of Martin Mahr and that Johannes, Andreas and Johan Philipp Mahr were her deceased brothers from whom she inherited the title to the other three.

Two years later Wrede sold the easternmost townlot, No. 160, to E. Krauskopf for $100, and on March 29, 1865, sold Nos. 157 (the corner lot), 158 and 159 to Peter Itz for $800.

From Peter Itz and his wife, Christine, ownership passed to Karl Itz and a brother of Mrs. Karl Itz, Ludwig Evers, by deed dated October 23, 1867. In this deed reference is made to "some buildings" on the property and still to be erected, for which Karl Itz and Ludwig Evers agreed to furnish material, money and labor, with the Peter Itzes retaining the right to live there with the grantees to get possession after the death of the older couple.

Ludwig Evers and his wife, Pauline, and Karl Itz, partitioned their three lots on August 6, 1887, with Ludwig Evers and his wife taking the corner lot, No. 157, and Itz the other two. In this deed reference is made to Susan Street -- the street now known as Milam Street.

The corner lot has remained in the same family ever since. In a partition of the Ludwig Evers property after his death, one of the daughters, Lina, Mrs. Hy. C. Keyser, received the Northwest ½ of Townlot 157. Lina Keyser died November 1, 1936, and her daughter, Lillie Bierschwale, wife of Walter F. Bierschwale, inherited this Northwest ½ of this lot on which this building stands. On March 30, 1972, Mr. and Mrs. Bierschwale deeded this property to their daughter, Lucille, and her husband, Fred E. Dietel.

Mr. and Mrs. Ludwig Evers farmed and ranched in the northwestern part of the county, but in their old age moved to town, settling in the little log and rock house which was adjacent to this place.

A simple floor plan was followed by the original builders of the structure. Downstairs there was one large room, with a thick stone wall dividing it from the smaller back room. Underneath this is a large cellar.

At one time the steps led up along the east wall on the inside of the building, but these have been removed and an outside stairway put in their place.

The upstairs was originally one large room, which was later divided with frame partitions, but these were removed by later tenants. When the building was renovated by Mrs. Keyser, the front was knocked out and show windows added and additional windows were added upstairs. There are no openings of any kind on the west side of the building.

At one time the John Knopp family lived upstairs and he operated a saloon downstairs, selling groceries and also some staples, too. During these years this place also figured in the "beer war," a fact mentioned in Knopp's obituary. At that time Probst was brewing beer here and selling it for 10 cents a glass. Knopp imported it from San Antonio and sold it for 5 cents. Tales were told long after of the rush on his bar.

Once a doctor who felt that goat's milk would cure most people's ills occupied the building and kept a lot of goats here to supply the demand. It was not great, however, so he did not stay long. A dentist office, a millinery store operated by Mrs. Louis Henke, Otto Schneider's grocery store and Schneider Produce, Walter Knopp's grocery store, Haversack Wines and W-K Electric were other tenants.

Now that the Gallerie of Fine Arts' owners, Mr. and Mrs. Karl B. Guiney, occupy the building, visitors can see and buy their art and gifts attractively displayed in one of the city's oldest buildings.

———

WILLIAM C. HENKE HOME

Carved in the limestone rock above the doorway of the old William C. Henke home at the corner of West Main and North Milam Streets is the year "1886", the year in which the house was built.

It is now owned by a native of Fredericksburg, Dorothea (Doris) Weinheimer Cotter, and her husband, John, who lived in San Antonio, but spend much time in Fredericksburg. They were two of the 1975 recipients of awards given June 12 by the Gillespie County Historical Society for their research in the history of this area and for their generous donations of books and the research data they have compiled on people, places and buildings.

The house has an interesting early history, and for almost 60 years it was in the William C. Henke family.

Townlot 156 on which it is built once belonged to Sophie Spaeth, the widow of Ludwig Spaeth who was murdered by the Indians in 1870 at age 39 while at work in the fields on his place near Enchanted Rock. Mrs. Spaeth was a daughter of Peter Behrens, who was granted Townlot 155 which adjoins 156 on the west.

No. 156 was granted by the German Emigration Company to P. Friess on the original list of allotments. Behrens acquired Friess's claim to the corner lot and on November 21, 1849, signed a paper authorizing the company to make title to Townlot 156 to Julius Splittgerber. On September 24, 1851, a deed was signed by the GEC conveying No. 156 to Splittgerber as assignee of Behrens.

Splittgerber and his wife gave Sophie Spaeth, widow of Ludwig Spaeth, a mortgage on this lot as security for a $1000 note, due in 1874. He defaulted on the note, so following a judgment dated October 26, 1876, and foreclosure, Mrs. Spaeth bought it at sheriff's sale for $120 on August 7, 1878.

Sophie Spaeth and some of her children, Heinrich, Louis, Frank and Mary, sold the Southeast one-half of Townlot 156 for $350 to William C. Henke on April 4, 1885, with the provision that her minor children, Jacob and Wilhelm, would quitclaim their interest when they became of age, and they did so December 27, 1890.

William C. Henke was one of seven sons of Fredericksburg's pioneer butcher, Heinrich Henke, who founded the first Henke Meat Market "downtown" at the corner of East Main and South Lincoln. Five of these sons followed their father's trade and went into the butcher business. Richard and Hugo con-

Nos. 158 and 159. Of interest is the fact that in this deed reference is made to the street that is now North Milam as being named "Susan Street."

Karl and Henrietta Itz, after he became too "infirm" to farm, moved permanently into this house in town and were living here when they celebrated their golden wedding anniversary October 5, 1906. Their children, in secrecy, planned a celebration at this home on Main Street in their honor. In the October 10, 1906, edition of the Wochenblatt, there is a short story telling about their anniversary, however, over two months later, for the December 19 issue, the paper ran a complete story with a picture of the couple. Reference is made to the celebration being a "rare event" and it probably was in those days because people's longevity was not what it is now and one or the other of a couple rarely lived long enough to celebrate a 50th wedding anniversary.

For the celebration, since the couple was so "special," the news story stated, Klaerner's Kapelle (Band) came to serenade in the evening. Earlier the choir of the Evangelical Church (as Bethany Lutheran was known then) and the Concordia Choir came and sang "several appropriate songs." The guests "were served with excellent food and drink. The table groaned under the weight of the delicacies."

Karl Itz died January 31, 1908, but his widow, Henrietta, continued to make her home here until she died September 27, 1923.

Two of the couple's sons, Rudolph and Charles Itz, inherited this property. A larger, two-story, stone building had been built adjoining the old log cabin on its east side and here Rudolph Itz conducted a saloon and his family lived in part of it until 1918.

The Rudolph Itz family and others used the little house as a "Sunday house" after their mother's death whenever they came to town from their homes in the country.

Charles Itz and his wife, Louise, and the children of Rudolph and Emma Itz, sold this property to Paul Pfiester October 26, 1944. He made considerable renovations in the two-story Rudolph Itz building, but fortunately did not alter the little old house. Pfiester sold this property to Krauskopf Bros. November 14, 1949, and they used the old house for storage. Koock acquired it February 13, 1975.

When the carpenter crew he hired began restoration work on this old house it was like pealing off layers. The different stages of construction were easily discernible.

The oldest part is the one room log cabin, built rather high off the ground, so the cellar below it had "windows" in the back and two side walls -- about a foot or more above ground. There were also several shelves, some open and others with doors -- in recesses in the thick stone walls. The floor is dirt.

Steps of stone to the cellar were placed at the front west corner, and next to them steep, short steps led to the front door. This room had one window flanking the front door and a window in the east wall which has been made into a door way because the logs are so deteriorated. There was also a door in the back and the west side wall.

As restoration progressed, the mode of building the earliest log cabins was clearly visible. So often they were in such a hurry to get their homes built that they did not take the time to strip all the bark off the logs, and such is the case with many of these logs in the little room. The ceiling beams are pegged, and the long, stout pegs can be seen as new beams replaced those that had rotted. This roof was repaired with some cypress logs which Ty Cox located and had "ripped" (sawed into boards) at a mill. Windy Goff, head of the restoration crew, cut them in two to use as the roof supports which were later covered with cedar shakes.

Behind the log cabin is a small room with solid rock outer walls, and the back of the log cabin serving as the fourth wall of this room.

Through the doorway in the west wall of the log cabin, you step down into the later rock addition to the house. The larger of the two rooms, in front, had apparently once been partitioned, and later a room of frame construction was added at the front. This has been torn away, leaving the aged limestone which blends well with the adjoining logs.

How fortunate for Fredericksburg -- that through all these years -- this little log cabin built by an early settler and its rock additions have been left untouched while many similar "jewels" have been torn down because they were considered "too unsightly." Its survival is almost as fantastic as that of one of the men who once lived in it.

William Faulk Koock and his wife sold this property to his brother, Tim Koock, October 15, 1976, and "Antiek" is no longer located in the log cabin.

EVERS BUILDING—NOW GALLERIE OF FINE ART

Because its early history is so closely interwoven into that of the old Itz home in the same block, the story of the corner building at 342 West Main Street adds its interesting chapter to the history of old homes along Fredericksburg's Main Street.

Now occupied by an art gallery, the building has been used for many purposes, but was built as a combination home and store.

Following publication of the story on the Itz home, some interesting information came to light when a great-grandson of the man to whom the corner Townlot on which it is built called at the Standard office. He was Chester Schneider of Prairie Mountain Route, Llano, who was a grandson of George and Catharina Schneider, and a great-grandson of Martin Mahr, the father of Mrs. George Schneider, and to whom the German Emigration Company originally granted this lot.

Mr. Schneider pointed out that the family name was "Mahr" -- spelled with an "a". He knew from family history that Martin Mahr and his three sons died in the cholera epidemic, leaving only his grandmother, Catharina, the daughter of Martin Mahr, as their survivor. An uncle, Philipp Klaerner, reared her, and from the very early Probate Records in the county clerk's office, interesting information on Martin Mahr's estate was learned.

Philipp Klaerner was appointed administrator of the estate, and his account showed that April 3, 1847 he paid $10.75 "for

goods and boards for a coffin." The inventory showed four Townlots on San Saba Street (now Main Street) rented to Frederick Pape, valued at $50. Among the other items listed were 12 yards linen cloth, $1.50; 11 yards cotton cloth, $2.30; 3 bed sheets, 50 cents; 1 watch, $5; 6 pewter plates, $1; 6 teaspoons, 30 cents, 1 spinning wheel, 20 cents; 1 cow and calf $10; 1 steer, $4; and other household items. There was also a claim against the German Emigration Company for $108.63.

Klaerner's account also showed that May 8, 9, 10, 1847, he paid $3 for labor done on lots; May 17-20, mending fence, $3.50; on July 3, 1847, for "15 days going and coming to bring a cow from Santa Clara," $15; October 18, for 3 load bricks, $3.75; Oct. 21-28, repairing the house, $4; for boards, $3; and on November 11, two doors to the house, $2; nails and boards for the door, 35 cents, hooks and hinges, $1.50; November 12-17 for six days work, $6.

January 1 to May 1848 he was allowed $16 for boarding minor (Cath. Mahr -- later Mrs. Schneider); two trips from Llano to be sworn in as guardian, $6; and on December 17, 1848, $4 for making a trip to San Antonio to get the claim of Cath. Mahr recorded in County clerk's office.

Among his receipts for May 1847 to November, 1850, were $12 house rent; $4 rent for the hut; $24 for house and hut; and additional sums of $8, $6.55 and $4 for rent.

The term "hut" used here is English for the German word "Huette" used often in

24

faces for 100 feet on the Market Square and runs for 200 feet along East Main Street. This Townlot was originally granted by the German Emigration Company to Christian Wahrmund, as an emigrant, and the deed to him by the company was dated December 17, 1849.

Christian Wahrmund sold it to Zenas Nash October 13, 1850, for $100, and reference in its description is made to its being bounded on the southwest by San Saba Street and on the northwest by the "Plaza or Public Square." Nash is listed on the 1850 U.S. census as being a merchant from Massachusetts. He sold this Townlot for $150 to Chester B. Starks December 16, 1850, who had just two months before bought the two corner lots on the opposite side of the street, where Main Book Store and Jack's Emporium and other buildings now stand.

Starks was also a merchant, but from New York. He is said to have operated the second store in Fredericksburg (J.L. Ransleben had the first). The store, however, was probably on the other side of the street, because the first building on the Publishing Company's side of the street was the small residence Starks built on the corner (present-day Sears).

Starks sold the entire Townlot to Emil Wahrmund on April 1, 1858, for $800. It was to remain in the Wahrmund family until title passed to the Publishing Company in 1963.

An interesting sidelight on the title to this Townlot is that in three generations there were three Emil Wahrmunds who married women with the given name of Auguste. There is now a fourth generation Emil Wahrmund, who still owns part of the townlot -- the building in which Hill Country Community Press and Sears are located.

The first Emil Wahrmund and his wife, Auguste Sander, lived in the small stone house at the corner and conducted a general merchandise business in the larger stone house next to it.

The little corner residence was about a gate's width away from the larger building which housed the store on the east end and living quarters on the west end. At first the sign above the store read simply, "E. Wahrmund" and later the sign, according to another photograph, read "E. Wahrmund, Dry Goods and Groceries."

The earliest photo shows part of the front porch of the store covered with things they had for sale, such as farm tools. Next to it were bales of cotton lined up on the sidewalk. The photo taken a few years later showed they had "cleaned up" the area in front, taken the cotton bales away, placed a porch railing around the residential part of the store building, and planted oleanders and other plants in nail kegs and wooden tubs which added to the decor of the sidewalk. The building fronts came to the property line at the sidewalk.

Mrs. Wahrmund had her large garden at the side of the store building. In the days before banks, she kept their money in a churn, buried it in the garden. Some of the money she secreted below the bed of lettuce. They also had a large vineyard at the present-day site of Standard Service Company.

Their stable was in the large rock building to the rear of Sears where Gerald Schmidt's law office and Kilman Studio are now located.

The first Emil Wahrmund was born June 3, 1828, in Wiesbaden and came to Texas with his parents on the "Talisman" in 1846.

He married Auguste Sander in 1847, and they had seven children: C. E. Wahrmund, who was generally known as Emil (the second one); Adolph; August; Emma, Mrs. A.L. Patton; Mathilde, Mrs. H.B. Meckel; Lina, Mrs. Alfred Basse; and Louise, Mrs. William Basse.

Emil Wahrmund I died March 4, 1901, and his widow on February 10, 1910. In her will she bequeathed the townlot on which the buildings were located to the son, C.E. (Emil II) Wahrmund "in appreciation of his services and faithful care of his father during his long illness."

Christian Emil (the second Emil) Wahrmund married Auguste Feller and their children were Herman Arthur; Henry Emil (the third Emil); and Theresa, who married A.F. Moursund. The father deeded the corner lot to Herman Arthur Wahrmund July 1, 1913, but he died during the flu epidemic of 1918, leaving his mother, brother and sister as heirs. The latter two deeded their interest to the mother.

The C.E. Wahrmund family lived uptown on West Main Street in a long low building that stood where part of Crenwelge Motor Sales car lot is now located. They had a combination store and residence there, and when they gave up their business downtown, other businesses were conducted in the present-day Publishing Company building, including general stores run by Emil Gold, August Gold, Adolph Gold, and at one time J.O. Ernst had a piano store there.

At one time there was a saloon in that area now occupied by Hill Country Community Press, and underneath the Standard's building was a huge cellar used for storing the beer for the saloon. When the company leased the building from Mrs. Auguste Wahrmund (C.E.'s widow) this cellar was filled with rock and sand, and extensive remodeling was undertaken to ready the premises for the company by May 1, 1923.

Auguste Wahrmund died March 15, 1944, leaving the Standard's present-day property to Mrs. Therese (Mrs. A.F.) Moursund. Mrs. Moursund died April 1, 1950, and her husband September 12, 1953. Their two children inherited the property -- Lorene, who never married and lived in Austin, and Andrew, who lived in Eugene, Oregon. Their uncle, the late H.E. Wahrmund (the third Emil whose wife was Auguste Reeh), looked after their business interests as he owned the adjoining property at the corner and that behind it.

The Fredericksburg Publishing Company bought the building which they had been leasing since 1923 and the adjoining Saenger and Ochs building from them on July 8, 1963. Both are now deceased.

That summer remodeling was begun with an open house held in the completed facilities on Saturday, March 14, 1964.

Here every Wednesday the Standard is published, there is a commercial job printing plant in back, and an office supply store and newspaper offices in front. The newspaper press, owned jointly by Hill Country publishers, is located in the building next door.

On April 29, 1974, the Publishing Company also bought the building that now houses the automobile showroom of Standard Service Company which the Moursund heirs owned, and plans are to use it for future expansion.

Though the facade is new, there's a lot that's old here in this building on Main Street -- and as history is preserved in the old newspaper pages, so is history made anew each week as events are chronicled that took place here during the preceding seven days -- current events that become historical events for the generations to come. Some day there may even be an "old" look again for the facade of a building that is older than it looks.

H. BIERSCHWALE HOME

The small leather-bound ledger H. Bierschwale kept on the expenses of building his limestone rock house in 1872 is still intact and belongs to his great-grandson, Elmer Bierschwale, who now owns the house. The home is located at 209 West Austin Street, only half a block away from the Market Square.

Before ownership of Townlot 100 on which it is built passed to H. Bierschwale, this lot and the adjoining two lots belonged to three immigrants named Lehmann. No. 100 was granted by the German Emigration Company to Samuel Lehmann; No. 99 to Lehmann (no first name given); and No. 98 to Carl (Charles) Gottlieb Lehmann.

The Lehmanns died and Ernestine Lehmann, the widow of Carl (Charles) Gottlieb Lehmann, married Frederick Brandenberger. P. Buchmeier was agent-in-fact for Daniel Lehmann, and administrator of the estate of Moritz Lehmann, deceased. In the deeds made by them and as heirs of Samuel Lehmann to August Hennersdorf, H. Bierschwale and Conrad Ahrens Sr. in 1868 and 1869, the wrong lot numbers were listed in some of the deeds, so those three owners entered into an agreement October 12, 1872, in which H. Bierschwale rightfully got title to Townlot No. 100 on which he had by then built his house.

While he generally wrote his name "H. Bierschwale," he was also known as Henry or Heinrich. He was born September 7, 1828, in Gadenstadt, in the Kingdom of Hannover, Germany. His obituary in the Wochenblatt states that as a youth of 17 he came to America in 1845, landing at Indianola in 1846 and coming from there to Fredericksburg. When he could not find suitable employment here, he went to San Antonio "seine Schulkenntnisse zu ergaenzen" (to replenish or complete his scholastic or classroom knowledge). He returned to Fredericksburg and taught school at first in what was referred

Mr. and Mrs. Elmer Bierschwale, Owners

to in the obituary as "the Llano area."

He married Margarete Treibs January 13, 1853.

He was one of the first teachers in rural schools of Gillespie and Mason Counties, and was named Justice of the Peace of Precinct No. 1 when the county was first divided into four precincts October 18, 1852. This precinct included "residents of Castell, Leiningen and surrounding areas" as those parts of Mason and Llano counties were then a part of Gillespie. Among the schools he taught in were Squaw Creek, Hilda and Beaver Creek.

He was teaching at the latter school during the August 1865 murder of Heinrich and Johanna Kensing by Indians ·in that area. He and his wife took into their home one of their orphaned children and also two children named Korn who were also orphaned by Indians.

In the next few years, he must have made the decision to move to town, buying a townlot in 1869. He made plans to build a substantial home on it. While they were building the house, they lived in a little log house on Main Street where part of Crenwelge Motor Sales' car lot is now. When the new house was

finished they moved into it.

The first entry in the ledger was made May 3, 1872, and was for $120 paid "Kneese in advance for rock, etc." Other May entries were on the 15th for slaking lime, $5; the 25th "paid Kneese for Wm. Fritze, $100."

June entries (no date given) included digging foundation, $4.50; hauling sand, $2.25; and then on June 3 came the first entry for "one gal. of whisky, $2." Throughout the ledger for the duration of building were similar entries for one gallon of whiskey. This may seem strange, but in those days that was often part of the compensation for services performed.

Even the historical marker on the David Crockett Riley home in the Crabapple community reads: "Workmen were paid 50 cents and a pint of Crockett Riley's whiskey (home distilled) for a day's work."

Some of the entries included the following: June 23, Hennersdorf, for hauling sand, etc., $7; July 11, H. Walter for hauling timber from saw mill, 76 cents; July 22, 1224 feet of lumber, $48.96 and freight on the same day, $36.72; August 20, Peter Schuch for plate irons, $5.25; screws for plates, 60 cents; August 30, Basse for timber, $24.40; September 1, Walter for hauling shingles $4.50; one door lock, $3; paid C. Itz for hauling 5 packs of shingles, $7; F. Kneese for 570 feet of lumber, $40.

Also, September 4, Krauskopf for roofing etc., $40.30; September 9, white lead, oil, nails, etc. $6.50; September 14, Langehennig for logs, $12; F. Stucken for lumber, $31.75; September 19, Wm. Wahrmund, shingles, $40; September 26, E. Wahrmund for 1 pack of shingles, $7.50; October 12, Wm. Wahrmund, white lead, oil, glass, locks, nails, $12.75; December 5, Krauskopf for glass, etc., $16; February 8, 1873, Hotopp for one pack shingles, $7.

On March 13, 1873, is the final entry: "paid J. Schneider balance for carpenter work, $7.75." Jacob Schneider and H. Cordes must have done most of the carpenter work, and Geo. Peter most of the masonry work and whitewashing as there are frequent payments to them. On October 20, 1872, there is the entry, "Geo. Peter, balance for masonry work and whitewashing, $75.00."

At one place he showed total expenditures by October 29, 1872, of $1122.13, and a few entries followed between November 1872 and the final one on March 13, 1873.

On the next page he made this notation: "Compilated up to October 29, 1872," with these totals: hauling and quarrying rock, $231.20; digging foundation, slaking lime, haul sand, etc., $41.50; masonry work, including whitewashing etc. $310; pine lumber, $125.68; postoak lumber, $56.15; shingles, $72; Cordes for work, $60; whisky, $26; nails, glass, locks, paint, etc., $50.35; roofing, etc., $40.30; paid carpenter work, $100.

This made for a total of $1113.18 (or $1122.13) that he spent building this house. Wonder what it would cost in 1976?

What kind of house did Bierschwale get for this money?

The original structure had one large room in front where the parents slept and back of that was their kitchen. Upstairs there were two bedrooms. The stairway to the second floor leads out of the kitchen. The kitchen originally had a cooking fireplace with a knee-high hearth. In later years this was closed, and the two sisters, Emma and Elise Bierschwale, who lived here after their parents' deaths, used it as a "cooler" for potatoes, eggs and other staples.

The two bedrooms on the second floor or "half story" are amply ventilated with two large and one small window in each of the side walls. In the roof of the back room is a large square opening that they would push aside at night to let the cool air in. In the south or back wall are also two openings in the rock wall that could be "unplugged" to provide still more circulation.

The H. Bierschwales had nine children, of whom two, Henry and Mary, died around the age of one year. Those who grew to maturity were Bertha, Mrs. Edward Houy; William, Louis, Emma and Elise, who lived in Gillespie County, and Harry and Charles, who lived in Mason County. He served as County and District Clerk from 1870 until 1898 when he was succeeded by his son, William.

H. Bierschwale died March 9, 1912, and his wife died May 9, 1918.

The brothers and sisters deeded this house to Elise Bierschwale on February 2, 1916, and she and her sister, Emma, continued to make their home here. Elise died May 15, 1951, and she left the house to her sister, Emma, who lived here until her death June 19, 1960. Her nephew, Walter Bierschwale inherited it from her. He was a son of one of her brothers, William Bierschwale. Mr. and Mrs. Walter Bierschwale deeded the house to their son, Elmer, and his wife, Harriet, March 30, 1972.

Although no Bierschwales are living in the old house now, and it is occupied by renters, the present owners are very appreciative of the old home built by his great-grandfather. It is rare that an owner has the record of what it cost to build a house 104 years ago, but that somehow makes this old home just a bit more "special" than others.

Kathryn Nell Harrison, Owner

KANTER-KLECK HOME

One of Fredericksburg's over-100-year-old homes awaiting restoration is the Kanter-Kleck home at 216 East Austin Street. Since the death of its previous owner, Manuela (better known as Lella) Kleck, it has been unoccupied and now belongs to Kathryn Nell Harrison, who bought it from Miss Kleck's heirs.

The old home holds memories for many women, who as young girls, took sewing lessons there from Miss Lella. In those days there were no home economics classes in school and patterns were not as readily accessible or of as great variety as now. When girls were old enough, or showed an inclination to learn, their mothers made arrangements with Miss Lella to teach them how to adapt patterns, cut and sew their garments.

They often brought their own treadle sewing machines from home, or if that was not practicable, Miss Lella had several in her home that the learners could use.

The house is built on some of Fredericksburg's unnumbered townlots. These were parcels of land, mostly along the two creeks, irregular in shape, that were not numbered by the surveyor when the original plat of Fredericksburg was made.

This parcel was part of Sur. No. 128, patented to John H. Herndon, assigneee of H.C. Thompson. Herndon never legally surrendered his claim to John O. Meusebach or the German Emigration Company, and in the middle 1800's many of the legal holders of townlots on it found themselves having to pay him token sums for quitclaim deeds. Herndon went bankrupt and the unassigned parcels in this 640-acre survey were bought by Christian Doebner at bankruptcy sale on July 6, 1869.

Doebner sold unnumbered lots containing approximately 30,000 square feet to Anton Maier August 10, 1869, who in turn sold the property to Henry Kanter June 12, 1871. Kanter was listed on the 1860 census as a cigar maker and on the 1870 census as a laborer. He built the original part of this house, the two rooms of fachwerk construction on the eastern side, shortly after he got title to the land. The front room was a bedroom and the back room the kitchen.

Kanter married Dorette (Dorothea) Zenker August 16, 1879. After his death, his wife and children moved to Tom Green County. His widow petitioned the probate court for permission to sell the Fredericksburg property, stating she needed the money to support and educate the children.

The house and lots were sold to Victoria Kleck, whose husband had built the White Elephant Saloon, on November 26, 1892, by Dorothea Kanter, administrator of her

143

husband's estate, for $225 cash. Victoria Kleck deeded it to her son, Sylvester, April 11, 1893, with the provision that he was not to sell it during his lifetime.

In that deed reference is made to the creek behind the house as being "Little Baron's Creek," however, it is now known as "Town Creek." Sylvester Kleck was appointed sheriff of Gillespie County May 24, 1869, by the military government and also served as tax collector. He held the office until his successor, Alfred Hunter, was elected in 1872. The Sylvester Klecks also at one time operated a cafe on the present day site of the Goodyear Store.

The Sylvester Klecks added the other rooms to the house. This addition consisted of a passageway (durchgang) between the old rooms on the east and the two new frame rooms on the west which were used as bedrooms. The front of the passageway at first was open, but the back was closed, having a door and window. The passageway was later closed in front, too, with a door and windows in the wall -- providing a hallway for the house.

The floor of the passageway was lower than the old rock rooms and the two new frame rooms. As the years went by, the fachwerk part of the older rooms was covered with boards in front, and the stairway that led along the east wall to the small door in the attic was removed.

After the death of their parents, Manuela and her brother, Fred Kleck, a bachelor, continued to live here, with the other heirs deeding their interest to them September 26, 1922. After Fred's death, Manuela Kleck got sole title to it by deed from his heirs dated May 6, 1939.

Manuela died January 4, 1966 and her heirs sold this house to Kathryn Nell Harrison by separate deeds dated May 8, 1969, and July 17, 1969. She is the daughter of Oliver and Nell Betty Harrison of Corpus Christi who own the Walch home two blocks east of this house, also on the banks of Town Creek.

Changes have taken place in the immediate vicinity of the Kleck home. The creek has eroded the once gentle slopes so they are now steep high banks. The extension of North Lincoln Street is overgrown with weeds and unused. There was never a bridge over the creek for vehicular traffic, although at one time there was a foot bridge across the creek at this point.

Some day other changes will take place here, too, when the house is restored. Perhaps one day still other changes will be made, too, on the property adjoining it on the east where abandoned and junked autos line the once beautiful creek bed.

WEIDENFELLER HOME

One of the city's oldest homes, the Loth-Weidenfeller home at the corner of West San Antonio and South Bowie Streets -- has been unoccupied for many years, awaiting restoration by an appreciative owner. It is destined for a new life now that it belongs to Timothy Koock who has owned it since October 17, 1975.

Not only does he plan to restore the house that is still standing, but he wants to restore the addition in back that was torn down many years ago.

Tim is a native of Austin and a brother to William (Guich) Koock who restored several buildings in the complex near his restaurant, "Oma Koock's." Tim and his wife are now living in Fredericksburg and hope to make their home in the old house once it is restored.

The house is built on the north corner of Townlot 378. This lot was granted to "Voges," according to the original list of allotments. Apparently he never laid claim to it or died, because the German Emigration Company deeded it to Peter Staudt, assignee of "Christoph Voges, an emigrant," December 2, 1852. Staudt may have owned it earlier, because county records burned in 1850, and replacement deeds were often made for some of the records which were destroyed.

On that same date, Staudt as assignee of C.L. Ervendburg, also got a deed from the company to Townlot 403 which adjoins No. 378 at the south corner of the block at South Bowie and East Creek Streets. The two lots were to stay in the same family for the rest of the century.

Peter Staudt, who came here from Germany, married Catharina Weber. They had three children: Peter A. Staudt; Catharina, who married Anton Kunz Sr.; and Elise, who married Caspar Fritz. Peter Staudt died in 1852, according to a proof of heirship recorded in the county clerk's office. His wife married Anton Loth May 24, 1853. Loth had come here from Germany, but his first wife died on board ship on the way over. He had one son, John Loth.

Anton and Catharina Loth had three children after their marriage. They were Anton Loth Jr.; Maria, who married Christian Leyendecker; and Gertrude, who married Peter Maurer. Anton Loth Sr. died June 30, 1869, and his wife, Catharina, died February 12, 1899.

After her death the children partitioned the two townlots by deed dated August 21, 1899. Different ones got small parcels, with Peter A. Staudt finally owning the 100 by 127 feet on the corner which he deeded to John Lott March 20, 1900.

This was the same John Loth who was a son of Anton Loth Sr., however, he changed the spelling of his name, according to one of his daughters, Mrs. Otto Meurer, who was interviewed for the Standard's 1954 series of old homes.

The John Lotts lived on a ranch in the White Oak community, so during the eight years they owned this old home, they used it as a "Sunday house" staying there when they came to town for the weekend to shop and attend church or when someone was sick. Mrs. Meurer recalled, too, that her mother often stayed here with the children when they attended school at St. Mary's.

Mrs. Meurer could not say for sure who built the house, or when the oldest part of it was built, but she said this was the only place the Anton Loth family lived, so the oldest part of the house was probably built by Staudt, and after his widow and Anton Loth married and their family increased, they added the rest of the house.

John Lott sold the house to John Weidenfellerr October 29, 1908, and it was to remain in the Weidenfeller family until 1974.

The John Weidenfeller family also lived in this house. They had five sons and two daughters, of whom one of the girls died in childhood. Around the mid-1920's, the Weidenfellers built a new home immediately east of the old house, and after that the back part of the house was torn down.

The part that was left standing has one large front room, probably the oldest part of the house. Its walls are constructed of heavy, square cut logs, meticulously dove-tailed, and all numbered with Roman numerals. They were probably fitted together where the logs were felled and hewn and then numbered so when they were put in place where the house was to stand there would be a minimum of trimming and fitting. The inside walls were plastered and whitewashed.

There is only a door in the front wall and a small window in the west and east wall of the front room. The low front porch has a flagstone floor.

The exterior side walls of the front room are covered with weather-beaten shingles, put there many years ago to waterproof the walls. The back room, or lean-to, was added later and is of solid rock construction.

The window in the west wall of the front room may at one time have been a fireplace because the construction below the window still is of solid rock.

Behind the back room of the house was a "durchgang" which connected the house with the kitchen in the back. The west wall of the connecting room was of rock construction and the other side of lumber. The kitchen walls were built with logs and mortar, and it had a big cooking fireplace in the south (back) wall. The roof sloped in the opposite direction of that of the main house, with the ridge running from north to south, whereas the house roof line runs from east to west.

Ownership passed to three of the John Weidenfeller children, Frank and Anton Weidenfeller and Emma Sahm. Frank died August 6, 1967, and the other two deeded the house and a parcel of land 34 by 127 feet to Kenneth Knopp December 21, 1974. He had plans for restoring it, but sold it to Tim Koock about a year later.

Now an interesting future faces this old house of the past.

Mr. and Mrs. Lee Ethel, Owners

CARL HENKE HOME

Several things that are distinctive add special interest to the Carl Henke home at the corner of North Llano and East Travis Streets which now belongs to Mr. and Mrs. Lee Ethel of Dallas.

First of all, it was built by and for a long time was owned by Carl Henke who was the first boy born in Fredericksburg. (The first child born was a girl.) His birth date was April 8, 1848, exactly one month before Fredericksburg was two years old.

It was the first rock house built on the north side of Town Creek.

Some of the timbers used in it were milled by the Mormons at Zodiac on the banks of the Pedernales River in the Rocky Hill Community.

Travis Street was the northern boundary of the Townlots, one of which was allotted to each emigrant in the new colony. All blocks north and northeast of Travis Street were among the Ten-Acre Outlots which were allotted, one to each emigrant, as his "farm."

The house is built on the corner of Outlot 281 which was originally allotted to Christian Klein II, who also received as his share Townlot 527, one of those across the street from this Outlot.

Klein never received title to his lots and there is no record of whether he sold his interest or whether he died, because the deed from the German Emigration Company to Outlot 281 and Townlot 527 was made to Johan George Weber as assignee of Chr. Klein. The date was December 2, 1852, at which time he also received title to Townlots 525, 526 and 528. County records were destroyed by fire in 1850.

Johan George Weber and wife, Katharina, sold Outlot 281 and the four Townlots to Johan Kleck October 24, 1853, for $275, of which $100 was cash and $50 was due December 27, 1853, with $125 due December 27, 1854.

Kleck sold the same four Townlots and Outlot 281 to John Schmitt on November 25, 1861.

Carl Henke, a stonemason, built the house for Schmitt, with the original structure having only two rooms, a loft and outside stairway, in 1874. These are the two rooms along the North Llano Street side with the small porch in front of them. It was typical of the first solid limestone rock homes built here. It had 2x8-inch ceiling beams and 2x8-inch rafters milled at the Mormon sawmill. The roof was shingled with hand-hewn cypress shakes. The loft with its original pegged cypress window remains today as built over 100 years ago. The front two rooms are being restored exactly as they were when first built.

John Schmitt had appointed Carl Henke as his attorney-in-fact, so when the house was sold October 18, 1883, for $400 cash, the deed was made to Henke's wife, Mina Henke, nee Crenwelge, whom he had married July 1, 1882. It was to remain in the Henke family until March 1972.

The Carl Henkes added more living area to the back after they moved here. A "dur-chgang" separated the house from the rock kitchen. This was later enclosed to form the dining room and a porch along the east side was enclosed still later.

The Carl Henkes had four sons, twins who died in infancy, also, Max T. Henke, who later owned this place, and Adolph Henke, who now lives in California.

When Max and his bride, Cora Schaper, were married in 1911, two large rooms and bath were added along the west side of the house. The rooms were constructed of 6x6x24 solid concrete building blocks, and have beaded ceilings 11 feet high. The doors all have movable transoms above them for good ventilation in the rooms.

The entire building is now roofed with standing-seam tin, the earliest part dating back to 1895.

The original hand-dug and rock-lined well is still in use.

The rock wall of the old rock and log barn, built at the time of the house, is now incorporated into the present two-car garage.

Carl Henke built many houses that are still standing today. He laid the cornerstone for and helped build Holy Ghost Lutheran Church. Mr. Henke died January 8, 1928, and his widow on December 2, 1949.

Max T. Henke died May 23, 1967, and his widow sold the house to Ray Bellinger March 9, 1972. Bellinger, an antique dealer, lived here until his death, and from his estate title passed to the Ethels, a Dallas couple, November 11, 1974.

They spend a lot of time here, and are taking their time with restoring the house, doing much of it themselves, and hoping one of these days to make their permanent home here.

Dr. and Mrs. J. Hardin Perry, Owners

PETER PLETZ HOME—NOW PERRY GUEST HOUSE

His house was small and the July night was hot, so Peter Pletz decided he would sleep out under a tree. This was not unusual, for many in the olden days did that in the summertime. But for Peter Pletz this night in 1863 his outdoor sleep was to be fatal. He was shot to death by two of the Haengerbande or mob members who committed so many outrages among the Germans during the Civil War.

Peter Pletz built the little house that is now the guest house of Dr. and Mrs. J. Hardin Perry, and the tree under which he slept may have been one of those that surround it.

John Peter Pletz and his wife, Anna Maria, came from Breitscheid, Nassau, Germany, on the ship, Auguste Meline, sailing from Bremen. When he declared his intention to become an American citizen on November 11, 1849, at the age of 48 years, he stated that he arrived at the port of "Indian Port" on December 18, 1845, and an account of that ship's passenger list showed it arrived in Galveston December 31, 1845. He was naturalized and became a citizen November 1, 1852.

The ship list shows five children arriving with them, however, the two boys and a daughter must have died before 1850 as they are not on the census list for that year and when Pletz died, there were only two daughters as legal heirs, in addition to his wife. And, one of these daughters, Wilhelmine, is listed as "William," a male, on the 1850 census, one of the obvious errors the census taker of that year made.

As an original emigrant, the German Emigration Company gave him Townlot 269 in the original allotment, although his name is given as "J. Blatz" on the list, but this is an error, too as title turns up in the Pletz name. Since each emigrant also received an Outlot, or ten-acre lot, as his farm, Outlot 580 was granted to Pletz, although the official list shows the name again as "Blatz."

The Perry property includes Outlot 580 and Block IV, the latter one of 19 "Blocks" laid out on the original plat of Fredericksburg. These were irregular-shaped tracts of varying acreage, in between the Outlots surrounding the townlots. Block IV was one of the Blocks and Outlots totaling an acreage of 3,360 acres which M.A. Dooley, a Louisiana promoter who operated in Fredericksburg in the early years, bought from the German Emigration Company for $1,000 cash December 24, 1852. This must have been a legitimate sale for the witnesses to the deed were H. Willke, the surveyor, and John O. Meusebach, founder of Fredericksburg, although the deed was not acknowledged until June 1, 1853. Dooley deeded what remained of this property for $1700 to Oscar Basse September 20, 1871,

148

however Peter Pletz had the legal title to Block IV by this time. He bought it October 19, 1852, at a sheriff's sale.

The oldest part of the house that Peter Pletz built was the one-room log cabin and the kitchen with cooking fireplace of solid limestone rock. This was probably erected in the late 1840's or early 1850's. The limestone rock addition at the side of the cabin was added later.

Pletz lived here with his wife and two daughters, working as a laborer and later as a wagoner. He also had an orchard of fruit trees near his home here. Life in this new land was to come to an unhappy end, however, during the Civil War days. According to an account published in 1924 in "German Pioneers in Texas," this is what happened:

"Sam Doss and Sam Tanner were indicted in 1865 for the murder of Peter Pletz in 1863. This was a typical crime for a mob murder outfit. Pletz had a little home and some fruit trees near town. It was hot weather and Pletz was sleeping under a tree near the house. Doss and Tanner invaded the little orchard late at night. Pletz was aroused and got up to see what was going on and was murdered."

The indictment in the District Clerk's office shows that it happened on the night of July 23, 1863. It states the two men, maliciously and with intent to murder "held the six-shooter pistol loaded with powder and leaden bullets against him" and that he died instantly of the shots fired. No further details are revealed in the records, however, the grand jury indictment signed by Julius Ransleben lists as "witnesses" the names of Joseph Whitley, Sinclair Colbath, J.B. Lacey and Silas McDaniel. Doss and Tanner evidently made a complete get-away as no further action was taken and the case was finally dismissed against Samuel Doss, who had "left the county" and "witnesses' whereabouts are unknown." Sam Tanner had also been indicted for other murders along with J.P. Waldrip, the Bantas and others.

Though his life came to a tragic end, life went on for his widow and two daughters, who in the meantime had been married, Wilhelmine to Michael Pfiester, and Ernestine to John Dechert. On January 26, 1868, they divided the property owned by their mother and their deceased father.

The Pfiesters got one tract of 15 acres of Outlot 580 and another tract of 12 acres of Block IV located on "Barons Creek, near the town of Fredericksburg." This is now the Perry property. In turn, the Pfiesters and Decherts released their interest in Townlot 269 which became Mrs. Pletz's sole property, paying her an additional $50, $18 cash and the rest in one and two-year payments. The Townlot which adjoined this (at the east corner of West Main and South Acorn), the Pletz heirs sold to Carl Cammert, with the provision that Anna Maria Pletz was to get the "crop of wheat raised on it the present year."

The Pfiesters made their home on the Pletz acreage until their death, however, following Mr. Pfiester's death, his widow deeded part of it to their daughter, Bertha Pfiester, who later married Edward Kott. After Mrs. Pfiester's death, this daughter deeded her interest back to the other children, and then joined the other heirs of Michael and Wilhelmine Pfiester on August 18, 1924, in a partition of this property. They were William, Edward and Emil Pfiester; Bertha, the widow of Henry Pfiester (one of the brothers), and Caroline, Mrs. August C. Jordan.

Finally ownership of all the little tracts passed to Reuben E. Jordan, a son of the August Jordans, and a great-grandson of Peter and Anna Maria Pletz. He sold it to Dr. J. Hardin Perry and his wife, Victoria (Nooky), on August 18, 1948, exactly 24 years to the day after the Pfiester partition.

Within the next few years, the Perrys began restoration of the house into a guest house and later built the new two-story residence near it out of stones from the old St. Mary's Rectory.

The cooking fireplace in the Pletz kitchen had been poured shut with concrete, which the Perrys eventually got out with great difficulty. It has a knee-high hearth, but any cooking that is done in there now is on a small built-in efficiency unit which has stovetop, oven and sink cleverly concealed in an antiqued wood enclosure.

They added a small bay window in the kitchen where a door had been, providing better light and a good view. There was once a wood partition wall in the back which they removed and added a small bath at the other end.

Both front rooms are furnished as bedrooms, and among these furnishings are two "Kleiderschranke" (wardrobes) in the bedrooms and a kitchen safe, all hand-crafted by Gottfried Ottmers, an early-day cabinet maker.

There never was a stairway to the loft, with

early residents using a ladder to reach it. Now the heating and air-conditioning units are located here.

The lovely yard between the guest house and the Perry home would probably please early residents. Peter Pletz had fruit trees, but the Perrys have grapevines which bear good grapes. There are lots of flowers, too, and the Jordan boys who were sent by their mother, Caroline, to water "grandmother's potatoes" by carrying buckets of water from Barons Creek often had to give preference to watering her flowers instead of the potatoes.

Mrs. Rodolph Smith, Owner

KRIEGER-GEYER HOME

Rodolph and Roberta Smith lived on a ranch, but owned a little house at 512 West Creek Street in Fredericksburg that they often used as their early counterparts did -- a place to eat, spend the night or relax while in town. It was not built to be used as a Sunday house originally, but that's how it's often referred to by others.

It was built as a home for two of the first immigrants who came here with the colonists from Germany. The property that the Smiths owned is all of Townlot 405, originally granted to George Geyer, and 25 by 200 feet of Townlot 404, which was the lot Adam Krieger received from the German Emigration Company as his allotment.

There must have been some bond between them -- either kinship or friendship. Geyer, a single man, and Krieger and his wife, Eva, came to Texas on the same ship, the Hamilton, according to a ship list published in Pioneers in God's Hills. This shows their common point of origin to be Bingen, Germany. The two lots they were given by the German Emigration Company adjoined each other.

No record of Geyer turns up again, so presumably he died during the early epidemics that hit the colony and Krieger inherited Geyer's claim to the lot or the deed from Geyer to Krieger was lost or never recorded.

The house stands on the common boundary line of the lots, so they probably built it as a joint venture. When The Peach Tree Gift Shop released the third in their series of historic Fredericksburg plates fashioned of Armetale, it was of this house, known now as "The Krieger-Geyer house."

When the Smiths bought this property in 1968 and began work on restoring it, they made several interesting discoveries.

The oldest part is the front room at the west end and is of the fachwerk type of construction -- upright and crosswise timbers, with the space in between filled with rocks, twigs, grapevines, grass and mortar. The Smiths saved some of the grapevines which were used to "bind" the other material together. They are displayed in an old pitcher on a kitchen shelf.

In their restoration, they exposed the timbers and found them to be marked with Roman numerals. This was done by the builder after the trees were felled, de-barked and cut into the desired lengths needed for the house dimensions. To protect the rock filler, Smith used a "wash" he made using thin cement and other ingredients, and it has held beautifully.

This room has the original floor joists exposed. Since subsequent owners had covered the original wood floor with layers of linoleum and it had deteriorated badly, all the flooring was removed with the exception of the floor joists. The room probably had a dirt floor originally as it was packed hard and rocks surrounded the fireplace at floor level. The space between the joists was filled in with similar flat stones, and now makes an interesting appearance.

The rockwork around the fireplace was exposed after the plaster was chipped away to show the type of construction used between the timbers. The other masonry is covered with a wash similar to that used outside.

The original hardware is still on the casement windows, and even some of the old glass panes remain. The original front door was stripped of 12 coats of paint to reveal the mellowed wood. The furnishings, including an old schrank with unusual drawer locks, add interest to this room.

The room behind it and the two at the side are of solid rock and later construction. The front room was probably added in the second stage of construction. The same window flanks its front door -- identical to the ones on either side of the front door in the first room. This room is now used as a bedroom.

Reconstructed Log Cabin

A small room behind it was made into a bathroom by the Smiths. The only structural change they made was making an entry into the bath from the front bedroom and closing up the entry between the bath room and the kitchen.

The kitchen is on a lower level than the original front room and it still has the original random-width boards in the floor. The windows in this room, three of them, have the "six over six" panes, a feature not generally found in homes before the 1880's, leading the Smiths to believe the kitchen was added much later. Also, the methods used in cutting and shaping the rocks and the woodwork are much better than the cruder means evident in the front rooms.

An old Darling brand wood cookstove was electrified by Mr. Smith and makes a nice addition to the kitchen, along with a dry sink, an old ice box, a typical old-time kitchen table and chairs, and other small accessories.

Though known as the Krieger-Geyer house, the family that owned the house the longest was that of Carl (or Karl) Henke Sr. and his wife, Dorothea. Henke contracted to buy it from Krieger January 27, 1868, paying $200 cash and agreeing to pay $200 a year later and the final $300 two years later. He paid it off sooner and got a deed to it February 15, 1869.

Dorothea Henke died January 16, 1876, and two of the couple's children, Dorothea and Carl, died in infancy. Mr. Henke was joined by the couple's two surviving children, William, and Anna, who married Henry F. Jordan, when he sold the house to Maria Mosel, widow of J.N. Mosel, April 5, 1906. Mr. Mosel had died February 18, 1904, and this made a nice small home for the widow.

After Maria Mosel died September 10, 1911, one of her daughters, Lina Mosel, who was single, acquired it on January 23, 1912, from her sister and brothers, Emma, Mrs. Louis Dietz; August, Theodor, Arthur and Louis Mosel.

Miss Mosel sold 75 off the west side of Townlot 404 to Ernst Weinheimer April 21, 1913, but the rest of the property remained intact to the present day. She sold the house and the remaining property, 25 feet of Townlot 404 and all of Townlot 405, to Christian Staudt Sr. January 5, 1920. Staudt and his wife, Anna, sold it to Mrs. Rosa Fritz, wife of August Fritz, December 27, 1941, who in turn sold it to J.F. Johnson and wife on April 13, 1945. The Johnsons conveyed it to Eug. H. Kramer and his wife October 10, 1945, and the Kramers to John R. Crouch and wife, Helen Stieler Crouch, July 1, 1966. The Smiths bought it from the Crouches October 10, 1968.

Some of these owners lived in the house, some used it as a town or Sunday house, and others rented it out to tenants.

The Smiths put the outside stairway to the loft, as it made for easy access to the heating and air-conditioning units placed there.

Originally the house had a small narrow stairway that led to the loft from the first room built, now the living room, but this was removed by someone before the Smiths acquired it.

Behind the house is an old log cabin now that the Smiths erected there after it was given to them as a Christmas present from Col. and Mrs. Robert Mitchell. It stood on property the Mitchells now own in Comfort and was built by Edward Steves. Later it belonged to Herman Ingenhuett who married Mathilda Real.

It was used as a smoke house in later years, but now its fireplace has been reactivated, and it is often the center of interest when Mrs. Smith's mother, Mrs. Fritz Stieler, churns butter here or prepares other tasty goodies when tour groups come through.

In addition to finding this a useful and practical house in town, the Smiths were gracious in opening it to the many tour groups that came through here under the sponsorship of the Gillespie County Historical Society. Thousands have gotten a glimpse of yesteryear in this charming little house and the log cabin behind it.

Mr. Smith died November 29, 1976, but his wife, daughter and son-in-law, Laney and Dick Bristol, are carrying on the tradition of conservation and preservation he practiced.

MEINHARDT-PFEIL HOME

Many of the old homes in Fredericksburg that are comfortable homes for their owners in 1976 were once used for widely different purposes. A blacksmith shop that is now a home? Yes, that's the case with the Hagel home at 125 West San Antonio Street.

Here at one time G.A. (Adolph) Pfeil had his blacksmith shop, but its history goes back even farther. It is built on Townlot 354 which was granted by the German Emigration Company to "Pape" as shown by the original list. Later references to his name indicate he was H. (Henry) Pape, and the deed by the company was made to Albert Meinhardt as his assignee. The date of the deed is December 21, 1849, so Pape probably died during one of the epidemics that hit the new colony. His widow, Doris, (whose name is given as Dorothy in some references) married Meinhardt. She

had two children, Henry and Doris (also referred to as Dorothy) Pape.

On the same date Meinhardt also obtained from the company other lots, including the Townlot and Outlot assigned to him individually and to others as assignee of deceased persons.

The Meinhardts built the oldest part of the house, although the year is not known. The daughter, Doris, first married August Julius Arlt December 12, 1866, and later married G.A. Pfeil on February 15, 1874. They were divorced and Doris Meinhardt, by then a widow, and her daughter, Doris Pfeil, made a deed to the corner 50 by 200 feet of Townlot to Adolph Pfeil on March 7, 1879. Pfeil married Bertha Ruegner, the daughter of a stonemason who lived at the east end of this block, on October 9, 1879, and they had six

Mrs. Benedict Hagel Sr. Estate, Owner

sons.

Pfeil, who is best remembered for his cotton gins, early in his life operated a blacksmith shop at this place. The Hagel living room and kitchen originally was one large room which they partitioned after they bought the house. This is where Mr. Pfeil had his blacksmith shop and the entrance to the room is very large, since at one time it was the entrance to the shop. Now there are two large panels, the tops of which have glass panes, flanking each side of the wide door. In the stone arch above the door is a large glass transom.

Next to this room is a narrow room with a window facing the street and another in the back wall. The Pfeils used it as a hall and "treppen zimmer," as the stairway led up out of this room to the upper story. The Hagels partitioned the back half and made a bathroom out of it. They left the steps as they were, with a door on the enclosed stairwell. The door has an interesting iron latch which still works well.

The large room at the east side of the house was the Pfeils' bedroom, and the Hagels used it for the same purpose. It has a conventional-sized door.

The second floor is also interesting. It is divided into two rooms. The steps come up into the room on the east side. The windows in this room are so much larger than those in many of the "half-story" houses. There are two large ones in the east wall, and one smaller casement window in each the north

and south wall. In the room at the west end, there are only two large windows in the west wall. The light and air these windows admit make the rooms comfortable for sleeping.

Behind the original part of the house are two smaller rooms, added by the Pfeils, the first of which used to be open at the east and was used as a woodshed and washhouse, and the other a smoke house. The Hagels closed up the wall, but left the floor built of large stones intact.

The history of the house does not end with its early use as a combination blacksmith shop and home, because Pfeil also operated a soda water factory here for a while.

Later he moved with his family out to the Palo Alto community where he operated a gin near the site of the Kramer gin. It was here that he lost his arm in a gin accident.

They moved back to town and for a while he operated a light plant at the present site of the Schoolside Lunch Counter near the Public School campus.

He also had the Pfeil gin in the area where the Allen Keller residence now is located. This area had been set aside by the German Emigration Company as "Orphan Children's Land" and is so known on the public records.

G.A. Pfeil died January 26, 1926, and his widow, Bertha, who inherited this house, then their homestead, deeded it to one of her sons, H.P. (Henry) Pfeil September 19, 1935. She died October 4, 1939, and after her death, the house was sold to Reuben E. Jordan on

153

November 27, 1939.

In a trade of property, Jordan deeded this house to Lorence Feller June 1, 1945, who in turn deeded it to Benedict Hagel Sr. June 16, 1945. Hagels, who had owned the Central Hotel building which is now part of Fredericksburg Clinic, wanted this house as a residence.

Mr. Hagel did not get to enjoy ownership of it and living there very long, however, as he died September 25, 1946. But, for his widow it was a comfortable home and a convenient place for her children and grandchildren to visit -- in the center of town and just one block off Main Street.

The Hagels' children numbered eight and included the following: Appalonia, Mrs. Bruno Fritz; Ben C. Hagel Jr.; Edward Hagel; Agatha, Mrs. Frank Jenschke, who is deceased; Johanna, Mrs. Carl Jenschke of San Antonio; twin daughters, Marie, Mrs. Emil Sauer of Doss, and Cecelia, Mrs. Bill Cartwright of San Antonio; and Josephine, Mrs. Warren Crane, San Antonio.

The pretty flowers and potted plants that enhanced the porch and tiny front yard are gone now, just as is Mrs. Hagel who tended them so lovingly. She died February 11, 1977, but the Hagel corner across from the Courthouse Square with its old home is still one of the city's special attractions.

Mrs. Dolly Nabinger, Owner

WUNDERLICH-FRITZ HOME

In a block that has several interesting and historic old buildings, the home of Mrs. Dollie Nabinger located at the corner of South Crockett and West Creek Streets has a story that is as fascinating as any. After Mrs. Nabinger and her late husband, John Earl Nabinger, bought the house in 1962, they made a few changes inside that added comfort and convenience, but also preserved as much of its charm as possible.

Adding beauty, too, inside are Mrs. Nabinger's oil paintings, several of which hang in her home, while others are awaiting delivery to art patrons who eagerly seek her work. She works in her studio at the northeast corner of the house -- where large windows were added to admit the north light artists need for their work.

Built on the corner of Townlot 427 which was originally granted to Johan Peter Wunderlich and deeded to him by the German Emigration Company on December 2, 1852, it stayed in his family until almost the end of the century. Wunderlich, a blacksmith and carpenter, was one of the men who helped build the Vereins Kirche.

He built the oldest part of the house -- the one-story rock part at the north end. He and his wife and their three sons, lived here. A small log addition was in the back which later owners, the Fritzes, tore down after they added the two-story addition.

Wunderlich died in 1897, forty-eight hours after the death of his wife, Elisabeth, according to a proof of heirship of record, but it does not state the cause of death. One of their children died in infancy, and their three surviving sons, Henry, William and Adolph, inherited this property. They sold it to Casper Fritz October 16, 1899.

Fritz, a farmer, wanted to move to town because his wife was constantly plagued with poison oak while they lived on their farm. She improved considerably in town, however, washing her husband's clothes after he returned from visiting his sons on their farms, still gave her mild attacks.

The Fritzes added the two-story frame addition at the south end of the house. They built it two stories high, so there would be enough room in the back yard for the family cow and the horse. Mr. Fritz kept a horse so he could hitch it to his buggy and go out in the country to see his children, as he loved to go out to their farms.

The rock part of the house was originally one large room with a door at one end in the front and two casement windows adjoining it. The back wall had a door and a casement window, however, the window was taken out by the Nabingers to provide an open area between her studio and the living room.

At one time the large front room had a partition wall added by later owners, but the Nabingers removed this, providing a large living room. The fireplace at the north end of the room had been closed up, but the Nabingers removed it and with just a little extra repair work, it now works great to provide warmth and cheer to the room. Lining the wall around the fireplace are bookshelves made out of wood used in the partition wall they tore out.

Behind this room was a porch which had been enclosed by previous owners into a kitchen. Mrs. Nabinger uses it for the same purpose, but converted the north end into her studio.

The two-story addition the Fritzes added had a hall with door opening under the porch.

There was one large room downstairs in the front which the Fritzes used as their "gutes zimmer" (parlor), however Mrs. Weinheimer, from whose heirs the Nabingers bought it, used it as a bedroom. This room is now Mrs. Nabinger's bedroom, too, and behind it part of the hall was converted into closet space by the Nabingers.

The upper story is one large room, and has three large windows in each the front and back walls and two in the south wall. Here was where Mrs. Fritz liked to sleep -- a change in the habit of having the boys sleep upstairs.

Mr. Nabinger, while he was living, used this room upstairs as his workshop and hobby room. There is a loft above the oldest part of the house, but it is not used.

Part of the rock wall that once enclosed the entire yard -- just like that at the Kerrville Road corner of the block around part of The Peach Tree's property -- is still there. At one time this extended across the front of the house and along the side and back where it was eight feet high. Wunderlich, the original owner, built it this high in back to keep his oxen safe from being stolen by the Indians.

Mr. Fritz died April 14, 1911, and his wife, Elise, on March 22, 1932. Their children were John Fritz; Lina, Mrs. Frank Schmidtzinsky; Jacob Fritz; August Fritz; Carl Fritz; Anna, Mrs. Henry Weinheimer; Bertha, Mrs. Joe Besier; Edward Fritz; and Elise, Mrs. Max Keller.

The executors of Mrs. Fritz's estate deeded the house and lot to Mrs. Weinheimer October 1, 1932. She and Mr. Weinheimer made their home here until his death December 17, 1937, and after that she continued to reside here until she died April 11, 1961.

Their children, Eugene, Hilmar, Albert and Edmund Weinheimer, and Laura, Mrs. Gustav Jenschke, sold it to the Nabingers March 30, 1962. The Nabingers bought it, thinking they would do a little "fixing up" on it and then use it as a weekend or summer home when she would come to the Hill Country to paint. For years, while they lived in Harlingen and Nacogdoches, she had come to the Hill Country to paint landscapes in oil.

Mr. Nabinger, who had not been in the best of health, found himself feeling so much better every time they came to stay at their house in Fredericksburg, that they finally sold their home in East Texas and moved here, making the improvements as his health permitted.

The little barn in the back was renovated,

adding cedar shakes for the roof and a carport at the side. The terraced yard and garden in back utilize the old rock horse trough as a planter, and the smaller rock chicken watering trough as a "watering hole" for Mrs. Nabinger's cats.

After the Nabingers moved here, their daughter, Virginia, and her husband, the Belton Mullers, became so enchanted with Fredericksburg, that they finally bought an old house here which they renovated and now is their home and gallery. Like her mother, Mrs. Muller, is also an artist. Another daughter, Jean Fairchild, lives in Dallas.

Mr. Nabinger died January 5, 1972, but this is still "home" to Mrs. Nabinger.

Now from this old home, Mrs. Nabinger is a purveyor of the beauty of the Hill Country as she paints in oil the beautiful landscapes that have gained her a statewide reputation. For years she was under contract to one of Houston's leading galleries. Now that the owner is dead, the children and friends of patrons who bought her works still seek her out here in Fredericksburg, and almost as fast as she finishes her pictures they are spoken for.

Dr. and Mrs. W. Oliver Harrison, Owners

WALCH HOME

The 400 block lying between East Austin and East Schubert Streets has undergone many changes in the years since Fredericksburg was founded. Here at one time Johan (John) Joseph Walch had his farm while he and his family lived in the southwest corner of the block. Until about twenty-five years ago, it was an area almost completely devoid of trees.

The corner lot where he lived in the houses he built now belong to Oliver and Nell Betty Harrison of Corpus Christi. Dr. Harrison has been the minister of a large Christian Church

in that Gulf Coast city for almost 35 years, and his wife, the former Nell Betty Anderson of Pecos, is a college classmate and close friend of Mrs. J. Hardin Perry.

To them the old Walch place is now a pleasant Hill Country retreat, but following his retirement, the Harrisons plan to spend more time here.

Where once this part of the block was entirely treeless, now you can hardly see the houses for the trees on the Harrison property. Most of them were planted by Mary Louise Denman, who owned it between 1950 and until

First Walch Home

June 30, 1967, when she sold it to the Harrisons. Mrs. Denman bought the property from Lois Cunningham Irby and her husband, Arthur Irby, of Beaumont on March 23, 1950. The Irbys had bought it from the Walch heirs July 18, 1947.

In the years following the death of her husband, Mrs. Denman took consolation in immersing herself into the work of remodeling the Walch houses and in landscaping not only the yard surrounding them, but in planting trees and shrubs in the creek and across the street from her house as well.

When the Walch heirs sold this property in 1947, it was a little more than 100 years after their grandfather, John J. Walch had come to Fredericksburg and received this corner lot from the German Emigration Company as his Townlot allotment.

Thanks to the old time way of writing up anniversaries and obituaries of prominent persons in the journalistic style of years ago, from those appearing following the Walchs' golden wedding anniversary and his death, much was learned about the original builder of these houses. The slight variance in dates shown there and the ship lists of immigrants may be typographical errors.

Walch was born February 24, 1828, in Marxheim, Germany. With his father, Peter Walch, and a younger sister he sailed from Antwerp to Texas aboard the "dreimaster" (three-masted) ship, the "Washington," leaving September 9, (or 29) 1845. On November 25, 1845, they arrived in Galveston,

but were stranded there for over a week on a sandbar, and then were loaded onto a "schooner" that was supposed to take them to "Indian Point," their destination in Texas, within 12 hours. They were caught in unfavorable winds, however, so the trip took six days.

Finally, after 70 days of sea travel, they were on land, but had only brush arbors or huts for shelter as they waited for transportation to take them to the colony. Later they got tents to live in, and finally on July 14, 1846, left for New Braunfels -- a trip that took them four weeks.

On May 17, 1847, Walch, his younger sister and father arrived in Fredericksburg. Each of the men were given a Townlot on Austin Street. One, No. 477, was listed simply as being granted to "Walch" while the other one on which the houses are built, No. 476, was given to Johan (John) Joseph Walch, although illegible handwriting showed it as "Kloch."

They first built a "blockhaus" (log hut). This stood on the lot that is now vacant and adjoins the Harrison property. Then both men went to work for John O. Meusebach, the founder of Fredericksburg, at his place at Comanche Spring. The newspaper story says it was because of a scarcity of food here that they sought work elsewhere, doing stonemasonry work on Meusebach's house. J.J. Walch later worked as a "Knecht" or farmhand for Meusebach.

Still later he went to Austin with some "comrades" and worked for a while in a brick factory for $12 a month and his board. Soon he returned to Fredericksburg and worked as a stonemason.

John J. Walch married Wilhelmine Gaertner June 28, 1851, with the Lutheran minister, Rev. B. Dangers, officiating. They were married in the house that is now the Harrisons' guest house and it was here, too, they celebrated their golden wedding anniversary in 1901. This limestone rock house had two rooms, one of which had a fireplace at the northwest end and was used as a kitchen.

Next to it was their smokehouse and in front of it their "wash house". The latter did not refer so much to its being a laundry room as being one in which they "washed up" themselves bodily.

The John Walches had 11 children, of whom eight were still living at the time the last of the two old people died. Mrs. Walch died April 17, 1911, and he July 20, 1914. The surviving children were Ida Doerfuss of Chicago; Minna (Wilhelmine) Weber, San Antonio; Anna Ludwig, Devine; Ernestine Mergenthaler of Shiner; Rosa Rosenthal of Comfort; Christine Staats, Fredericksburg; and two sons, Felix and Eugene, both also of Fredericksburg.

One thing that was recalled about the elder Walch for the 1955 series on old homes, was a characteristic he had that might be likened to a modern lifestyle, however, for a different reason. He wore a gold earring in one ear to protect the sight in his one "good" eye. He had lost the sight of his other eye when a stone chip flew into it while working as a stonemason. In those days it was considered good luck to wear "Gold ins ohr" (gold in the ear) and he wore his earring until shortly before his death when he asked his son, Felix, to remove it and gave it to his granddaughter, Geraldine Weatherford.

When their son, Felix Walch, planned to get married, they deeded to him on May 24, 1904, the Northwest one-half of Townlot 476 and the Unnumbered lot adjoining it. He inherited the other half and adjoining property from his parents. This Northwest half had on it the original part of the two-story structure. It was first built as a barn, with lean-to, and in the latter part of the 1800's the second story was added. He remodeled it into a home.

He married Ida Jung November 22, 1904, and she died July 4, 1905. On February 8, 1910, he married Helene Schandua, who survived him, dying March 1, 1935. Mr. Walch died November 16, 1933. Their three children were Geraldine, Mrs. J. H. Weatherford, Margaret Walch and Francis Walch.

Originally their house had a living and a dining room downstairs, with the stairway leading up under the porch to the two bedrooms upstairs. They had their kitchen to the east of the stairway -- forming an L-shape. After the death of their parents, the Weatherfords made some changes in the house, such as putting the stairway inside, adding a bathroom upstairs and other alterations.

When Mrs. Denman did the house over, she made additional structural changes and added the frame addition in back which served as her kitchen, and maid's room and bath. The Harrisons changed the kitchen arrangement, making an extra doorway to the carport, adding a small breakfast room with glass wall and converted the maid's room into a small bedroom and bath.

The two rooms downstairs had the partition removed by Mrs. Denman, who used the homemade bricks to construct a fireplace in the corner of the combination living-dining room. At the far end of the dining room are shelves which the present owners used to display copper and pewter plates and objects and other bric-a-brac.

The Harrisons also rebuilt the stairway, taking out the wrought iron railing and adding a more traditional one of wood.

The two large bedrooms upstairs are ideal for when their children and grandchildren come to visit or when they have more house guests than the little guest house will accomodate.

Their children are Mike, who is married, has three children and lives in Pecos; Bill, an attorney in Corpus Christi; and Kathy, who lives in Denver, Colo.

The upstairs porch is screened with green shutters for privacy.

The old cistern with a "well-type" top, wheel and oaken bucket is under the front porch. A ripple-limestone terrace ties the big house in with the guest house. A swimming pool in the back yard provides summer recreation.

Surrounding the front and sides of the place is a high rock fence, made a few feet higher when Mrs. Denman owned it. Ivy covers its walls and bamboo cane at the east side provide more privacy. It is an ideal place for this couple from the city to come and relax and will be an even more ideal place to spend some of his retirement years, although they plan to maintain a home in Corpus Christi after he is no longer active as a minister in that city.

Mr. and Mrs. M.L. Bogisch, Owners

J.J. KNOPP HOME

One hundred years after Johann Joseph Knopp bought the land on which he built his little stone house at the corner of West Schubert and North Milam Streets, Martin Bogisch and his wife, Maurine, became its new owners. By the time they acquired it, however, much had been added to Knopp's little house, and since then they have done even more.

Early in 1971 the house was declared an official Texas Historic Landmark and the marker below the medallion gives a capsule history. It is significant that the marker was placed early in 1971 because it was 100 years before, in 1871, that Knopp bought one-half of Townlot 22a on which he built the house, and it was later in 1971 that the Bogisches bought it from Mrs. Marschall D. Altgelt, who had placed the marker.

The inscription on the marker reads: "The Johann Joseph Knopp Home. Built of native stone in 1871, soon after Knopp and his wife, Katherina (Stein) came to America. From Germany they traveled six weeks by clipper ship to Indianola and by oxcart to Fredericksburg. They bought this homesite for $70 in gold. Knopp was a stonemason; family farm, a mile from this home, was worked by the wife and children, (of the 15 children born to the Knopps, nine reached adulthood). House, restored in 1939, was extensively remodeled in 1968."

Its history begins with the acquisition of Townlot 22a by L. (Lewis or Louis) Haasper, assignee of Fr. Samse, to whom the German Emigration Company had originally granted it. He sold it to Christian Crenwelge on November 28, 1860, for $17. Crenwelge at the time also owned the land to the east of this on which he built his home and which is now owned by Dr. and Mrs. P. O'B. Montgomery Jr.

Crenwelge and his wife, Elisabeth, sold the corner half of the Townlot 22a to Knopp for "$70 in gold coins," as specified in the deed dated December 8, 1871. On the same date he sold the other half to Friedrich Probst for $60.

Johann Joseph Knopp and his wife, Katharina, gave Johan Kallenberg, a stonemason, a mortgage on the lot for $500 which was "to be invested in the premises mortgaged and to be expended for labor and materials thereon." The mortgage was dated January 6, 1872, but the note for $500 was to bear 10 percent interest from December 4, 1871, so that was when he started building the house.

Knopp bought the other half of the lot from Fredericks Probst and his wife, Lina, on February 9, 1894, paying him $115 for it. The Knopps made their home here, rearing nine children to adulthood. They were Franz, Edward, Fritz, Joseph and John Knopp; Katharine Fritz; Maria, Mrs. Alvin Olle;

Bogisch Garden House

Theresia, Mrs. Christian Fritz; Amalia, Mrs. Henry J. Weber.

Mr. Knopp died January 31, 1917, and his wife followed him in death later that same year on December 14.

When John Rosenbach bought the property from Mrs. Knopp's estate, the deed dated September 10, 1920, stated that it was "property occupied by Katharina Knopp at the time of her demise."

Rosenbach's widow, Eve, sold it to Albert Petri November 16, 1923; and Petri and wife, Barbara, conveyed it to Arthur Fischer July 30, 1929. Albert Keidel bought it from Fischer December 14, 1937, and not long after that began the first of four restoration and remodeling projects the house was to undergo. His sister and her husband, Dr. and Mrs. J. Hardin Perry, lived here for many years, and during their occupancy, the back wing of the house was added.

They used the front room as a living room, with the room behind it separated by a small hall with the kitchen on the west side and a bath on the east side. The room behind that was widened with a glass wall on the east side and a glass roof over the extension.

Behind it was their bedroom. When the back wing was added, it provided an additional bedroom at the extreme east end, and another bathroom, storage space, closets and a darkroom.

The Perrys moved away from the house and Keidel sold it to J. G. Milholland June 29, 1956. A ten-foot strip along the east end of the lot had been sold earlier to Mary Louise Denman who bought the property the Montgomerys now own.

Milholland and wife, Kathryn, sold it to her uncle, Frank R. Thies of Charlotte, N. C., March 31, 1958. He sold it to Mr. and Mrs. Fred H. Wagner on May 16, 1960, and they lived in it for several years before selling to Mrs. Altgelt January 24, 1968.

Mrs. Altgelt made major changes in the house, taking out the front bathroom to enlarge the kitchen, enclosed the small side porch, put in carpeting all over the house, converted the darkroom into another bathroom and closed the side door with glass brick.

She sold it to Martin and Maurine Bogisch on November 17, 1971, when she moved away from Fredericksburg.

The Bogisches were living in San Antonio at the time, but spent a lot of time up here and gradually began what turned into a major restoration project. They undid a lot of what Mrs. Altgelt had done, and with the help of Albert Keidel gave the house the "country charm" it now has. They took out all of the carpeting, exposing the tile floors again, put a new wood floor with an "old" look in the living room, and put paneling above the fireplace, staining it with Early American Mimwax. Identical paneling was put on the other side of the door around the space that had once been a window, but is now a cabinet. When the cabinet doors are closed they match the paneling above the fireplace.

The kitchen and breakfast room follow behind the front room. The country look is repeated in the antiqued built-in cabinet, little round table with old chairs in the breakfast room and the tiling of the kitchen.

In the next room, once the carpeting was removed, the attractive red Mexican tile floor, together with the little corner fireplace and glass roof (now topped with bamboo slats) and glass wall set off the room and its furnishings to its best advantage. The door to Milam Street which had glass brick in it, now has a window with stationary shutters and screens.

The former bedroom is now Mr. Bogisch's office and den. This was the back room of the original Knopp house. The back rock wall of the old home forms one wall of the bathroom that was once a darkroom when the Perrys lived here. Now its striking decor is enhanced by an antique hatrack that holds guest towels.

At the back corner of the house are large closets, with one holding the washer-dryer, and next to it is a second bath. The walls of this bath are covered with decorative wallpaper made even more so by painting out part of the design and using cutout vines and flowers from another wallpaper design as runners.

The master bedroom is at the far end of the wing, with one feature the closet doors in a subdued red finish achieved by means of Mrs. Bogisch's antiquing. Several pieces in the home were personally refinished or antiqued by her.

The narrow outdoor stairway along the east side of the front part of the house leads to the attic bedroom which has dormer windows in the roofline to the south. Matching single antique beds and some other old pieces add interest, and for convenience a lavatory in an old-fashioned washstand and commode are concealed behind a decorative screen.

They have gotten the yard started on the plan they hope will soon "take shape." Cyclone fencing in places is now concealed temporarily with bamboo for privacy until the ivy they have planted will completely cover the wire. When it has, they will remove the bamboo.

The garden house utilized the old native stone barn that is now a charming place. This took imagination and careful planning. The rock walls of the barn were left intact, but additional rooms were added, using native stones, old railroad ties for cross timbers, Mexican tile for the floor, leaded glass in the narrow slots of the north barn wall, and the exposed ceiling is finished in the same Early American Mimwax that was used in the main house.

There is a "garden room" with glass roof, built-in trellis at one end with a fountain in front of it. The doors behind the trellis can be opened to the garden view in back. This adjoins the living room which is an extension of the north and east walls of the barn. Tones of yellow in the furniture upholstery in the living room are repeated in the antiqued yellow cabinet that conceals the FM-stereo music system.

The entrance to the garden house is through glass-enclosed French glass doors which open onto a rock terrace.

The floor drops down near the west end of the barn for a small dining room separated from the diminutive kitchen with its big fireplace at the far west end. A recessed wall space holds fireplace wood. Built-in kitchen appliances and the small sink are concealed behind wood panels and the white oven door is decorated with hand-painting to make it look like tile.

From the living room, narrow steps wind to the second level where a small balcony concealed behind bifold doors from the view below provides headspace for the double bed. An interesting touch to the bathroom is the antique wash basin that is now used for the lavatory. An opening was sandblasted in the center and then it was placed on an antique washstand. There is a closet under the eaves, and a high window under the roofline of the former barn throws natural light onto the winding stairway.

Although the Bogisches were intending to use this place as a weekend and vacation retreat when they first bought it, they found themselves getting so interested in it that they kept spending more and more time here and finally decided to move to Fredericksburg permanently. They were no newcomers, however, to the city.

Bogisch lived in Fredericksburg many

years ago when he managed Mutual Lumber Company (now NBC, Inc.) and later was associated with Security State Bank before moving away from here to go into banking in Yorktown and later in San Antonio. His wife, the former Maurine Newberry, lived in Fredericksburg during her grade and high school years.

Now Fredericksburg has gained two more residents who are not only appreciative of the architectural beauty and possibilities of its old buildings, but who have used their time and talent to restore and remodel the 100-year-old Knopp place into a beautiful home.

Dr. and Mrs. Philip O'B. Montgomery Jr., Owners

CHRISTIAN CRENWELGE HOME

Christian Crenwelge's old home overlooking the banks of Town Creek has seen a "lot of living" in the years it has been there. Now Dr. Philip O'Brien Montgomery, a Dallas pathologist and associate dean of Southwestern Medical School, and his wife, Ruth Ann, own it. It has become a Hill Country home for them and their four sons, Philip, Will, Carter and Harold since 1965. It is located at 307 West Schubert Street.

Through sensitive restoration and remodeling by Albert Keidel, an earlier owner, and the Montgomerys, the house remains today much as it was in its early days, but additional space has been provided and modern conveniences have been added, all in a harmonious style of construction.

The house is built on Townlot 22b which the German Emigration Company allotted to John Peter Kuhlmann and deeded to him November 18, 1852. Kuhlmann also laid claim to an Unnumbered Lot (one of many irregular tracts scattered throughout Fredericksburg, especially along the two creeks) which adjoined it. The official map did not have 22b numbered either, however, it was the one which adjoined 22a on which Johann Joseph Knopp built the home that the Martin Bogisches now own.

When Kuhlmann sold Townlot 22b and the adjoining Unnumbered Lot on February 8, 1855, to Philipp and Christian Crenwelge for $53, reference is made to the fact that "both of said lots are not numbered on the map of the town of Fredericksburg." The description, however, refers to the boundaries as being Lot 22, Schubert Street, a "branch" (referring to Town Creek) and Townlots 56, 57 and 58.

The value they placed on the unnumbered lot which adjoined the creek is interesting as shown by the stipulation in the deed: "In case the lot herein described as being only 'part of

162

Reconstructed Log Cabin

a townlot' should be claimed by the German Emigration Company or by any other person and the said Philipp and Christian Crenwelge be evicted therefrom, then I will pay them $20 and no more."

Christian and Philipp Crenwelge came from Bruchweiler in the Kingdom of Prussia (Germany), the same town from which Frederick and Wilhelm Crenwelge also originated. Their declarations of intention to become U.S. citizens indicated that at that time they spelled their names starting with a "G," but all later records show it spelled with a "C."

Christian, at age 20, arrived in New Orleans January 1, 1854, and Philipp, at age 19, arrived at the same port December 20, 1854.

Both were single, so they built their home on the lot they bought from Kuhlmann. Christian married Elisabeth Margaretha Mohr on February 16, 1860. (They obtained their license December 28, 1859). Philipp sold his half interest in this property on October 15, 1861, to Christian who made his home here with his wife and they reared their family here.

Christian Crenwelge farmed a ten-acre lot near Cross Mountain, but also had a molasses press in an old building across the street from his house. Across the creek on the east bank there was a lime kiln which he owned and which later belonged to Heinrich Hopf, his son-in-law.

The 1860 census lists him as a cabinet-maker, age 26, and his wife, Elisabeth, as being age 18. Their family grew in size during the next decade, as the 1870 census (which lists him as a farmer) shows five children. Two others were born to them, six of whom grew to adulthood. They were Minna, who married Charles M. (Carl) Henke, the first white boy born in Fredericksburg; Caroline, Mrs. Heinrich (Henry) Hopf; Emma, Mrs. Henry Cordes; Bertha, Mrs. Richard Tatsch; Theodore Crenwelge; and Henrietta, Mrs. S. C. Zettner.

At the time of the 1954 series on old homes, Max T. Henke, a grandson of the Christian Crenwelges, recalled some details about life in the house. He said he believed his grandfather built the front two-story solid rock part of the house first, adding the kitchen and storeroom behind it later. Some doubt this, thinking the older part to be the one-story log house and fachwerk kitchen. It would be more logical to have added the larger house as the family grew.

The two-story part of the house originally had two rooms downstairs, with the front door in the room at the north which has a window in the north wall and a door leading into the kitchen. The room next to it has a window in the east and south walls and door leading into the room behind it. Albert Keidel removed the partition wall and the fireplace is now the center of interest in this large room which the

163

Montgomerys use as a living room.

Behind it is the kitchen of fachwerk construction (timber-stone-masonry). The storeroom, with walls constructed of logs, is now a dining room and has been enlarged to include a bathroom and an alcove with casement windows in the outer walls. The alcove has a stone floor which at one time was a kitchen floor in an old Fredericksburg home. The dining room has a wet bar in a closet. Among its furnishings is an old organ which Mrs. Montgomery often plays.

Exposed ceiling beams, old wood floors and plastered walls are typical of the early homes built here.

There is now a stairway across the front leading to the balcony or narrow porch and the large room on the second floor which was a "bunkhouse" for the Montgomery boys before their parents erected the log cabin on the back of the lot. A small bath was also added on the second floor in the early restoration by Keidel.

After Mrs. Crenwelge died, he and the six children sold the property to John Weinheimer on June 28, 1906, for $800. Weinheimer, a single man, died and his parents, the George W. Weinheimers, inherited it. They deeded it to their daughter, Eleonore Becker, February 9, 1910.

She sold it to Hugo Wiedenfeld March 31, 1915. She stated in an affidavit at that time that her husband had abandoned her ten years ago and did not contribute to the support of her and the children so she had to sell the property "to get in possession of money to support the family."

Wiedenfeld sold it on June 12, 1920, to Friedrich Probst. Probst died September 15, 1935, and the administrator of his estate sold it to Albert Keidel May 7, 1937.

Keidel, known for his interest in preserving Fredericksburg's early-day architecture, did the first remodeling of the old home. He lived here for a while and later rented it to various tenants during his ownership. He sold it to Mary Louise Denman July 12, 1951, who also rented it out. From her, ownership passed to Milton M. Moseley and his wife, Johnnie, July 23, 1964.

The Moseleys sold it to the Montgomerys April 27, 1965. They expanded the garage at the back of the lot into a master bedroom suite which has a bath with glass roof.

A hall with utility closets for the washer and dryer and storage connects the bedroom and bath to the Crenwelges' smokehouse which is now a guest bedroom. The cellar is still there, too, below this bedroom, with entry to it by way of a trapdoor. An old trunk stands over the trapdoor.

The Montgomerys acquired additional property towards the back and reconstructed an old log cabin on it. It was carefully dismantled at its original site in the country and moved to its present site where stonemasons and carpenters put it up, adding a fireplace.

Now the house has an historical medallion and marker which was unveiled by Grace (Mrs. Lynn) Milam, the mother of Mrs. Eugene McDermott, Dallas, on Saturday, November 13, 1965.

Through the years the boys, and their parents have spent a lot of time here during holidays, over weekends and parts of their summers when they were not traveling or in school. Overlooking the banks of Town Creek, it's still a retreat for the parents when they come to the Hill Country from Dallas where both are active in civic, medical and community circles.

McADOO WHITE HOME

Christian Crenwelge bought two un-numbered townlots at a sheriff's sale November 7, 1872, for the sum of $5.25. These two lots now belong to McAdoo White and his wife, Libby, and they have developed the property as one of Fredericksburg's choice homesites, complete with major creek beautification.

Their home at 312 West Schubert Street on the corner of its intersection with North Milam Street on the banks of Town Creek, was built when Crenwelge owned the property, and through the years many people owned and lived in it before the Whites bought it.

The sheriff's sale at which Crenwelge bought the house was to satisfy a judgement J. J. Giddings had obtained against the German Emigration Company. The unnumbered lots, many of them irregular in shape and not of uniform size, were mainly the plots along the two creeks that flow through town. These were not allotted to settlers and technically remained the property of the German Emigration Company. Most of them were not considered of much value, so when these two were put up for sale, Crenwelge bought them because they were situated across the street from property he owned and where he lived. His home is that now owned by Dr. and Mrs.

Philip O'B. Montgomery Jr.

In those early days West Schubert Street, because of the meandering of the creek, was not the well-traveled thoroughfare other streets were, as there was no bridge over Town Creek.

Crenwelge farmed and also operated a molasses press in an old building which he erected on what is now the Whites' property. When the Whites landscaped their grounds, they came across remains of the foundation of an old building.

Crenwelge built the little frame house, probably around 1903, as indicated by tax records. It is known for sure that it was there when the Crenwelges' daughter, Henriette, married S. Carl Zettner September 19, 1905, because they lived in the house, according to Mrs. Max T. Henke. Known also as S.C. and Charles Zettner, he was the pastor of Bethany Lutheran Church in 1905, for a period of less than a year, according to church records.

After Christian Crenwelge's wife, who was Elisabeth Margaretha Mohr before their marriage February 16, 1860, died he and the children sold the homestead across the street in 1906. On December 11, 1907, he and the children and their spouses sold the house and two lots across the street to Lewis K. Smith.

The children were Emma, Mrs. Henry Cordes; Caroline, Mrs. Heinrich Hopf; Minna, Mrs. Charles (Carl) Henke (her husband was the first white boy born in Fredericksburg); Bertha, Mrs. Richard Tatsch; all of Gillespie County; Henrietta, Mrs. Charles Zettner, then of Williamson County; and Theodore Crenwelge of Bexar County.

Mr. Crenwelge then made his home with a daughter and son-in-law, the Carl Henkes, until his death.

Smith and his wife, Clara, sold the house and lots to Valentin Novian on October 14, 1911. In a deed of trust given by Novian and his wife, Anna, reference is made to the Whites' house as being "the old Crenwelge place." The Novians lived here for a while, but later claimed as their homestead 95 acres 12 miles southeast of Fredericksburg. They used this place in town as their Sunday house for a number of years.

Novian gave the house and two unnumbered townlots as security for indebtedness to J. B. DaCamara of Webb County. He later deeded it to him April 1, 1936.

The house in the meantime became a "rent house" with a succession of tenants, longest of them being the Max F. Beckmann family who lived here from the 1930's until the late 1950's.

Mr. DaCamara Sr., a well-to-do resident of Laredo, died April 22, 1944, and his widow, Emma Hale DaCamara and their only child.

J. B. DaCamara Jr., sold this property to Peter Jenschke June 26, 1944. Jenschke and his wife, Mathilda, deeded it to their daughter, Elenora Jenschke, May 17, 1956, together with some property on Austin Street.

In the deed they reserved the right to live on the conveyed property until their deaths. Mr. Jenschke died August 3, 1957, and Mrs. Jenschke June 22, 1963. On January 16, 1967, Miss Jenschke sold the property to Edward J. Hagel, and he sold it to Joan Hubbard and her parents, the Douglass Hubbards, on March 4, 1972.

The Whites bought it from them May 28, 1974, "sight unseen," and after they moved to Fredericksburg began their project of making the house into a livable home, erected the adjoining guest house and undertook their creek beautification program.

At the time the Whites bought this house, they were living in Oregon where they had ranching interests and he was in the contracting business, building expressways, airstrips and the like. They had visited in Fredericksburg often when her father was living on the ranch he and her brother, Robert Sechrist, owned. Mrs. White had expressed a desire to own a "Sunday house" type of home in Fredericksburg, and her brother found this for them.

Used to living in a much larger house, Mrs. White admits she was dismayed when she first saw the tiny house they had bought and the condition it was in, but with a lot of work, renovation, restoration and remodeling they made the tiny little white frame house into a beautiful home with the help of Carlos and Marvin Weigand.

The original beaded walls had been covered with sheetrock, some of which they took off to expose the beading on one wall in the living room, a wall in the dining room and another wall in the bedroom. The rest of the walls are papered in distinctive patterns, with the painted woodwork in each room highlighting one of the predominant colors in the paper. The ceiling was torn out, exposing the wood beams which were painted in the same color as the other woodwork. The doors were stripped of their many coats of varnish and paint to reveal the lovely old wood.

The wood dining room floor looks old, but is new and was put in place with square nails which are exposed. Other floors are carpeted. Mrs. White began collecting "primitives" long before that was the "in" thing and has some lovely tables, schrank, kitchen safe, ice box with fancy trim and brass hinges, and innumerable useful and decorative items. She's glad now because the things she brought with her to Fredericksburg, together with the old pieces she acquired here, blend in so perfectly in this diminutive little cottage that fills their need now that their four children are married.

Some structural changes were made to make the bathroom more accessible than it had been, and the entire structure was stabilized throughout. The outside stairway that had become rickety was taken down, and duplicated in every detail with a new one. They use the loft for storage and to house the heating and air-conditioning system.

The privacy fence at the west side of the house encloses a small patio complete with white wrought iron furniture and their entire property on both sides of the creek is enclosed with a white board fence.

They built the guest house of cedar siding and are letting it age, and then will seal it with a silicone coating to preserve the wood. It has a laundry room, Mr. White's office, and a garage on the ground floor. Upstairs there is one large bedroom with distinctive fur-nishings, a big closet, tiny coffee bar, and bathroom.

It's a great place to put up their out-of-town children and grandchildren when they come to visit. The White family includes two sons, Kelly, who has apple orchards in Washington; Tom of Houston; two daughters, Sherrill Myers of Orange, California; and Mrs. Robert Kohfield of Fredericksburg. They have ten grandchildren.

The loft holds the air-conditioning and heating system, but outside the loft door, there's a pulley wheel just like those used on barns long ago to hoist the hay into the upper loft.

The little log cabin that stands between their white frame home and the cedar cottage is one they brought from Tillie Lehne which had been built by her grandfather, J. N. Mosel, one of Gillespie County's earliest Commissioners, on his farm in the Liveoak Creek community near the Harper Road. It was dismantled there and erected on its present site.

The old low cypress fence in front of it was a gift from a San Angelo friend and had been used in front of his boyhood home. On it is an old weathered mailbox that had been on one of the homesteads that was a part of the 13,000-acre ranch the Whites had owned in Oregon.

There's even a working cistern at their back door and Mrs. White uses the rain water on her plants. A wooden well frame with iron wheel and wooden bucket sits atop the rock-lined dug well. There's also a windmill on the premises, giving the premises an old-fashioned look.

The rock-lined creekbed, the rock retaining wall on the east side of the creek where the Whites acquired a bit of additional property, the ducks peacefully swimming in the impounded water of the creek, the willow trees and the sloping green lawn all add up to a vista of rural contentment in the midst of a busy little city.

Some people are credited with having that special something that is best described as "charisma." Well, here's a house that can best be described that way, too. The Whites' little white frame cottage has the charisma that sets it aside as a distinctive example of what can be done with a plain little four-room-and-bath house.

RAUSCH HOME

Near Main Street stands a nice example of an 1890's native stone home built by William Rausch, a local stonemason and carpenter. Located at 107 South Lincoln Street, it now belongs to Mr. and Mrs. Harry Mayer, who bought it from the William Rausch heirs.

The corner townlot fronted on East San Antonio Street for 100 feet and ran parallel for 200 feet to what was once known as "Gartenstrasse" (Garden Street) and which is now South Lincoln. It was called this then because it led to the "Company Gardens" of the German Emigration Company.

According to the official allotment list it was originally granted to Fr. L. Rudolph, but the deed from the German Emigration Company was made to A. (August) Rudolph December 2, 1852. He and his wife, the former Anna Marie Wulle, sold it to Adolph Lungkwitz September 3, 1856, for $110. Lungkwitz also obtained a quitclaim deed from J.H. Herndon, to whom the survey on which it is located was patented, on November 10, 1859.

The Lungkwitzes built their first home here. Adolph Lungkwitz came to Gillespie County from Germany in 1852 in a family group that included his widowed mother; a sister, Theresa Lungkwitz; his brother, Herman Lungkwitz, an artist, and his wife, the former Elisabeth Petri; her brother, Richard Petri, also an artist; and a sister, Marie Petri.

Adolph Lungkwitz was a silversmith, tinsmith and goldsmith who used his skill to produce the practical items the settlers needed, such as bullets, cooking utensils and other household items. He also found time to create decorative things like the beautiful bow and arrow transom in his second home -- that located on East Main between Keidel Clinic and the Kurt Keidel home. He even made jewelry and flat silver that was passed on from one generation to another.

Lungkwitz and his wife, Elise, contracted to sell Townlot 325 to William Rausch February 26, 1894, with Rausch paying $20 cash and executing a note for $860 payable to August Arlt. After the note had been paid, Lungkwitz and his wife were to execute a deed to Arlt (which they did on November 29, 1897), and then Arlt on November 28, 1904, passed the title on to Rausch.

Rausch tore down the old Lungkwitz home that stood where he built the present L-shaped limestone house. He and his wife, the former Olga Schmidt, a sister to Albert Schmidt, who lived next door with his family, lived in this house for most of their married life with the exception of several years they spent in San Antonio during the time of World War I where he also did carpentry work.

They had three sons, Erwin C., William O. and Arno Rausch. After the death of their parents, the heirs, Erwin and William and their wives, and the widow of Arno Rausch deeded the house and lot to Harry A. Mayer July 24, 1943. It has been home to them ever since. They have one son, Gilbert Mayer, who worked for Kelly Field in San Antonio for over 30 years and is now a ranger at Galveston Island State Park.

The Mayers sold the southwest half of their lot to Dr. Werner Keidel Jr. April 30, 1947, as a site for his dental clinic.

The house has a pretty front paneled wood door with glass pane in the upper half. The bottom half has a carved wreath in one of the panels. Flanking the door are two panels with glass in the upper half.

At either side of the hall are two large rooms, the one on the north side being their living room and the one on the south side their dining room. Behind the living room is a large bedroom.

The back porch became a kitchen when it was enclosed with frame construction. A tiny washhouse, with open side to the east, was also added at the back in later years. A bathroom was added at the east end of the hall.

The steps to the upper floor ascend out of the front hallway. Architectural interest of the house is centered on the window arrangement in the upper floor.

At center front is a tall gable with large casement window, and next to it, under the eaves, are small half-size windows. The room at the south has a large casement window in the south wall and a smaller one in the east wall.

The larger of the two second story rooms is that along the north side of the L and it includes the dormer window in front.

Adding interest to their home is the Mayers' yard filled with flowers, shrubs and well-kept lawn. Now retired, Mr. Mayer takes great pride in keeping up its appearance and it's a pleasant oasis in the midst of Fredericksburg's downtown business section.

KOLLETT HOME

What did the labor cost in the summer of 1885 to build Joseph Kollett's stone house at the northeast corner of West San Antonio and Bowie Streets?

$121.30 is what Joseph Moritz, the stonemason who built it, charged for his services. But Kollett, a well digger by trade, had rendered $7 worth of services in digging a well for Moritz, so that amount was credited on the bill, making a total of $114.30 for which Moritz had a lien against Kollett's house.

The story and a half stone house at 516 West San Antonio Street, now belongs to Mildred W. Bolding, but interwoven into its early history is the story of Joseph Kollett, a pioneer well-digger of Fredericksburg.

Townlot 289 on which it is built and the adjoining Townlot 290 were assigned by the German Emigration Company to "Muller" (should probably be Mueller) on the original list of allotments. Title to both passed to Peter and Margarethe Petsch. After their deaths their children partitioned this property by deed dated November 9, 1889, however, Joseph Kollett and his wife, Catharine, one of the Petsch children, already were occupying the corner two-thirds of Townlot 289. They had been married April 25, 1876.

The Petsches' only son, Peter, received the corner thirty-three and one-third feet, but in the partition deed it is stated that Joseph Kollett had paid him the equivalent of $35 in money for his interest, so he relinquished his claim to that portion to Kollett. This was the part on which the stonemason Moritz had built the house in 1885. Catharine Kollett received as her share the adjoining thirty-three and one-third feet, and this frontage of sixty-six and two-thirds feet stayed intact during the years.

The other children, in addition to Peter and Catharine, were Margarethe, Mrs. F. Gentemann; Anna, Mrs. Joh. Speyer (Speier); Elizabeth, Mrs. Christian Jackmuth; and Maria, Mrs. Anton Weinheimer.

Joseph Kollett hired Moritz to build the house on the corner of this property. According to Moritz's account filed in the Mixed Records of Gillespie County August 4, 1885, claiming a lien against the house for the amount of money due him, he stated he performed the following services during May,

June and July of 1885, in erecting the stone house on the corner 33 by 100 feet fronting on San Antonio Street: "Erecting 96½ rods of stonework at $1.20 per rod, $115.80; making top to two chimneys, $3; whitewashing stairs and ceiling, $1.50; hauling water, $1.50; total, $121.30; credit for four days work in well, $7;" which left a balance of $114.30 due Moritz.

The house he built for Kollett and his family had one large room downstairs with a frame partition wall. They used the smaller room on the west side as a kitchen, and the steep, narrow stairs led out of this room to the second floor. The larger room on the east side was the Kolletts' bedroom and sitting room. The front door opened into this larger room. There was also a window in the east wall of the bedroom.

The second floor was used as the children's sleeping quarters and it has one average-sized window in the east and west walls for good cross ventilation.

The Kolletts had six children, of whom one died in infancy. The other five were Theresa, Mrs. Albert Metzger; Mrs. Anna Robitzsch; Albert, Peter and Friedrich Kollett.

Mr. Kollett made his living as a well-digger. In those days there was no well-drilling equipment available, so the job had to be done by hand.

Mr. Kollett would use a pick and shovel to dig the deep round hole. A helper or helpers were needed, because as the hole he dug grew deeper, someone had to be on hand to lower him into the hole. This was done by means of a large reel from which the ropes were slowly unrolled as he descended into the well, seated in a box at the end of the ropes.

Some of the wells he dug were as deep as one hundred feet, because in some places that was how deep they had to go to assure an ample supply of water.

Once down in the hole there was always the danger of asphyxiation. Before going down into a deep hole, he would lower a candle, and if the flame went out, he knew there was "stickluft" in the bottom of the hole. This is the German word for the condition that existed when there was "stickgas" (asphyxiating gas, carbon dioxide) present, indicating a lack of oxygen needed by a human to survive.

As a further precaution, when he was working in a hole of considerable depth, he usually kept a candle burning, and when the flame went out, he would quickly signal the helpers to haul him up.

The buckets of earth he dug were also hauled up in the same manner as the hole grew deeper.

After there was a sufficient supply of water, digging operations ceased, and he began to line the well with rocks that were lowered into the well. No cement was used -- the rocks were just fitted together carefully, one on top of the other.

Even with all the precautions, well-digging was still a dangerous occupation as proved by

Kollett's untimely death.

While working on a well near Fredericksburg, the ropes broke as he was being lowered into the well, dropping him to the bottom of the hole. His neck was broken, and he was dead upon being hauled to the surface.

After his death, his wife continued to live here, and then one of her sons made his home here. For many years it was vacant, and finally the surviving Kollett heirs, Theresa Metzger, Albert Kollett and Wilbert J. Robitzsch, sold it on February 13, 1956, to A.O. Boening. Boening and his wife sold it to L.J. Durkop and his wife April 22, 1957. Neither of these couples ever lived here, having bought it for speculative purposes. The Durkops sold it on December 6, 1962, to Paul L. Desch and his wife of California.

The Desches made a few changes inside the house, some of which Mrs. Bolding "undid" after she bought the property June 21, 1971. She and her husband, A.P. Bolding, a disabled veteran of the Korean War, moved here later from Dallas. He is a resident at Knopp Nursing Home, and Mrs. Bolding lives in the house they bought at 607 W. San Antonio Street and have completely remodeled. They have one daughter who lives in California.

There's now a small bath in the east front corner of the house and behind that a kitchen, with a bookshelf as room divider. The frame partition wall was removed by previous owners. Mrs. Bolding renovated the kitchen to give it more of a "period" look, and with Schatzie Crouch's help, she found several nice pieces of furniture for the house. The whitewashed ceiling beams are exposed.

She plans to do more, including the taking out of the linoleum floor covering, hoping to find the old wood floor beneath it.

Chester Langerhans helped her with the flagstone patios in front and in back of her house. In the back, beams have been put up for what will eventually be a muscadine grape arbor when the vines she planted this year grow bigger.

Her garden tools are stored in the old outhouse that sits at the back corner of the yard. A fieldstone and picket fence encloses the yard and at the side of the house there's even one of Joseph Kollett's "dug" wells which has been enclosed with stone. It has an ample supply of water which she uses on her plants, pulling it up by means of a rope, well wheel and old metal bucket.

The old Kollett home is now a guest house for folks who come frequently to visit this couple from Dallas that now feels "very much at home" in Fredericksburg. Water supply no longer depends upon "hand-dug wells," but the story of how it was done by a man who first owned this house is an important chapter in this community's history.

PAPE-DANGERS HOMES

A log cabin, built by community effort for the family of Friedrich (Fritz) Pape soon after he arrived here with the early settlers in 1846, still stands today. Near it is a limestone rock home, part of which was built just a few years later.

Now the two old homes at 213 West Creek Street are owned by Robert and Dorothy Sechrist, through whose efforts they have been restored and furnished with period furniture, and are shown frequently on tours sponsored by the Gillespie County Historical Society and Commission. Both houses are also recorded Texas Historic Landmarks, following the unveiling of official markers on Easter Sunday, 1974.

Woven into the history of the two old houses are the stories of two people whose lives touched important facets in this community's history.

The houses are built on Townlot 442, granted by the German Emigration Company in its original allotments to Fr. Pape (also known as Friedrich or Fritz Pape), one of the 1846 colonists who settled Fredericksburg. Pape and his wife lost three of their four children on the long trip from Germany. His wife was ill for several months, and the small log cabin was hastily erected with help from others in the colony to provide shelter for her and the lone surviving child, Dorothea (Dorette).

Dorothea was to become the wife of Carl Hilmar Guenther, founder of Pioneer Flour Mills, San Antonio, one of Texas' oldest business firms. The Friedrich Papes moved to their farm on Liveoak Creek in the Wrede

Mr. and Mrs. Robert Sechrist, Owners

community and Guenther built his first mill in Texas on land he bought from them. Guenther and Dorothea were married October 7, 1855. Later his milling operations were moved to San Antonio after floods on the Liveoak washed out his dams. The Guenther family has been prominent in San Antonio business and social circles since he moved there in August 1859. Four more children were born to Papes after they arrived in Fredericksburg. Pape contracted to sell this townlot, together with the adjoining one to Burchard Dangers on June 1, 1850, for $250, due in July 1851, with the deed dated July 7, 1851.

Dangers' role in the community was a vital one. He was the Rev. Gottlieb Burchard Dangers, the second Protestant minister to serve this community and generally signed his name simply as "B. Dangers." A native of Langenhangen in the province of Hanover, Germany, he and his bride, Mathilda Max, left Bremen October 10, 1845, on the Johann Dethardt, coming to Fredericksburg in 1849. He served as the pastor of the Evangelical Protestant (Lutheran) Church from 1849 until his death November 12, 1869.

Three of the five Dangers children died in February 1861, within ten days of each other. Francisca, who later married Peter Kraus, survived, and another daughter, Augusta, was born in April of that same year. She first married a Mr. Schulz, and her second husband was John Sandilands of Galveston. At the time of the 1956 series, Mrs. A. B. Lange, a Dangers granddaughter, recalled family events as told to her by her mother, Mrs. Peter Kraus. Folks in the community talked frequently about the meaningful funeral orations Pastor Dangers preached for his own children.

Dangers built the stone house east of the Pape log cabin. It is not known for certain which part of the house was built first, as some indications are that the back two rooms, now the kitchen and bedroom, with the cellar below the bedroom, were built first. Reference is made to Dangers having erected a "rectangular" home on the lot after he bought it, and the mode of construction of it is more primitive. This theory is also given credence by the fact that the back room of the two that comprise the front and wider part of the house is so narrow. The porch of the house fronts on the property line, and the front room is of average size for that day, so when the second part was built, this middle room was, of necessity, narrower.

The ceiling beams, however, used in the front room show evidence of an early mode of construction, with several of them having notches in them that are hard to explain, except that they may originally have been cut to be used as upright beams in fachwerk walls, but when they were so straight and of such good quality, they decided to use them as ceiling beams. There are also places where the early method of filling wall and ceiling spaces with the homemade mortar combining grass, clay and dirt are visible in this front part.

What is interesting is that there are no

openings on the west side of the house except the door that leads out of the kitchen onto the side porch. The front door is the original door, however, Sechrist put the prettier paneled side to the outside when they renovated the house. It is flanked by two small windows, and a similar window is in the east wall. Mrs. Sechrist has pretty old-fashioned lace panel curtains hanging in front of them, and the room is furnished in the style of the typical old-time bedroom-sitting room with furniture that looks as if it had been there forever.

The narrow room behind it now has a compact bathroom in the east half, with the water heater and a very small refrigerator above it concealed behind louvered bifold doors.

The long narrow kitchen, with fireplace in the southwest corner of the room, has a wood cook stove in which Sechrist concealed an electric unit beneath the wrought iron stove lid. The "dry sink" has an inconspicuous removable board inside the top with a small stainless steel sink below it. This way, the house can be utilized by the present owners if they want to or have to spend time in town when they are unable to get to their ranch home because of high water or for other reasons.

The door between the kitchen and the back bedroom is unique in that it is constructed of two boards, one 14 inches and the other 18½ inches wide, with the cross-pieces fastened with diamond-head nails -- very rare. It does not reach completely to the floor, probably to admit heat from the fireplace into the back room. The wall that divides the kitchen and the back bedroom is made of logs and stone, and has two recessed shelves, one towards the kitchen and the other opening towards the bedroom.

The original kitchen floor boards are 12 inches wide. The door opening from it onto the side porch is also unique in that the screen door swings open against the outside wall in one direction, and the wood door with glass panes is hinged so it opens flat against the outside wall in the other direction. For security there is a solid wood door which is kept locked at all times when the owners are not there.

Steps under a trapdoor lead from the side porch into the well-built cellar with rock-lined walls and domed ceiling. Ventillation is provided by the slanted windows in the two outside walls.

This old rock house was home to several families after Rev. Dangers' widow, then living in San Antonio, sold it on January 1, 1873, to John Raulz. They made their home here, until Mr. Raulz died February 2, 1897, and his wife, Margaretha, passed away March 6, 1915. The property was left to their son, John Raulz, and the children of their deceased daughter, Maria Heinemann. The couple also had a daughter, Helen Fasel, who lived in St. Louis, Mo. John Raulz, John and Henry Heinemann, Magdalena and August Hahn, Mary and Charles Schmidt and Anna and Felix Maurer sold the property for $1200 cash to Moritz Hartmann October 23, 1916.

The Hartmann family lived here in the years that followed, however, on May 30, 1939, Hartmann and his wife, Anna, deeded it to their daughters, Christine H. Noble, Mary H. Mechler, Katherine H. Meurer and Otillia H. Christilles. Three of the sisters quitclaimed their interest to Mrs. Noble, who lived here for a number of years, but then joined her in the deed to Robert M. Flenniken and wife, Katherine of Dade County, Florida, April 23, 1959.

The Flennikens made some changes, such as putting jalousies in place of many of the old windows, however, fortunately they stored them carefully, so when the Sechrists bought the house and set about the task of restoring it as faithfully as possible to its original form, they put the old windows back in place.

The Flennikens lived here for several years, but finally moved away again and it was sold to John Russell Crouch II and his wife, Mary Louise, on April 5, 1971, who a year later on June 16, 1972, sold it to R.J. (Bob) Sechrist.

The Sechrists began their restoration work, with Bob doing a lot of it himself, together with the help of Boyce Fischer and some other help. One of the biggest tasks was getting rid of the concrete that had been poured to close up the cooking fireplace in the kitchen, but with care they got it back in its original state and it looks just like it did when it was built for use back in the 1800's.

Many who have come to Fredericksburg to go on the old homes tours have gotten a glimpse into life as it was lived here from the time of the colony's founding to the present day restoration period through their visits in the Pape Log Cabin and the Dangers Stone House.

Mrs. Enid Collins, Owner

WUNDERLICH HOMES

The transformation undergone by the two old homes at the corner of West Liveoak and Post Oak Streets since Enid Collins bought them in 1970 is just great. She preserved the old, and the new that she added was sensitively and esthetically done to retain the feeling of "old Fredericksburg" combined with modern comforts and dramatic, artistic touches.

The oldest house is a one-room log cabin which had the adjoining kitchen in back built of limestone walls. The small addition behind this was added by an owner prior to Mrs. Collins, and for the time being she is leaving it there for storage.

Next to it is the two-story limestone home built in 1892, the date carved above the front door. It originally had only two rooms downstairs, divided by a frame partition wall, with a door leading out of each room to the front porch and another out the back. One window was placed in each room under the porch which faces east and the north and south walls.

The upper floor was reached by the outside stairway which Mrs. Collins has there to retain its authentic look, however, she had added a stairway inside, too, for convenience. A prior owner placed a stairway inside which she removed, along with the partition wall, so the entire first floor of the original house is now one large living room. The wooden stairway leads up in the southwest corner of

the living room to the second floor.

Behind this she built a large frame addition painted in a soft olive color which goes well with the old limestone. Immediately behind the front room is a large dining room-den with a huge stone fireplace. Carrying out the "open feeling," the kitchen next to it has appliances and facilities blending with the "old" by means of the shelving, cabinets, furnishings and decorative touches.

The hall leads past the laundry room and a small guest bathroom to the spacious bedroom which Mrs. Collins also uses as a sitting room. There's room enough, too, for her quilt frame which she always has up for some of her creative work.

Her dressing room in a recessed area of the bedroom has wallspace literally "hung" with many of the personal adornments that are part of her always distinctive attire -- belts, chains, necklaces and other accoutrements and accessories.

With her artistic talents, this lady who created the famed "Collins" ladies handbag line and the company's related accessories for women and the home, was just bound to have her own home filled with something unusual, decorative and distinctive wherever the visitor's eyes may roam.

Adjoining her bedroom is a large bathroom --over 12 by 13 feet, with sunken tub at one end and a skylight which admits daylight for the many plants and hanging baskets she keeps in there. In the wintertime she moves most of them inside, and it becomes a garden-bathroom!

On the second floor two bedrooms were created with a bathroom and closet space separating them. Period furniture, including beds covered with patchwork quilts add special interest. The small four-paned windows under the eaves of the roof above the porch roof remain in place.

The outside stairway on the north side leads to a door in the wall of the north bedroom, and the inside stairway comes up into the south bedroom.

Outside of her home in the back is a small open porch with terrace furniture, barbecue pit built into the wall, and almost as many decorative touches as there are inside the house. The brick terrace leads to the log cabin, the little log smokehouse behind it, and to the old barn in back, picturesque with its weathered board and stone walls.

Majestic oak trees on the back of the lot, pecan trees and a lawn in front, rock terraces with simple landscaping, and a gravel driveway add natural beauty to the place.

What a contrast to the stark surroundings and practical buildings erected by the early settlers of this part of present-day Fredericksburg that was then "farming country."

Built on Ten-Acre Outlot 128, it was originally granted by the German Emigration Company to M.A. Dooley, an early-day "promoter." He acquired many of these Ten-Acre Outlots, one of which was given to each colonist as his farm plot, together with a number of Townlots. He sold most of those that were in his name to Oscar Basse September 20, 1871. Basse sold Outlot 128 and adjoining Outlot 129 to Peter Wunderlich for $50 on February 19, 1874.

Wunderlich used this as farmland, as he had a house in town he had built on the townlot the company granted to him which is now owned by Dollie Nabinger. He was by trade a blacksmith and carpenter and in 1870 was listed on the U.S. census as a laborer.

Peter and Elizabeth Wunderlich had three sons, Henry, William and Adolph, who are listed with them on the 1870 census. After Adolph married Martha Schumann October 15, 1883, his uncle, Lorenz Schmidt, helped him build the little house on the Outlot that was then "out in the country."

His father deeded the two Outlots to Adolph December 4, 1884, and it remained in his family's anme until 1956.

When the little house became inadequate for the family, Adolph built the nearby two story house. He and his wife had five children, Hilmar and Eddie Wunderlich; Emilie, Mrs. Chas. (Carl) Kammlah; Ida, Mrs. Edwin Heimann; and Alma, Mrs. Ernst Siggel.

Mr. and Mrs. Wunderlich deeded this place to one of their sons, Hilmar Wunderlich, June 24, 1914, but retained the right to live in the house on Outlot 128 during their lifetime. He died December 12, 1935, and his widow continued to make her home here. At the time of the 1955 series, she was an invalid and her daughter, Mrs. Emilie Kammlah, made her home here with her mother. Mrs. Adolph Wunderlich died March 9, 1956.

Hilmar Wunderlich, then a widower, and his daughters and their husbands, Julia and Silas Foster and Anita and Carl Townsley, sold this place to George W. Davis and wife July 5, 1956. A succession of owners followed. The Davises sold it to Andrew R. Hartman August 12, 1960, who in turn sold it to Olive Eiband February 12, 1965. Her brother, Clyde Cook, lived here and added the workroom behind the old log cabin and made a few other changes.

Title passed from Mrs. Eiband to Nell Anderson Harrison (Mrs. W. Oliver Harrison) on July 12, 1969, who then sold it to Enid Collins on December 30, 1970.

Now these houses that were once "out on the farm" are distinctive "town houses" for Mrs. Collins who often shares their distinctive beauty when they are open on tours for the public.

A.W. MOURSUND HOME

The old home built in the 1880's by one of Gillespie County's most revered pioneer citizens, a lawyer and judge, A.W. Moursund, in the midst of a wooded area northwest of the city is still standing today. Not only is it still standing, but it has been remodeled into a beautiful comfortable home, and the wooded acreage in the middle of which it stood when first built is now one of the city's choice residential sections.

Mr. and Mrs. Jerome Annis have owned the home at 302 North Kay Street since they bought it from Mr. and Mrs. James Bender on December 13, 1965. The Benders made the initial renovations after buying it January 2, 1957, when it was placed on the market by the developers of the addition, Oakcrest Manor, laid out on the Moursund acreage.

The builder of this old two-story limestone home, along plans credited to Alfred Giles, eminent early-day Texas architect, was Albert Waddel Moursund, better known as A.W. Moursund. He was the "dean" of lawyers in early-day Fredericksburg and the entire Hill Country. While not many are left who were his clients, there are a lot who recall their parents talking about "Judge Moursund" and his handling of their legal affairs.

The house is located on Outlot 587, one of the Ten-Acre Lots granted to the settlers of Fredericksburg for their "farm." Outlot 587 was given by the German Emigration to "Wilh.

Horlen" and the adjoining No. 586 to "Hch. Lang." Lang and Horlen, in the same deed, sold their two lots to Jacob Weinheimer December 1, 1855, for $50--$25 for each ten acres of land! Jacob Weinheimer sold it to August Schuller for $100, but failed to sign a deed, so his heirs on May 22, 1884, made a deed to Schuller. They were George, Anton and John Weinheimer; Elizabeth and John Dietz; Anna and Joseph Petsch and Sophie and B. Meckel. Although August is listed as the grantor in that deed, Charles Schuller and wife, Laura, deeded it to Anton Loth on that same date, May 22, 1884. Earlier in that year, January 6, 1884, Charles Schuller had deeded these two Outlots, along with other property to his wife, Laura.

Anton Loth and wife, Anna, sold Outlots 586 and 587 to A.W. Moursund November 1, 1886, for $725 cash, and he began construction of the home. By this time Moursund was established here in the legal profession and also held public office. His story -- and that of his home -- merit re-telling for the benefit of future generations.

Moursund was born May 13, 1845, in Tromso, Norway. He decided to "seek his fortune" in the new world, and his ticket from Throndhjen, Norway, dated September 21, 1869, took him via Quebec to New York. His destination was the State of Texas.

He was mustered into the Texas Frontier

176

Forces, Capt. A.W. Cox, Company B, at Austin, September 8, 1870 and mustered out at Austin May 31, 1871. The company was stationed at Fort Davis and operated against the Comanches and other hostile Indians from Mexico. He attained the rank of sergeant.

On August 13, 1872, he filed his declaration of intention to become a citizen and was naturalized February 1, 1876.

On June 10, 1873, he was licensed to practice law by the District Court at Austin and he practiced in Blanco until he moved to Fredericksburg.

Moursund married Henrietta (sometimes written Henrikke) Marion Mowinckle of Oak Hill on June 4, 1874. Courtship in those days was no simple matter, for he rode the distance from his home to her's on horseback, usually taking all night to make the trek.

He was appointed County Judge of Blanco County on October 23, 1876, to fill a vacancy. In December 1880 he was elected to the State Legislature from Blanco and Travis Counties and two years later was elected to the same body from Comal, Gillespie and Blanco Counties.

The family moved to Fredericksburg in 1883, and at first lived in the Charles F. Priess home which stood where the McFarland home which now belongs to Holy Ghost Lutheran Church is located. They lived there until their two-story rock home was built on the two Ten-Acre Lots he had bought.

He was elected District Attorney for the 33rd Judicial District on December 15, 1884. On February 27, 1885, he was appointed District Judge of the same district to fill a vacancy caused by the resignation of Judge Townes. In December 1886 he was elected to the judgeship.

He was once in partnership with A.O. Cooley, one of the earliest Fredericksburg lawyers, and they had their offices in the Maier Building now occupied by Main Book Store. Moursund's office for the many years that followed, however, was upstairs in the first Gillespie County courthouse which became the post office after the second courthouse was built in 1882. That building was razed when the new post office was built.

With five children, the Moursunds decided to build a large home that would adequately house their family and be in keeping with his station in life.

The hard limestone rock for the house was quarried a few miles from town, with A.W.

Petmecky and his helper, Thompson, doing all of the rock work. The lumber was hauled in from Austin and Bastrop.

Three more children were born to the couple after they lived here.

The oldest son, Andrew Fleming Moursund, was born June 3, 1875, in Blanco. He became an engineer and was for a long time District Engineer for the Texas Highway Department. His home was in Fredericksburg. The second son, Anton Norwall Moursund, was born March 26, 1877, at Oak Hill in the home of his mother's parents. He became a prominent lawyer in San Antonio and was at one time a Judge of the Fourth Court of Civil Appeals.

The third son, Ernest Marion Moursund, was born June 20, 1879, in Blanco and he became a civil engineer for the railroads.

The fourth son, Albert Waddel Moursund, born in Blanco February 17, 1882, made his home in Johnson City where he was associated with a bank and conducted an abstract of title business.

The fifth son, Walter Henrick Moursund, was born in the Priess house August 13, 1884, and became a medical doctor, serving as Dean of Baylor University Medical School for more than 30 years. His home was in Houston.

The sixth son, Rolf Christian Moursund, was born in this old home May 8, 1888, and lived in Fredericksburg until his death.

Finally, the Moursunds had a daughter, who was born November 27, 1889. They named her Henrikke Magdalene, and she married E.L. Malsby, a prominent Mineral Wells businessman.

The "baby" of the family was named after a famed Norse hero, Leif Erikson Moursund. He was born October 5, 1892. His home was in Austin where he was associated with a railroad company.

With this large a family, the house the Moursunds built served them well, and it was the center of happy family activities and entertaining. Though some changes have been made, basically the house remains the same.

Their main entrance was through the large front door with glass transom and glass sidelights. This led into the central hall. The large room on the left was the family parlor and music room. It has two large windows in the east and west sides of the room, and one of the five large fireplaces is located in the southwall. This is now used by Mr. and Mrs. Annis as their formal living room.

On the other side of the hall, the front room

with its bay window (three tall windows) was used by Judge Moursund as his study. In later years, when the old couple no longer cared to climb the stairs, this room was used as their bedroom. It is now used by the Annises as a music room. It also has a fireplace, and a door leading to the front porch. Originally another door led out on the small north side porch, but this has been made into a window. The little side porch was enclosed by the Moursunds in later years, and then the walls were removed, with lattice work now in place at the front. The roof of the porch has a railing to form a balcony on the north for the upper floor bedroom door. This door has also been made into a window.

The middle room on the north side has another bay window (three windows) and was used by the family as their dining and everyday sitting room. The fireplace in this room is faced with cream-colored tile. The Annises use it as a dining room. The center of interest is a large, tilt-top inlaid Austrian table over 300 years old that was in Mrs. Annis' family.

Behind it is the large kitchen, which in the years after the children left home, was also used as a dinette.

In back of the hall was a small open service porch which was later enclosed for a utility room and bathroom. There was another small service porch in front of the kitchen door leading out north side. Here is where the Annises have added a den. There is a back porch on the southwest end.

The bedrooms upstairs were large and well-ventilated. On the north side, the front bedroom was the daughter's room and was in later years used by their family servant. It was also heated by a fireplace.

The middle room on the north side was used by Judge and Mrs. Moursund and the young children in the family. It, too, has a fireplace. Mr. and Mrs. Annis now use this as their bedroom. The large bedroom at the northwest corner was used by the older boys. As the boys left home, the younger ones moved into it. It was heated by a wood stove.

The large room across the hall on the south side was originally divided into two bedrooms by a frame partition. The one in back was a guest room and the front one was used by the servant girl (dienstmaedchen). Later, Judge and Mrs. Moursund used this as their bedroom and turned their middle bedroom into a guest room.

The large open porch upstairs was a favorite place for the sons in the family, and later, too, the grandsons when they came visiting and slept there in the summertime.

In the back there was also a small porch which was later enclosed and turned into a bathroom with an overhead water tank. Originally, however, the main bathroom was in the tankhouse situated outside the kitchen door.

Their main yard was enclosed with a picket fence. There were several large grape arbors and the yard was filled with shrubs and flowers. Ivy crept up the walls of the home, but has now been removed. Nearby were fields, a large plot southwest of the house was their fruit orchard and the plot west of the house was the family garden. The wooded area east of the house was used as pasturage for the buggy and saddle horses and calves. There was also a tennis court. The wooded area northwest of the house was used for pasturage by the milk cows and other horses.

In the center of these two areas stood a large two-story barn. There was also a large buggy and saddle house just south of the barn. Part of this building shaded a "dug" well which was later abandoned and the building was removed and turned into a garage.

Life here was good, but like all things, it came to an end for Judge Moursund when he died December 29, 1927. His wife continued to make her home here until she died May 18, 1942.

On May 26, 1955, the Moursund heirs sold the property to Leo Blanchard Jr., Patrick Dooley, Richard Hoerster and William Schroeder, who developed the acreage into Oakcrest Manor, a residential subdivision. Schroeder and Hugo Kallenberg, a partnership, acquired the home property and sold it to James M. Bender January 2, 1957.

The Benders re-decorated the house, leaving the varnished beaded ceiling, but made no major structural changes. After several trips to Fredericksburg to look for a place to live, Mr. and Mrs. Annis were shown this home when it was placed on the market by the Benders. They fell in love with it right away, and just a few months after buying it moved in here in 1966. They were living in Coral Gables, Florida, at that time. Now they are enjoying life here in Fredericksburg in this lovely old home.

———

Mr. and Mrs. Chester Langerhans, Owners

THE OLD MILL—NOW APARTMENT HOUSE

Customers who drive up to Langerhans Florist and Nursery do not realize that the house immediately north of it at the corner of South Elk and East San Antonio Streets is one of Fredericksburg's historic old buildings. Just like you can't tell what's in a book by its cover, so it's impossible to tell from the outward appearance of this house that it was once an early day steam mill.

It is now owned by Chester Langerhans, who has just finished converting it into a two-apartment unit. Owners prior to him gave this venerable old building a "new" look during those years when the thing to do was to fix up an old building to look as modern as possible.

Located on Townlot 593, which the German Emigration Company deeded to Georg Friedrich Holekamp May 27, 1850, ownership passed to Franz Gross who deeded it to Friedrich Kiehne Sr. for $18 on October 23, 1854. In the deed reference is made to its being bounded by Houston and San Antonio Streets. Houston Street is now known as Elk Street.

Kiehne, who had also acquired the adjoining Nos. 594 and 595 from the original grantees, Seiler and Neuroth, sold the three townlots to Fredericksburg Actien Mill Company February 6, 1867. This was a stock company whose shareholders were mostly farmers. Although in some later transactions the name

is spelled "Action," the word was a derivative of the German word, "Aktien," meaning a share, or stock in a company.

The deed stated the company was formed for the purpose of erecting a building for a steam mill.

Overlooking Barons Creek, this was an ideal site. Among the shareholders were William Kramer, J. Kallenberg, F. Lochte, F. Rahe, H. Mueller Sr., F. Kiehne, August Koennecke, Wm. Koennecke, Carl Koennecke, Math. Bonn and Caspar Hoffarth.

A resolution was passed on July 14, 1867, for the purpose of raising $5,000 capital, and was signed by Wm. Keidel, president; and H. Ochs, secretary. July 16, 1868, Keidel was still president, F. Wilke was treasurer and R. Radeleff, secretary. The building was apparently finished by then as they resolved to borrow an additional $1,000 for which the lender was to have a second lien against the mill.

The trustees of the mill company, W. Kramer, Aug. Koennecke and C. Brockmann, sold the building and all equipment to J.T. Johnson for $15,500 on July 15, 1871. He was a brother of Sam Ealy Johnson, grandfather of the late President Lyndon B. Johnson and Josefa Johnson Moss, a later owner of the building. J.T. and Sam Ealy Johnson were partners in many of their business ventures

179

and it was recalled in 1955 that he was a "silent partner" in this mill.

J.T. Johnson's partner of record, however, was C. (Charles-Carl) Basse with whom he entered into a co-partnership agreement July 18, 1871, three days after buying the mill. It was for the "purpose of carrying on the business of millers at the steam mill."

In the agreement reference is made to the fact that Johnson was leaving on a trip up north, and provisions were made for business transactions while he was gone. This was probably when he was making one of the cattle drives he made each year from the Stonewall-Johnson City area.

Johnson sold the three lots and the mill to Charles Basse January 13, 1873. Financial troubles, however, beset the milling operations, requiring frequent refinancing and finally it was acquired on May 27, 1876, by Charlotte Basse at a trustee's sale. Mathilda Basse and Henry (Heinrich) Henke had assumed payment of some notes, and on May 5, 1879, Henke, by trustee's deed, acquired the three lots and "the mill and all machinery thereon."

Henke was already conducting a butcher shop at the corner of East Main and South Lincoln Streets and had a farm on the Pedernales. Since he had several sons who were old enough to work, they assisted in running the mill. Besides milling grain, they also ran a saw mill here.

Fritz Langerhans, who was a boy at the time the Henkes ran the mill and lived nearby, in 1955 recounted some of his recollections about the mill.

The two-story limestone rock building had a small third floor used for storage. The thick stone walls of the first two floors withstood years of use and later of neglect and vandalism during the long years the building was vacant in the early part of this century.

On the west side towards the creek there was a large opening near the southwest end where the boilers were. In the middle of the first floor in the east wall was the large, main doorway. On each side of this were two large windows. Upstairs in the east wall were five large windows. The north wall facing on San Antonio Street had a small doorway near the northwest corner and a window to the east of it. Above them were two windows on the second floor.

Chester Langerhans recalled that when he helped his father, August Langerhans, do some of the initial remodeling, they knocked out some of the stones in the west wall to make the small windows that are there now and closed up the large opening. The other windows in the house were closed up part of the way from the top, making them a lot smaller.

At the southwest corner of the building was a large stone platform with immense wooden timbers which "cradled" the boilers which were filled with water from nearby Barons Creek. The steam they generated ran the machinery for the flour mill and also for the saw mill.

There was a deep trench dug at the east side of the building in which the saws for the saw mill were located. Folks would drive their wagons up from San Antonio Street and the logs would slide right off the wagons into the saws that cut them into lumber.

Farmers brought the wheat and corn they grew on their farms to the mill where it was ground into flour and cornmeal. This was a slow process and they often had to wait all day, but most of them left their grain and called for the flour or meal when they came to town on their next trip.

From the wheat that was milled, the farmer took home three by-products. The "Kleie," or "shorts" was a mixture of the coarse coverings of wheat kernel which was fed to farm animals animals; the "nach mehl" was a coarse flour mixture which some people used to bake bread; and the refined flour was used for general baking.

Tragedy befell the mill one summer, probably in 1884, according to some recollections, when the boiler exploded killing the miller and burning Henry Henke Jr., one of Heinrich Henke's sons, so severely that he was in bed for almost a year.

Water for the boiler was hauled from Barons Creek at the foot of the hill in large barrels on a wagon pulled by two horses. Henke was driving the team and had pulled up next to the mill when the miller and the fireman, a negro, began to put the water in the boiler.

The water from the creek was so cold and the boiler was so hot, that a tremendous explosion resulted. The fireman had seen the boiler begin to shake and made his way to safety behind a pile of cordwood, but the miller and Henke were severely scalded. Chester Langerhans recalls that his father told him that the negro was thrown by the explosion into the next lot but was not injured.

Henke repaired the mill and operated it for a few more years. Then it stood vacant, taking on a bleak and deserted look as time, the weather and vandals took their toll. Known simply as "the old mill," it became a landmark.

Dorothea Henke, widow of Heinrich Henke, deeded it to her son, Otto Henke, May 8, 1919, and he sold it to Wm. Borchers November 22, 1944. Henry Fernau of Hidalgo County bought it from Borchers July 30, 1945, and he undertook the initial remodeling of the mill into a residence. He sold it to Max Joseph December 20, 1947, and it was rental property for many years.

Josefa Johnson Moss and her husband, James D. Moss, bought it from Joseph July 28, 1955, and they made their home here until her death December 25, 1961. Her son, Rodney

White, inherited it. The present owner bought it from Donald S. Thomas, Trustee for Rodney J. White Trust, April 1, 1970. For several years Langerhans, who has his florist and nursery business next door, used part of it for storage. He and his son, Jimmie Roy Langerhans, spent two years "redoing" the entire interior. There is a large two-bedroom apartment on each floor with large living-dining room, kitchen, bath and hall.

What Chester would really like to do someday would be to make a roof garden on top of the building. He says the view one gets of the city and the meandering creek is great and he believes it would make an attractive sundeck and roof garden.

What a nice finishing touch that would be for an historic old building.

PATTON HOME

Mr. and Mrs. Albert Detjen, Owners

The first home A.L. Patton built in Fredericksburg for his family is still standing and now belongs to his grandson, Albert Detjen, whose parents made their home in it for many years.

The A.L. Pattons moved out of this house around 1897, when Patton built the large two-

story building on West Main Street which has his name carved in stone across the front. It was featured in the April 7, 1976, edition of this series. That story also covered the Patton family history.

Located at 107 North Orange Street, the house is built on part of Townlot 102 which the

181

German Emigration Company granted to "Dietz." The company deeded the townlot to Gottfried Bader, assignee of H.G. Dietz on December 2, 1852. He sold it to Ad. Stucken January 30, 1854, for $130. For the same price Stucken sold it to Karl Kranisch February 24, 1862. Kranisch and his wife, Katherine, sold it for $126 to Karl (Carl) Cammert February 2, 1867.

Cammert must have been the one who built the log house that was standing on this lot when the Pattons later bought it. Cammert sold it to Julius Kordzik January 18, 1870, for $500 cash, indicating there were improvements on it.

Kordzik sold this lot to Herrmann Mebus July 13, 1870, for $526, part of which was due at a later date, and on April 20, 1872, Kordzik was joined by his wife, Hedwig, in releasing the property. Charles (Carl) Mebus acquired the other Mebus heirs' interests on March 9, 1876, and sold the house and lot to A.L. Patton by two deeds dated March 15, 1877, and September 15, 1877.

Patton had come to Texas from Independence, Mo., with his parents at the age of six years, but after living in San Antonio for a few years they returned to Missouri. When his father died, they came back to Texas again and A.L. Patton settled in Fredericksburg. He married Emma Wahrmund, daughter of the Emil Wahrmunds, on October 24, 1875. Their first home was in a log cabin that stood north of the house he built at 107 North Orange Street.

The first part of the house he built is the low, sloping section on the north side. The outside walls are constructed of thick limestone rocks. At first there were four rooms in here, and later they added another which they used as their kitchen.

As the family grew and Patton prospered in his business, the two large rooms were added at the west side and the interior walls of the older part were changed, forming a large hall.

The building trend of that period is seen in the very high ceilings of the newer part, as compared to the rather low ceilings in the oldest part of the house.

A.W. Petmecky and his helper named Thompson did the building work on the new addition. They were the same ones who built the A.W. Moursund home at 302 North Kay Street. Refinements of building style are evident, too, in the newer portion as seen by the way the rocks are artistically placed at the front corners of the room that faces the street. It also has a large bay with three windows, another elegant touch of that day.

After Mr. Patton built the large building on West Main Street, he moved his family into the living quarters on the second floor sometime around 1897. The lower floor was used for many years by the now defunct Citizen Bank which closed its doors in February 1932.

Mrs. Patton died January 8, 1927, and her husband followed her in death March 18, 1934.

They had five children, of whom only one is still living, Ruby, Mrs. Otto Burgdorf. Emmie (Emma), Mrs. Henry Detjen, who died this year, received this house as part of her inheritance in a partition deed dated March 3, 1938. The other children were Emil and Henry Patton and Elizabeth, Mrs. Anton Moursund.

Mrs. Detjen, after the death of her husband, continued to make her home here until ill health made it necessary for her to enter a nursing home. The house now belongs to her only child, Albert Detjen, who lives in Austin.

Mr. and Mrs. Walter McKay, Owners

HEINEMANN-MORITZ HOME

How a house grew from a modest little rock house into one of Fredericksburg's showplaces is the story of the home of Mr. and Mrs. Walter McKay at 714 West San Antonio Street.

Now over a hundred years old, that part begun in 1871 has been remodeled and added to by its owners, having undergone two major expansions by the McKays since 1945.

Built on Townlot 278 which is listed on the German Emigration Company's allotment as having been given to "Doeves," it was sold by Carl Doewes to Wilhelm Doebbler on September 30, 1853, for $16.

By the time F. Wilhelm Doebbler sold it to Martin Heinemann May 20, 1871, the value of the lot had increased to $100, the price he paid for it. Heinemann began construction of the little limestone rock home on the lot in 1871, completing the job sometime in 1874, the two dates found by McKay scratched into the rock.

After Mr. Heinemann died, his children deeded their interest to their mother, Maria Heinemann, on May 20, 1907. They were John, Henry and Valentin Heinemann; Magdalena (Lina), Mrs. August Hahn; Maria (Mary) Mrs. Charles Schmidt; and Anna, Mrs. Felix Maurer. After their mother's death, the three brothers deeded their interest in this and the adjoining lot to their three sisters on April 24, 1909. They were joined by their husbands in the deed to Joseph Moritz February 4, 1911.

Mr. and Mrs. Joseph Moritz were Mrs. McKay's parents, and the family made their home here. Her sisters and brothers were James J. Moritz; Rosie, Mrs. Howell Jordan; Louis A. Moritz; Robert Moritz; Elise Moritz; and Marie, Mrs. Frank Schmidt. Mrs. McKay was the former Auguste (Gugu) Moritz, the youngest in the family.

The McKays bought the house from them on January 13, 1945.

The McKays, with the help of Albert Keidel, made their initial expansion of the home in 1945, followed with further changes with his help in 1968. They are now permanently at home here, having made their home at intervals in Dallas where he had business interests then, during some of the years since they owned the house.

Originally the house had only two rooms downstairs with an indoor stairway which led out of the back room to the room on the second floor. There was a leanto in back of it with stone and frame walls, but this was removed when the original renovation was undertaken. At one time, too, a small frame bedroom was at the west end of the front porch.

The original double door with old-time wrought iron latch is still in place as the front entrance to what is now the McKay's formal living room. It is flanked by a small window at each side facing the street. Like so many early homes, there is no opening in the west wall which now has a large gilt-framed mirror as the center of interest.

A big bay window with French doors has been put into the east wall, making the room light and airy with the filmy white curtains that cover it.

The next room was originally a kitchen in the early days, and the stairway leads out of this with one turn to the second floor. This room is a den and family room now, cheery with the old fireplace in one corner which had at one time been closed up, but is now functioning well. The west wall, which originally had no opening, has a high small window placed with a slant in the side walls. It took some doing on the part of McKay to get the proper slant he wanted, but the effect creates a pleasing natural light.

The old home had a "wand-schrank" (wall cabinet) which originally faced into the front room, but now opens into the den, leaving an uncluttered wall in the living room.

The one room on the second floor is used as a bedroom, and has a bay window that is an extension of the one below it. In the north wall is a large dormer window put there for added light, ventilation and aesthetic effect. A small bath is at the west end of the room.

Behind the family room is a hall which leads to the side door on the west and to the dining room on the east. The wall that separates the hall from the kitchen at the northwest corner of the house has storage space on both sides. The kitchen was remodeled in the 1968 project and has additional storage space below the counter that separates it from the dining room.

The dining room is a pleasant place, with part of the south wall featuring sliding glass doors which lead to the formal garden at the front. Here pastel-colored statuary depict the four seasons in each of the four figures.

Plants, beds, the lawn and trees lend a formal air to this garden. One of the trees is a giant old cedar where Mr. Moritz used to hang the hog the family butchered and underneath which he had the huge pot in which they rendered their lard.

The organ sits by the front garden entrance. Along the same wall is an equisite antique French sideboard, intricately carved.

Another counter serves as a low partition with built-in TV between the dining room and the large garden room which extends to the north into the large back yard. All the walls are of floor-to-ceiling glass with sliding glass doors. This area, the dining and garden rooms, have a total of nine doors in all, leading in all directions!

An extension of the garden room is the patio enclosed on the west and east side with solid walls. The north wall is made up of plexiglass panes fitted in place in the fall and winter, which can be removed in the spring and summer, opening up the back wall to the garden.

Against the west wall stands an immense schrank which was made by an earlier owner of out of wood crates, but the patina of age has given it special beauty. It has a tiled bar built into it, and the McKays use it to display some of their choice smaller antiques.

Opposite it sits a more elegant piece of antique furniture -- a game sideboard, also intricately carved along the same lines as the piece in the dining room.

The view you get from here centers on the white gazebo at the center back of the yard, with a built-in barbecue pit and serving bar at one end of the terrace outside of the garden room. Near the back side door is a giant pecan tree which Mr. Moritz planted after they moved here.

Parts of the McKay home have been featured in several home magazines and newspapers, with the most recent having been a short piece in Southern Living devoted to the distinctive finish of the ceiling in the dining and garden rooms. The beams and boards were coated with a stain and then a product known as "cementicoat" was applied generously. This was allowed to dry thoroughly and then the beams and boards were put up by the carpenters. Just enough of the white flaked off to give the effect of old fashioned whitewash -- a pleasing touch for these open, airy rooms.

Mrs. McKay says the garden room is the only one in the house large enough to hold the entire family when they are all home at the same time. Their children include a son, Walter McKay Jr.; and three daughters, Elaine Knaggs, Carolyn Blew and Waldeen Wunderlich. They also have nine grandchildren -- three girls and six boys, which makes for a "full house" when they are all home.

From the dining room a hall leads along two smaller bedrooms to the large master bedroom at the end of this wing. Along the back side of the hall are closets and two distinctive bathrooms. The first one, Mrs. McKay's, has feminine touches while his is more masculine. His also has an entrance to the back garden through a sliding glass door, and there are bougainvillea vines growing out of the beds in the floor, vining up along the lavatory and dressing table to the plexi-glass ceiling. Even the shower has a plexi-glass ceiling to give the entire room an ' outdoorsy" feeling.

There's more, too. The garage has a guest room, complete with bath; there's a large red barn in back, and a side yard at the west end.

Across the front a cedar stake fence with stone pillars gives privacy to the yard. Once visitors are inside the house, they are sur-prised how large it is, because from the front it looks like one of the city's typical small rock houses.

Two white American Eskimo dogs, beautiful but ferocious to intruders, are watchdogs who are very devoted to their master. They have automatic watering and feeding places arranged for them, so they are the "caretakers" when the owners are gone. And woe be unto anyone who tries to get past them!

It's almost as if the dogs share the pride in the old home which it is worthy of as a good example of what planning such as that done by the McKays with the help of Keidel can do in making a little rock house into a large, liveable, beautiful home.

CHARLES JUNG HOME

One of Fredericksburg's newest restorations of an old house is that done by Mary Ann and J.N. Castleberry Jr. of San Antonio at 108 East Schubert Street. The old Charles Jung-Christian Staats house has belonged to them since March 11, 1971, and their restoration and enlarging of it became a reality this summer and fall with the expertise of Albert Keidel evident in the beautiful effect they achieved.

Not only is the interior construction and decor warm and inviting, but the nice part about this house is that none of the front exterior lines of the original house were changed -- only such construction details were added that enhanced its beauty and symmetry.

The two-story, almost square, house Charles Jung built in 1871, was retained for the sake of its architectural beauty and aesthetic quality, with the addition enlarging it built towards the back. By not ruining the basic lines of the house from the front and side, this addition provided more room, but did nothing to detract from its lines.

Flanking the front doorway are wooden pilasters (flat architectural members of wood as opposed to columns which are round), in keeping with the squareness of the house. Around the roofline is a crown molding, dentils and cornice painted a warm beige. The dentils (a series of small projecting rectangular blocks) add special interest.

There had never been a porch or a balcony in front of the door in the middle of the second floor. Now there's a balcony supported by disguised steel beams with wood floor and a railing that came from an old Fredericksburg home with cutout detail seen in numerous old buildings here.

Nice detail shows up in the lintels above the windows and doors with their keystones and flat arches. The shutters were stripped and stained with a traditional green.

The front room has a fireplace in the northwest corner. The old ceiling was taken out, revealing the whitewashed beams and boards which serve double duty as the floor for the second story rooms. This is the Castleberrys' living room.

The small room behind it, a part of the original structure, was at one time the kitchen. Very steep steps led out of it to the second floor. The same stair treads were retained, but the stairway was rebuilt so that it would not be so steep -- adding about four or five steps.

New construction begins with the breezeway behind the original house which has an open look to it, the east and west walls being entirely of glass. There are two sliding doors in the wall to the east and another one on the west side. The west wall is a little smaller because the half-bath or powder room is at this side.

185

To hide the view towards the west side, a picturesque lattice work enclosure was built which will be a small garden area with plants and vines. The lattice enclosure is painted in the same soft beige shade which matches the rest of the painted exterior woodwork.

While the entire house is centrally air-conditioned and heated, there is a ceiling fan in the breezeway which will be used as the dining room. The back wall of the house with the warm look of the old limestone was left exposed. Behind the dining room, the kitchen area was built with the interior having hand-made Mexican brick filling out the "fach-werk" of old cedar posts and beams obtained from an old barn and house in the New Braunfels area. The ceiling utilizes the old boards which were part of the leanto kitchen, smokehouse and washhouse that were built adjoining the rock house in later years.

The first part of the kitchen is intended to be a replica of a kitchen of the 1870's, with an old woodstove fixed up with gas for cooking, a kitchen "schrank," a dry sink and a small round table and two chairs as a spot for coffee.

The working kitchen is at the far back, with narrow walls at the side of the same brick and fachwerk separating the two areas. The stainless steel sink has a working area and counter top faced with Mexican tile in an off-white shade with a light brown design. The dishwasher is built into this area and the refirgerator in the corner is inconspicuous behind the wall in the "working" kitchen.

A circular stairway with post and steps handcast of concrete lead to the small basement beneath the dining room which has the heating system and large hot water heater concealed in a closet behind wooden doors. From the small room at the foot of the stairway, a doorway-hole has been made into the walls of the old rain-water cistern. A ladder leads down into the cistern which has now become a wine cellar.

The cistern is interesting in that when it was first built it was dug into the hard caliche that forms the subsoil in this area. It is cylindrical in shape, like a big distilled water bottle, and since the caliche walls were so hard and impervious, only a thin layer of plaster (two inches or so) was used by Jung in finishing it off. It stored the rainwater efficiently which the family used as their drinking water and for washing clothes and dishes.

A small utility room at the side in back completes the addition and first floor plan.

The stairway leads into the back room on the second floor which at one time was the Jungs' second bedroom. Now this room will be used as a study with sofabed to accomodate family and guests. At the west end of it is a bathroom, complete with old-time water-closet (commode which has the tank up high against the wall with pull chain for flushing). The shower area is tiled with white and blue Mexican tile and sitting in the middle of it is an old-time tin bathtub which has been stripped of all paint, with the old wooden edge around the top adding interest.

You can take a bath in the tub, with waste water draining into the shower floor, or you can stand up in the tub for a shower. If you want to, you can even lift the bath tub out of the shower area entirely.

The lavatory is a large white antique wash-basin which has the drain drilled in the middle of it and then it is attached to an old washstand. The brass faucets are put in place so the water falls into the basin.

The front bedroom is the "beauty spot" of the house. The plastered walls are painted white. Then panels were cut from wallpaper with a design featuring flowers and birds and were pasted onto the walls. The area where the headboard of the bed will be is outlined with these panels, while others are placed on the rest of the walls in artistic fashion. The entire west wall of the room was made into a large closet, and each door has a panel of the cutout wallpaper design. Outlining the panels are matching borders cut from the coordinating wallpaper which lines the deep windows.

The predominating colors are turquoise blue and tan, with the same shade of tan repeated in the wide molding and the blue in the antiqued beaded ceiling with its finishing coat of antiquing glaze.

The house is built on Townlot 528 which the German Emigration Company granted to Joh. Geo. Weber and was deeded to him by the company December 2, 1852. Weber acquired three additional townlots east of this lot to the corner and also the Ten-Acre Outlot north of them.

He and his wife, Katharina, sold them to Johann Kleck on October 24, 1853, giving a release January 27, 1855, after he paid off the full purchase price. Kleck sold the same lots to John Schmitt November 25, 1861, who by his attorney-in-fact, Carl Henke, sold the four townlots in the block to Friedrich Kutscher March 1, 1869.

It was from Kutscher that Charles Jung bought Townlot 528 for $100 on March 27, 1871.

Jung had come from Germany when he was five years old with his aunt. He lived in San Antonio and after his marriage went to Fort Concho where he built some of the rock houses. He was a stonemason, and two years later moved to Fredericksburg.

He built the two-story rock house at 112 East Schubert Street for Fritz Kneese now owned by Charles and Lola Sherfesee of Wichita Falls, and the two-story rock house at 106 East Schubert Street now owned by Oliver and Josie Kowert. Having earned enough money to build himself a home, he built this house that the Castleberrys now own.

The limestone rocks came from the Cross Mountain area, Jung's daughter, the late Mrs. Christian Staats, recalled him having told her. Charles and Anna Jung had ten children, five boys and five girls. They were Mathilda (Tillie), Mrs. Christian Hahne; Dora, Mrs. Henry Doell; Mary (Maria), Mrs. Charles Kensing; Clara, Mrs. E.A. Lutes; Alma, Mrs. Christian Staats; Charles, Adolph, Willie, Andrew and Emil Jung.

One of these boys started a fire when he was a curious youngster that fortunately did no great damage to the house. His mother had emptied the shucks out of their mattresses where they slept on the second floor so she could wash the ticking. He had picked up some matches while playing nearby at Central Park (now the Turner Hall property). While his mother was downstairs, ironing with some of the girls, he decided to see if the shucks would burn. They did!

Mrs. Jung did not notice the fire, but her husband who was coming in on his wagon from the country saw smoke coming from his house when he got to the corner of present-day North Llano and East Travis Streets. He tied up his team and ran for help. They formed a bucket brigade, drawing water from the well the Jungs shared with the Kneese house next door. Using a ladder to scale the outside wall and the stairway, they got the fire out before it did too much damage.

The house was home to the Jung family with the children moving away as they married. Mrs. Jung died February 8, 1919, and Mr. Jung died May 31, 1925. Their youngest daughter Alma Staats, and her husband had taken care of the couple in their last years, and he was living in the country with them at the time he died. She inherited lot, house and its furnishings.

The house was rented to different people, with one of the couples living in it being Mr.

and Mrs. Adolph Heep, who moved here after they were married in 1927. Mrs. Heep is a granddaughter of the builder, her parents having been the Charles Kensings.

In later years, Mr. and Mrs. Staats moved here. She died June 6, 1962, and her husband died March 23, 1967. Ownership passed to Lonnie Itz and wife, Velma, who bought it August 17, 1968, from the three Staats children, Victor, Elgin and Christian Staats Jr., their only heirs. It was a rent house for several years before the Castleberrys bought it.

Now the house is one of Fredericksburg's most attractive restorations. The Castleberrys, who live in San Antonio, plan to use it as their country home, and you can be sure it will bustle with activity when their entire family gathers here. Their six children are Jean Willis of San Antonio, Nancy Stevens of Austin, Elizabeth Rodgers of Midland, Cynthia Cockrill of Corpus Christi, Robert of San Antonio, and Annie, a student at Hollins in Virginia. They also have three grandchildren.

Mr. Castleberry is a lawyer, associate dean and professor of law at St. Mary's School of Law.

Mrs. Castleberry is very involved in the San Antonio Conservation Society, having served as vice president last year and for several years was chairman of the Night in Old San Antonio event which raises money for the Society.

Landscaping the yard is also in their plans, and since Rodgers, their son-in-law, is a landscape architect, he will help them. They will first clean up the premises and then plan to take their time doing the yard so it, too, will be an asset to the overall appearance of the place. There's a wrought iron fence in front of the house and the rest of the lot has a picturesque rock fence which will be good "starters" for his plan.

BASSE-BURRIER HOME

There's a lot that's different about the home Oscar Basse built for his family in downtown Fredericksburg over 100 years ago. For one thing, it sits far back from the street -- different from those which had their porches adjacent to the sidewalk.

Also, there's a low broad rock fence that completely surrounds the house on all four sides, with a lot of open space around the house.

The house was built by Oscar Basse, one of the sons of Fredericksburg's first Protestant pastor, the Rev. Henry Basse. He bought Townlot 601 on which it is built on September 20, 1871, from M.A. Dooley, an early-day promoter, then of the parish of Orleans, La. This conveyance included over 3,000 acres of land, most of it in Outlots (Ten-Acre Lots) and a few Townlots, including this one.

This lot must have appealed to Basse, as he chose it on which to build his house.

Unfortunately the 1870 census does not list Basse's occupation at the time, but he had done freighting work during the Civil War, and was also a salesman of lightning rods and arresters. In later years he and his family moved to San Antonio, and at the time of the 1954 feature on this house, one son, Edgar Basse, was still living in the Alamo city.

Oscar and Mathilda Basse, nee Pape, sold this house and adjoining Townlots and another fronting on Main Street to R.M. Burrier on May 1, 1901. Burrier was an early day merchant, among his businesses being the The Daylight Store at 115 E. Main (now Fabric Center) and partnership with F.J. Maier in the Burrier-Maier Company Store.

In 1954 one of the R.M. Burrier daughters, Irene, Mrs. Norman B. Olsen, was living in Fredericksburg and recalled life in the house. She said the top of the fence was one of their favorite places to play as children.

From the front gate in the fence they had a broad walk leading to the porch with beds of "flags" (iris) and roses lining it. The children watered the flowers, using buckets of water carried from Barons Creek which meanders south of their property.

There were thirteen Burrier children, three of whom died, but the other ten -- five boys and five girls -- grew up here. Four of the girls were married in this house.

The Burriers sold their property in this block to Chester R. Basse April 11, 1914, and then began a period of change in ownership, with none of the owners living in the house so it

Mr. and Mrs. Rodman Saville, Owners

became rental property. Richard Henke and Edward Kretzer bought it from Chester R. Basse July 9, 1914, with W. R. Burrier retaining the right to have access to the cistern on the property for one year. (The Savilles plan to make the cistern into a wine cellar.)

Henke conveyed his half-interest to Kretzer October 6, 1916, and on March 8, 1920, Kretzer sold it back to Richard Henke, who owned and operated Henke's Meat Market at the corner of East Main and South Lincoln Streets.

It was to remain in his name until after his death. His widow and only daughter, Helen, Mrs. Ralph Gold, conveyed it to the only son, Udo Henke, January 2, 1947.

For many years Hugo (Jackie) Henke (a brother of Richard Henke) and his family lived here, and from the late 1930's to the late 1950's the Alois Novians lived in it.

Then, for many years the house just sat there, unoccupied, almost with the air of a deserted house, while the roof and frame portions of its exterior deteriorated. But Rodman and Pamela Saville saw promise in the old house and the lot on which it is built, and they bought it from Udo Henke April 16, 1973. Shortly thereafter they started on their restoration project with the help of Boyce Fischer who did most of the structural work and Luther Rode who built their kitchen cabinets.

Fortunately, the limestone rock work of the house was so substantially constructed and most of the windows, wooden door jambs and frames were in very good condition considering the fact that the roof had leaked so badly. Now there's a new shingle roof, and the porch was completely rebuilt along the original lines, except it has a tile floor which replaces the decayed wooden floor.

The Savilles had all the plaster removed and the house, inside and out, after repointing now has the pretty limestone walls exposed. There is a wide hall through the middle of the house, flanked by two rooms at each side which are not much wider than the hall. The entire north wall of the hall was at one time open, then enclosed with boards and doorway in the center. This was removed and replaced with French doors that have small glass panes with matching glass-paned panels above the doors.

The Burriers used this large central room or hall as their dining room, because that much space was needed for the big table to hold the ten children and parents.

At one time there was a frame partition in the hall, but it is an open area once more. Just about the only beam that was good in the house is a large one that runs across the hall in back.

Upon entering the house, the room at the right in front is the parlor, the same use it has had throughout its history, but the Savilles added a large fireplace in the northwest corner. The room behind it on the right side was the original kitchen, and it is used for that purpose now.

There is a knee-high hearth in the fireplace that was used by the builders for cooking as

189

well as heating the room. There's a small window at the side of the fireplace. Now cabinets blend with the old kitchen schrank and the new appliances.

On the left side of the hall are two large rooms, originally bedrooms for the Basse and Burrier families. Renters used the back room as the kitchen, and now the Savilles use it as a large bathroom. Adding charm is the old footed bathtub which has shower curtains encircling it that hang from a rod suspended from the ceiling. The lavatory is placed in an old washstand, and there's a big kleider-schrank (wardrobe) in here for closet space.

The front room is furnished with antique bedroom furniture, most of it acquired in Fredericksburg shops.

The floors could not be salvaged, but the well-worn wooden thresholds of the doors from the four rooms into the hall were in good enough condition to preserve. The hall, the back two rooms and porch have floors made of large square D-Hanis brick which the Savilles personally stained dark for a pleasing effect.

Having finished the house, they took on the job of remodeling the washhouse, cowshed and chicken house at the rear west end of the

rock-enclosed portion of their property. Now, with some new construction added to the old, they will have a small bath, kitchen and large den when they get that finished.

The Savilles live on the Klein ranch in the Tivydale community which they bought a number of years ago. They moved there from Houston where he was a builder and real estate developer. She is from Santa Barbara, Calif., and they have a 5-year old son. Mr. Saville has three children by his previous marriage, two daughters who live in Houston and a son in college in Denver.

They use this house in town as a guest house and for entertaining. When their son goes to school chances are they will live in it at times, too.

Mrs. Saville's hobby is making "one of a kind" pieces of jewelry out of precious metal, such as gold and sterling silver, using the "lost wax" formula.

Not only has the Hill Country gained some new residents with the arrival of the Savilles, but Fredericksburg has one more lovely old home restored and preserved for future generations through their efforts.

GOTTLOB FISCHER HOME

Schubert Street has a number of restored old rock homes on it, among them the Gottlob Fischer home now owned by Oliver and Josie Kowert at 106 East Schubert Street.

They bought the house, with 90 feet of frontage on East Schubert Street, from Mrs. Alma Pfeiffer, the widow of Dr. Herbert G. Pfeiffer, May 10, 1973, and remodeled the house that year, moving into it in early 1974.

The original house was built in the late 1860's during the post-Civil War building period in Fredericksburg. Mrs. Christian Staats, the former Alma Jung, recalled twenty years ago that her father, Charles Jung, a stonemason built the Fischer home, as well as the Kneese home farther east on the same block now owned by Charles and Lola Sherfesee. Then he built his own home, that now owned by the J.N. Castleberrys.

For the three houses, he used limestone quarried in the Cross Mountain area.

Located on Townlot 529 which is shown as having been granted to "Johan Betsch" on the

German Emigration Company's original allotment list, it was deeded by the company to Johann Tatsch, as assignee of "Johann Poetsch" on December 2, 1852. He also acquired adjoining Townlot 530 as assignee of Peter Poetsch.

Johann Nicolaus Tatsch and wife, Anna Margaretha, sold both lots for $66 to Johann Gottlob Fischer February 26, 1855. Fischer paid $36 cash and promised to pay the $30 balance by December 27 of the same year. He paid the balance due and received a quitclaim deed dated December 29, 1855.

Gottlob Fischer (not to be confused with Gottlieb Fischer who farmed in the Pedernales community) was a carpenter so some of the finer touches in the woodwork of the old home are probably his own.

John H. Herndon, by virtue of his Letter Patent to the survey on which this house is located, also quitclaimed his interest to Gottlob Fischer in Townlots 529 and 530 which adjoined each other and No. 505 located across

the street by deed dated June 20, 1860.

After Gottlob Fischer's death, his widow, Christiane, married F.M. Henschel. The Henschels on November 9, 1883, deeded this property to her son, Louis Fischer, but on October 22, 1889, she revoked the deed for the reason that she felt it was not a fair or equitable division of the Fischer property. In the earlier deed she had retained the right to "full control" of the property.

Not long after that, on December 26, 1889, the Henschels and one of her sons, Louis Fischer, deeded Townlot 529 to two other sons, Adolph and Herman Fischer. Herman Fischer later deeded his half interest to his brother, Adolph Fischer, October 28, 1909, and it was to remain in his family's possession until 1938.

The Adolph Fischers lived here and also had a farm on the Llano Highway. After their death, their heirs partitioned the property, with two of their children, Otto A. Fischer and Emma Krueger, getting title to this place by deed dated August 17, 1937 from the two other children, Clara, Mrs. Felix Kensing, and Eugene C. Fischer, who was also the executor of the estate.

Emma Krueger and husband, W.F. Krueger of Guadalupe County, and Otto A. Fischer of Bexar County, sold Townlot 529 to Herman E. Schoenewolf on February 22, 1938. Not long after that on March 14, 1938, Schoenewolf and his wife, Clara, sold the townlot to Herbert G.

Pfeiffer.

Dr. and Mrs. Pfeiffer built their new home on the north end of the lot, facing Travis Street. Later, with the help of Albert Keidel, they did the initial restoration of the Fischer house, making it into a livable, attractive place by retaining its original lines, with only the addition of a breezeway and garage at the east side. The first renters to live in it were Dr. and Mrs. Lorence Feller, with numerous other renters following them until the Kowerts bought it in 1973.

Originally there was a two-room log house attached to the present house on the east end. This was torn down many years ago, and when the initial remodeling was done by the Pfeiffers, its outline could be seen against the side of the house, but the sandblasting to clean the rock done at that time erased its outline.

The Pfeiffers put a door in the east wall of the kitchen which led to the breezeway and garage. The door that led out back in the kitchen was made into a window and the sink was put below it.

The stairway originally led up out of the kitchen, but it was put in its present location, with a small hallway added at the foot of the stairs.

The Kowerts made some major changes in the house with the advice of Milton Moseley. The original lines of the house at the west were altered when the frame addition at the west side was added for a music room which houses the piano and organ. It is entered through double doors put into the west wall of the living room where there was once a window.

The larger of the two front rooms is the living room and has double front wooden doors which have a distinctive transom above them with a graceful design over the glass. The other front room is used as a dining room, with this room having one of the original built-in cupboards in the east wall.

The back room at the northwest corner of the house was once a bedroom, later an office, and is now used by Mrs. Kowert as her painting room.

The open, dark wood shelves put in when the house was first remodeled are still in the kitchen.

The breezeway was converted into a breakfast room and a large master bedroom of frame construction was added in front of it. This new addition, which includes the former garage, has a complete bath, while the half-bath near the kitchen was also retained. A

utility room and a hall which leads out to the car shed in back of the new addition were also added by Kowerts.

Upstairs are two bedrooms, with a bath having been added in the first remodeling when a picturesque dormer window was added in back under the low roofline. The attic also runs the entire width of the house in back, great space for storage.

Enclosing the lot on the west and east side is a concrete block fence which, when finished, will blend in with the surroundings. The driveway and entire back of the yard, with the exception of narrow flower beds, are paved with asphalt. The front, however, has an aesthetic touch added with the broad stone steps that were put where the driveway had originally been.

These steps, the limestone retaining wall for the front yard, and the mellow stone in the original building, highlighted by the late afternoon sun as it glistens in reflection on the small casement windows under the eaves, add a warm touch to the Schubert Street scene.

AUGUST JORDAN HOME

A young family in an old home is the delightful combination to be found at 209 West San Antonio Street. Fredolin and June Kaderli and their two children are at home since October in the old August Jordan home which they bought this summer and restored into a livable home.

Just one block off Main Street, in the center of the city, its architectural lines are so typical of the early homes built in Fredericksburg that it's nice to have it preserved for posterity "as is" without any major exterior alterations.

The house is built on Townlot 358 which the German Emigration Company granted to P. Hild as his original allotment. He died and Julius Schuchard was appointed guardian of his children. In an inventory of the estate recorded November 25, 1854, P. Hild was owner at the time of his death of this townlot valued at $40; a Ten-Acre-Lot valued at $10; and a certificate for 640 acres of land in the Fischer-Miller Colony grant.

Heinrich Hild of Gillespie County and Christine Hild Veltin of Bexar County, P. Hild's children, sold Townlot 358 for $35 to

George Weinheimer on October 15, 1866. Weinheimer built a log cabin on the lot (to the east of the present house) and when he sold it to August Jordan September 1, 1884, he received $300 for it.

August C. Jordan, born August 2, 1856, in Lamme Spring, Hanover, Germany, married Caroline Pfiester December 29, 1881. At first they lived in the William Jordan (his cousin) home next door at 211 West San Antonio Street. Two of their children, Alfred and Meta, were born there.

After their own home was completed, they moved into it and their other children, Emil, Erwin, Otto, Reuben, Edwin and Arthur, were born in it. Their rock home first had only two rooms on the first floor and a "durch gang" or "dog trot" connected the back to the log cabin. Later the porch and a back room were added, with a smokehouse and cellar behind that. Much later, the log cabin was moved behind the house, but part of it was destroyed in a fire.

Sheds built on the east and south side were used for stables, and the log cabin for storage. As the family increased, the house grew.

The so-called "grandma's room" was built in the "L" behind the porch on the southeast corner around 1914 or 1915 when Caroline Jordan's mother came to live with them.

August Jordan was a cabinet maker and carpenter, and much of his work is still to be seen around town. One of his daughters-in-law commented that one could almost tell the older homes with gingerbread trim that he had helped build.

In the parents' bedroom were two immense handcrafted wardrobes of solid walnut that he had made. A granddaughter, Joy Jordan Hudson, and a great-granddaughter, Karen Nunley Hubbard, have them now.

World War I found five of the couple's sons in the service, four of them seeing action overseas on the front lines. Erwin, Otto, Edwin and Arthur were overseas and Reuben was stationed at Camp Travis. During these trying times, family and friends found Mrs. Jordan, when not occupied with her housework and garden, piecing quilts, and holding to her faith that God would safely return her sons ... and He did.

She cared for her flower garden in front and at the east side of the house where the vegetables grew, too. A representative of the University of Texas Extension Service once remarked at a state PTA convention that she had to come to Fredericksburg to find one who swept between the rows of cabbage -- which was what Caroline did. There was once a white picket fence between the yard and sidewalk.

August Jordan died July 7, 1942, and his wife, Caroline, on February 4, 1943. Later that year, on August 23, 1943, Alfred and Nellie Jordan of Cook County, Illinois; Emil A. and Thelma Jordan, Edwin R. and Jewel Jordan, Travis County; Arthur F. and Annie Jordan, Hays County; Otto, Meta, Erwin and Laura Jordan, all of Gillespie County, sold their interest in the place to their brother, Reuben E. Jordan, a bachelor.

Reuben lived here with his single sister and brother, Meta and Otto, and after his death July 16, 1947, they inherited his interest. Meta died May 17, 1951, and Otto, who continued to live here alone, died on November 15, 1975. The surviving heirs conveyed the property to Fredolin and June Kaderli June 14, 1976, and they are now living here. Fredolin is the manager of the Fredericksburg branch of First Federal Savings and Loan of Austin.

The Kaderlis made few structural changes in the house, adding only a storage wall between their bedroom and the den which provided them with a large walk-in closet accessible from both rooms and shelf space along the entire wall of the den.

Their living room is the big front room entered through the old wooden door with attractive transom above it. The other front room is their dining room. The original wood floor was retained in these two rooms, with area rugs adding warmth and color.

Behind the living room is Mr. and Mrs. Kaderli's bedroom. This room was once a porch, and stone steps lead down into the small porch which was glassed in on the east wall and is used by Mrs. Kaderli now to store her plants during the winter.

Behind that is "grandma's room," as the Jordans called it, which is now Mrs. Kaderli's workshop. She is a free-lance decorator and has her sewing machine and worktable for cutting draperies in here. She can take the table down and use the area as a guest room.

On the west side of the house, behind the dining room, is the den, which in the very early days was the Jordans' kitchen. Later the Jordans used this as a dining room when the open space between their home and the smokehouse was enclosed, and then they used that room as their kitchen. It is still a kitchen for the Kaderlis, although they made a few alterations, changing the sink and enlarging the cabinets.

The Jordans converted the smokehouse into a bathroom, and that's just how the Kaderlis use it now, too. It has a cellar below it, and when the kitchen and hall floors were carpeted, they put the carpet down so the trapdoor to the cellar can be easily opened.

The original stairway, with an attractive bannister added, leads out of the dining room to the second floor. The first room belongs to their son, Christopher, 11, and it has bunkbeds. Their daughter, Nancy, 9, has her bedroom at the east end. A bedspread crocheted by Mrs. Kaderli's aunt for her the year she was born, is now used as the canopy over Nancy's bed.

Some of the original closet space on the second floor was rearranged, so that both children have ample closet space, and the small half bath that was under the front eaves was enlarged so there was room for a shower and tub. There is one small casement window in the west and east walls, but the south wall has several large dormer-type windows which admit lots of light and ventilation.

Here's a house that's unique in another way. They did not add central heat and air, but instead have a new ceiling fan in the living room, another in the bedroom, and are fixing up an old ceiling fan for use in the den. With the cross-ventilation and the thick stone walls, the house is cool in the summer and warm in the winter. Gas space heaters do a great job -- even on one of the coldest, windiest days of the year when this interview took place.

Beaded ceilings, woodwork painted white and in warm colors, old-fashioned lace curtains at some of the windows, opaque and gingham ones on other windows -- all these add charm to the old rock walls. These walls had once been plastered, but this was all carefully removed, the rock repointed inside and sandblasted outside. Original doors and hardware were retained.

All of this adds up to a charming old house, livable, comfortable and just right for a young couple and their two growing children.

As the Bicentennial year ends and they spend their first Christmas in this old home and a new year begins, the Kaderlis have much for which to be thankful, and Fredericksburg is lucky to have another old home preserved so tastefully for posterity.

Agnes and Edith Sagebiel, Owners

THE H.H. SAGEBIEL HOME

Lumber bearing the marks of the mill operated by the Mormon colony on the banks of the Pedernales River in the years 1847-1853 was used in building part of the Sagebiel home at 420 West Austin Street which now belongs to Misses Agnes and Edith Sagebiel. Their parents, H. H. and Eugenie Sagebiel, bought the place in 1920, but its history goes back much farther than that.

When the Sagebiels did some remodeling years ago, it was discovered that the timber used in the rafters under the roof and the floor joists bore the marks of the Mormon mill. The Mormon colony of Zodiac was located in the Rocky Hill community east of Fredericksburg on what is now Schmidtzinsky land.

The house is built on Townlot 49 granted to C. Kuhn (the "u" written with the German umlaut) and the name is given as "Kiehn" in a later reference. Several families lived here for twenty-year or more intervals, but is is not certain who did the building in its various stages before the Sagebiels bought it.

Adam Zimmer, listed as a farmer on the 1870 U. S. census, and his wife, Catharine, sold Townlot 49 (and No. 50 which adjoins it on the east) and Outlot 130 (ten acres) for $500 to H. Langehennig July 19, 1871. This purchase price indicates that there was a building on the lot.

Henry Langehennig and his wife, Minna, sold Townlot 49 only for $400 to Peter Knopp May 5, 1873, and Knopp and his wife, Elizabeth, transferred the Northwest one-half

to Peter Maurer for $250 on the same date. The Southeast one-half of the lot Knopp sold to Maurer December 24, 1875, for $150.

Peter Maurer and wife, Gertrude, sold the place to Henry Ellebracht April 6, 1897, for $700. The Ellebrachts were the third family to retain possession for over twenty years, as he sold it to Emil A. F. Hannemann January 31, 1920.

The room that is now the dining room of the Sagebiel home was once the reception room and office of Hannemann, who was both a Lutheran minister and a medical practitioner. When he bought this place he had plans to pursue the practice of medicine, but the call back to the ministry was stronger and he returned to that calling. Hannemann sold it to H. H. Sagebiel December 10, 1920, and it has remained in their family since that time.

Mr. Sagebiel was an attorney in Fredericksburg prior to his death November 26, 1938. Mr. and Mrs. Sagebiel had four children: Edith, who is in the title business with her sister, Agnes, a Fredericksburg attorney; and Victor, now Gillespie County judge. Elsie, who married Smith Malone, died, leaving surviving two daughters, now married, Candace Malone Woodruff and Robin Malone Budde.

The Sagebiels remodeled the old home into a very comfortable attractive home a few years after they bought it, and later made other changes, adding esthetic touches.

The front room on the west corner is the dining room and the stairway to the second floor leads out of here. Formerly the steps began in the kitchen which is behind the dining room. The original wainscoting in the living and dining rooms adds a distinctive touch.

The other front room is the living room, and behind that is a bedroom. It is obvious from the rock construction that the house was built in several stages.

Behind the kitchen is the entry to the cellar, located midway behind the kitchen and bedroom. The room above the cellar, the floor of which has a higher elevation than the adjoining rooms, was made into a cozy bedroom. Adjoining it was a porch and small room of frame construction which as removed, adding in its place a bathroom and sewing room of matching rock construction. Mrs. Sagebiel used the sewing room to indulge in one of her favorite pastimes -- that of turning out beautifully tailored garments.

The second floor above the front two rooms was once a large room, but the Sagebiels converted the west end where the stairway emerges into a library. Avid readers, book lovers and collectors, this provided them lots of space for their books. The east end was made into a bedroom, both rooms having high dormer windows under the gables. There is also one window in the west and east walls of the second floor. Between the two rooms, the space was convereted into another bathroom and closets.

Though the Sagebiel sisters, Agnes and Edith, who own the house following the death of their mother, September 10, 1970, reside on their farm east of Fredericksburg, they maintain this house in town and do not plan to sell it. If they ever decide to move back into town, their home will be waiting for them. And a lovely and historic one it is at that!

NIMITZ HOTEL—NOW ADMIRAL NIMITZ CENTER

A corner that is possibly interwoven with more colorful history than any other in the community is the site of the Nimitz Hotel at the corner of present-day East Main and North Washington Streets. Originally this was the corner of San Saba and Little Creek Streets, but when the city was incorporated, the street names were changed.

Much has been written and said about the Nimitz Hotel, famed frontier landmark, and the Nimitz family, but a complete history of the hotel has never been compiled. The hotel story goes back farther than Nimitz ownership, but unfortunately, there are many gaps in its early history. Piecing together bits of information, however, gives clues to its founding.

The Nimitz family name can be traced in ownership of five of the Townlots back to the 1850's. The two corner lots and part of the two that adjoin them still bear the Nimitz name, although ownership is in the Fleet Admiral Chester W. Nimitz Memorial Naval Museum Commission since June 15, 1970. It was placed in the Commission's name on that date by the Fleet Admiral Chester W. Nimitz Naval Museum, who had bought the hotel property from Henry J. Schmidt and his wife, Emily, September 22, 1964.

Now its restoration as the Admiral Nimitz Center is the biggest project facing Fredericksburg, with plans to give the exterior the same steamboat shape superstructure it had before it was "modernized" in 1926-27.

The hotel building is now the "depository" of many relics and memorabilia associated with the role Nimitz had in winning World War II in the Pacific and with his boyhood days in Fredericksburg and the Hill Country. His birthplace is just a block away and the old hotel was where he spent many happy boyhood days visiting with his grandfather, Charles H. Nimitz Sr., who added the steamboat shaped superstructure to the hotel sometime after 1888.

The elder Nimitz, Charles Henry, was born November 9, 1826, in Bremen, Germany, and at the age of 14 went to sea. He came to South Carolina where his parents in 1843 had settled at Charleston. They operated a hotel near Fort Sumter. After spending a little over a year with them, he came to Texas, and was with the first colonists who arrived in Fredericksburg on May 8, 1846. He married Sophie (Sophia) Mueller April 8, 1848. According to his obituary published in the Fredericksburg Wochenblatt, they were the cooks at Fort Martin Scott, an army post near the city, for a

Fleet Admiral Chester W. Nimitz Memorial Naval Museum Commission, Owner

period of time and he is also listed as a farmer on the 1850 Gillespie County census. The obituary says that after they left the army post he went into the Nimitz Hotel business, but does not state in what year. Some sources have claimed he went into the hotel business in 1852, but if he did, he must have done so as manager because it was not until June 5, 1855, that he bought Townlots 186 (the one on the corner where the hotel is built), 185 and 184, at a Sheriff's Sale for $385. The sale was in satisfaction of a judgment in favor of Henry and Herman Runge against Joseph Martin.

Joseph Martin, 36, is listed as an architect on the 1850 census and lived in the "household" of Gabriel Martin (spelled Marten on the census where many mispellings are noted), 30, a hotelkeeper. Others in the household were Julius Cunzen, 21, no occupation given, and Philip Tarmstater, 33, barkeeper. This "household" must be the building later known as the Nimitz Hotel.

Joseph Martin had contracted to buy those three townlots from George Willman of Fredericksburg on March 25, 1851, for $1945.74, paying $934 cash and promising to pay the balance by April 1, 1852. The deed states that, in addition to the three lots, the conveyance covered "buildings, improvements and household utensils" so the oldest part of the hotel building was probably built before that time. Willman was quite a land speculator, who in 1850 bought thousands of acres of land at tax sales. Martin gave John M. Campbell a conditional conveyance, similar to a mortgage June 9, 1851.

Earlier records, however, show that Townlot 186, the corner lot, was granted to Casper Mertz and Townlot 185, also facing on East Main, was granted to J.L. Ransleben. Ransleben bought the corner lot from C.C. Mertz of Comal County on March 15, 1854, for $80.50, so there are some early conflicts in the title transactions -- something not uncommon during early frontier days -- compounded here with the burning of the Gillespie County Clerk's records in 1850.

Whatever the title conflicts were, however, Nimitz did have title to the three townlots facing on Main Street and to Townlot 80 which he bought from Christian Staats March 1, 1866, at which time there was a "logs house" on it which Staats specified Nimitz was to "leave there to my sole use as long as I please." Nimitz also acquired the corner lot, No. 79, and John H. Herndon, to whom the survey on which these lots are located was patented, quitclaimed all his interest to Nimitz to Nos. 184, 185, 186 and 79 on December 2, 1858, and earlier had quitclaimed his interest to No. 80 to Ottocar Mueller who owned it at one time.

In a news story in the Fredericksburg Standard preceding the June 18-19, 1927, opening of the "new" Nimitz Hotel, reference is made to the original structure having been a "six-room adobe house." Here, too, are conflicts about the age of the hotel. In one place it is referred to as being 74 years old, which would make 1853 the date of its founding and in another place it is referred to as being 80 years old, putting its founding in the year 1847.

The earliest photo of the property shows the two-story structure with a big two-story porch that extended in the center front for several feet out farther than the rest of the porch along the entire front and east side. An illustration in an 1888 Wochenblatt shows the same structure, but with a one-story stone structure to the east of it, with an arched driveway between them. The one-story structure had a sign in front "Bar and Billiard Room."

In the early days, Charles Nimitz Sr. also had a brewery in connection with his hotel, and the vines growing across the porch shown on the oldest picture could have been hops, as they were needed to brew beer and they do grow on tall vines.

Nimitz' obituary says the superstructure he added to his hotel, in the fashion of a "Mississippi Dampfer" (a Mississippi steamer) made it a landmark along the route from older settlements in the east and south westward to El Paso and California. This superstructure was erected sometime after 1888, as it is not shown in the 1888 advertisement.

The big stone barn and the rock fence that enclosed the lower part of the property were added by Nimitz, and they had also a big garden where they grew vegetables for use in the hotel kitchen. A real luxury was the bathhouse that still stands, as it provided the only hot bath between San Antonio and El Paso.

The old hotel had a big ballroom, where social events of the late 1800's and early 1900's were great occasions. The old guest register, begun around 1873, is still in existence and the names of many famous (and infamous) men are listed.

Charles H. Nimitz Sr. and his wife, Sophia, had 12 children, of whom nine grew to adulthood. A proof of heirship signed by A.W. Moursund, pioneer lawyer, and Bertha Nauwald, one of their daughters, Sept. 1, 1926, lists their names, birth dates, and dates of death of some of them as follows: Ernest A. Nimitz, February 8, 1849; Bertha, Mrs. Charles Nauwald, November 3, 1850; Charles H. Nimitz Jr., May 16, 1852; Chester B. Nimitz, born September 8, 1955, who died March 4, 1884; Sophie, Mrs. Otto Wahrmund, May 12, 1857; Auguste, Mrs. Henry Schwerin, who later married Lee Mason, March 12, 1860; Lina, Mrs. E.O. Meusebach, February 24, 1862; Willie Nimitz, March 31, 1864; Meta, Mrs. Henry Wahrmund, December 13, 1867; Anna, who died "at a tender age;" Willie Henry Nimitz, born March 16, 1854, who died December 12, 1860; and Louis Otto Nimitz, born March 17, 1871, who died June 29, 1872.

The 1870 census shows the following persons had their "place of abode" at the Nimitz Hotel: C. H. Nimitz, 44, hotelkeeper; Sophia Nimitz, 44, keeping house; Ernst Nimitz, 21; Carl Nimitz, 18; Chester Nimitz, 15; (no occupation given for these three sons); Sophie Nimitz, 13; Auguste Nimitz, 10; Lina Nimitz, 8; Willie, 6; all four listed as "attending school": and Meta Nimitz, 2.

Others listed as residing there and their occupations were Wm. Kuhlmann, 52, hosteler; Chr. Schlaudt, 18, hosteler; Sophie Ottmers, domestic servant; Martha (or Metha) Niemitz, 66; Heinrich Mueller, 74; and Sophie Mueller, 72.

In the 1860 census, those listed in addition to Carl Nimitz, hotel keeper and beer brewer, his wife and children, were Julius Stieler, 28, mail rider; Philipp Braubach, 33; Franz Flistel, 40, servant; Fritz Jordan, 20, servant; Sophie Campe, 20, servant; and Minna Cramm, 21, servant.

Sophie Nimitz died February 7, 1877, and the inventory filed by her husband in the administration of her estate in the Probate Records gives some idea of the assets and furnishings of the Nimitz Hotel at that time. There were "35 complete beds and bedsteads and furniture in 10 bedrooms;" also 11 stoves and pipes, so there were probably only 10 guestrooms at that time.

The barroom figured prominently in the inventory, and included glasses, decanters, counters, stoves, tables, chairs, and a billiard table. There was also a piano, parlor furniture, pictures and "looking glasses" (mirrors) -- one in the bar and another in the hall. The dining room had six tables and 18 chairs; and the kitchen furniture included a cook stove, crockery and tables. There was also a mangel, an iron safe, one wagon, two horses and two ambulances (buggies or hacks). The community property of the hotel also included $500 in "book accounts" and $1130 cash on hand.

The elder Nimitz deeded the hotel property to his son, Charles H. Nimitz Jr., June 6, 1906, who continued to run it. His father continued to make his home here, although he was in ill health for his last years, and died April 28, 1911.

The younger Nimitz and his wife, Antonie, sold it July 29, 1926, to the fifteen men who formed The Hotel Nimitz Company, Inc., and completed remodeling it at that time. They were Otto Kolmeier, Alfred Schmidt, Max O. Schmidt, Otto W. Schmidt, Louis Kott, R. L. Kott, Hugo Basse, Wm. Habenicht, Albert E. Klett, Ed. H. Apelt, Edward Stein, Joe Stein, Frank A. Nimitz, W. J. Schroeder and H. H. Sagebiel. Of these 15, Edward Stein and Otto W. Schmidt are still living.

These fifteen individuals deeded it to the corporation October 13, 1926. In the intervening years, different ones sold their shares and eventually Henry J. Schmidt became sole owner, so he filed for a dissolution of the corporation charter which was granted October 10, 1947. He managed the hotel for many years, and was succeeded by other managers, but the hotel was finally closed in 1964. Mr. and Mrs. Schmidt sold it to the Fleet Admiral Chester Nimitz Museum September 22, 1964, and plans for its renovation were begun.

Throughout the years that followed many changes have been made in it, with the most notable taking place after Douglass Hubbard, a former restoration specialist with the National Park Service, took over as superintendent. Now it awaits funding for restoration of the exterior into the landmark it had become with its steamboat super-structure and its use as the Admiral Nimitz Center dedicated to not only Admiral Nimitz, but all servicemen who have served their country.

The addition of the Japanese Peace Garden behind the stone walls in the back of the hotel as a gift from the Japanese government as their Bicentennial gift to the United States added a true beauty spot. It was completed in April 1976 and dedicated on Founders Day, May 8, the 130th anniversary of the founding of Fredericksburg.

Hopefully, soon the funds will be available to restore the old hotel building, bringing to a climax the colorful story of this historic structure.

References and Acknowledgments

Gillespie County Clerk's Office
    Deed Records
    Probate Records
    Birth, Marriage, Death Records
    Miscellaneous Records

    List of Allotments of Townlots and Outlots by German Emigration Company to original colonists, Volume D, pages 388-399, Deed Records, dated December 23, 1852, and certified to by H. Willke, surveyor of the city of Fredericksburg and neighborhood, and L. Bene, Agent General of the Company.

Gillespie County District Clerk's Office
    Naturalization Records and Papers

United States Population Census of Gillespie County for 1850, 1860 and 1870.

Fredericksburg Standard
    Bound copies available from January 1, 1916, to date. Special reference to issues between April 14, 1954, and April 3, 1957, and to issues between April 9, 1975, and December 31, 1976; also January 26, 1977, and March 9, 1977.

Fredericksburg Wochenblatt
    August 31, 1888, edition; bound copies for 1890-91, and from January 1902 to December 1945.

"Fredericksburg, Texas...The First Fifty Years"
    This English translation of Penniger's "Fest-Ausgabe" published in German in 1896 for the city's 50th anniversary was made by Dr. C.L. Wisseman in 1971 for the city's 125th anniversary. Fredericksburg: Fredericksburg Publishing Company, 1971.

"Pioneers In God's Hills" - Volumes I and II, published by Gillespie County Historical Society, Fredericksburg, Texas, 1960, 1974.

"Alfred Giles: An English Architect in Texas and Mexico" by Mary Carolyn Hollers Jutson. San Antonio: Trinity University Press, 1972.

"Engelbert Krauskopf, Pioneer Extraordinary" by Bruce Kowert, Junior Historian, March 1959.

"They Buried Our Dead" by Bruce Kowert, Junior Historian, November 1959. (Schaetter Family)

"A Musical Star Over Two Continents" by Nancy Kowert, Junior Historian, September 1963. (Frank van der Stucken)

Mr. and Mrs. Raymond Kneese gave permission to use the sketch which appears on the cover of the book. It was made by Bob Williamson of the old Ruegner home which they restored for use as Kneese Law Office.

Mrs. Herwin Wehmeyer loaned Werner Weber's old photograph of Zion Lutheran Church's old Sunday School house.

AUTHOR'S NOTE: Gratefully acknowledged, also, is the help given by many people, too numerous to list here—through personal interviews or correspondence, during the 1954-57 and the 1975-76 series.

Wherever possible, footnotes were added in instances where changes in ownership or deaths occurred after the copy was set in type, but there may have been others of which the author was not aware as the book went to print.

Index

(Author's Note: The homes and buildings are indexed under all the names given in the captions to the individual stories, because through the years some of them were known by different names. The names of the owners are also included in the index, with "M-M" used as abbreviation for "Mr. and Mrs.")